ON THE RUN

ON THE RUN

The Story of
an Irish Freedom Fighter

A translation of Colm Ó Gaora's *Mise*
by Mícheál Ó hAodha

Edited by
Ruán O'Donnell and Mícheál Ó hAodha

MERCIER PRESS
IRISH PUBLISHER – IRISH STORY

MERCIER PRESS

Cork

www.mercierpress.ie

This book is a translation of *Mise* first published by An Gúm in 1943. Revised edition published in 1969.

© Irish text: An Gúm, 1969

© Introduction: Ruán O'Donnell, 2011

© Translation: Mícheál Ó hAodha, 2011

ISBN: 978 1 85635 751 7

10 9 8 7 6 5 4 3 2 1

A CIP record for this title is available from the British Library

Printed and bound in the EU.

Contents

*This book is dedicated to everybody
who died fighting for Irish freedom.*

Translator's Note

Given that an exact translation from one language to another is a literary impossibility, this book is, as far as possible, a translation from Colm Ó Gaora's Irish-language memoir *Mise* into English. The editors have included endnotes with the text where it was felt that certain points required further clarification for the modern-day reader or where the addition of such information served to clarify or add to Colm Ó Gaora's fascinating narrative. Every Irish-language place name that has an English equivalent was translated into English; where there are no officially recognised English-language equivalents the Irish-language place names, which continue to be used to these places in the Gaeltacht, were used. The English-language versions of all officially recognised Irish townlands cited here have been sourced from Bunachar Logainmneacha na hÉireann (Placenames Database of Ireland) – www.logainm.ie.

There are a small number of Irish-language terms left untranslated and in their original Irish-language forms. This has been done in the case of the names of organisations, individuals, books, songs, etc., that have always been known by their Irish-language sobriquets. In these cases translation to English was deemed inappropriate and unhelpful in terms of making the narrative more fluid.

MÍCHEÁL Ó HAODHA

Introduction

Colm Ó Gaora's memoir (*Mise*) establishes the depth of his commitment to the cultural and political transformation of Irish society in the late 1800s and early 1900s. The interplay of both these powerful tendencies was significant as it infused the historic period with the dynamism and momentum that yielded the independence of twenty-six of the thirty-two counties by 1921. If by no means centre-stage in such events, Ó Gaora was nonetheless a constant presence behind the scenes and his insights are those of a perceptive, well-informed activist. His narrative is imbued with evidence of his strong sense of history, heritage, location and destiny.

Accounts of the west of Ireland during the years of revival and revolution are comparatively rare. As such, Ó Gaora illuminates the historical record and establishes that the inhabitants of some of the most geographically remote parts of the country were fully conversant with the major issues in play. Numbering such men as Patrick Pearse, Eoin MacNeill, Éamonn Ceannt and Seán MacDiarmada amongst his associates, it is not surprising that Ó Gaora gravitated with them from the language movement into radical politics. Fittingly, he was sworn into the elite Irish Republican Brotherhood by Seán MacDiarmada at an Irish festival in Galway. He was present when Pearse, a man he had first encountered in Rosmuc in 1908, founded the Volunteers in Galway, in 1913, with Roger Casement.

This memoir provides one of the most important commentaries on the tense situation in Galway during the 1916 Rising and a gripping account of his imprisonment in Dublin when martial law was being used to execute many leading Volunteers. His recollection of being jailed in England for republican activities is one of the most detailed and compelling extant perspectives.

Ó Gaora's description of the re-organisation of the Irish Republican Army in Connacht and participation in the War of Independence provides much new information and analysis.

DR RUÁN O'DONNELL
Head of Department
Department of History
University of Limerick

Preface

There is something strange about writing an introduction to one's autobiography, particularly when one is still alive! This introduction is to explain the fact that this volume provides only the bare bones of the trajectory that was the early part of my life. There is probably nothing more real in this world than the truth 'as lived' and if this book functions to elucidate that truth then I will be a happy man. This book was not written to cast aspersions on anyone, whether living or dead. My intention in writing this account was to describe my own experience as an Irish child growing up at this juncture of Irish history and to describe this era in the truest possible terms. If there are omissions in the story there is good reason for this. It may even be the case that certain events are still too recent to express in their fullness or to do adequate justice to them. Quite a few books have been written about the better known people who were involved in Ireland's War of Independence but there are still relatively few that describe this period as written in the Irish language. As yet, there is no English-language book written about this subject to surpass Mitchel's *Jail Journal* and it was this book, more than any other, which inspired me – from my earliest youth – to write the account you are now reading. Many is the time that I have implored God to let me follow in the literary footsteps of a hero as noble as Mitchel. I am very grateful to the people who helped me see this book to fruition and any fault that lies with this volume is my own and nobody else's.

COLM Ó GAORA
Rosmuc, May 1943

1

Family and Birth

It is said about me that I was born on 29 January 1887. I have
no reason to contradict this version of events and I therefore
assume that this is true! I was the third son of six children born
to Seán Pháraic Éamainn Mhaolra Uí Ghaora and Máire Ní
Shúilleabháin, a daughter of Páraic Ó Súilleabháin who was
married to Máirín Pháraic Aindriú. The sister who was born
after me was the 'shakings of the bag'.

My father was a powerfully built man. He had blond, curly
hair and he had the education of the average man of his day. He
travelled the world when he was young and spent a good many
years working on a ship before qualifying officially as a shipmate.
I often recall him speaking of how it was on the island of Cape
Verde that he first heard of the death of President Lincoln. He
had other stories of his sailing days too and I remember him
describing how he was confined to port once for a full four
months when the St Lawrence River was frozen over with ice.
He sailed on a ship that had every shred of its sails blown away
on the Horn of Africa. My father told me that it was the local
healer who gave him the measles when he was small to inoculate
him against the disease, an act that probably saved him from
death when a measles outbreak occurred aboard a ship he was
working on in the East Indies.

I often remember him telling people that the British hadn't a hope of victory in the Straits of the Dardanelles during the Great War (1914–18). He had sailed through these Straits himself on a voyage to the Black Sea and he had seen the big guns lined up cheek-by-jowl on both sides of the Straits. 'It was so heavily fortified with weapons,' he said, 'that there was barely space for a man to pass between the cannons and guns.' On an island in the West Indies once, while loading sugar, he and his fellow shipmates had been forced to run for their lives when the slaves rebelled against their slave masters, who controlled the sugar trade. The fact that they were white and found themselves in a very volatile situation meant that the sailors had deemed it wise to beat a hasty retreat from the island. My father was in places where the heat was so intense that it split the trees, so that the sap drained out of them. In another country, he saw the ryegrass die in the fields such was the extremity of the cold weather there.

His travels gave my father the opportunity to educate himself about other cultures and get to know the huge diversity of the world beyond his home place. He could communicate and do business almost anywhere in the world then, as he was able to speak Irish, English, French and Spanish. Having given up his sailor's life on the big ships, he spent the rest of his life trading on the smaller boats which sailed regularly between Galway and Connemara. Anybody who spends their entire childhood and youth involved in a particular trade will always carry with them a special love for that trade for the rest of their lives. Such was the case with my father. His greatest pleasure in life was to be out on the open sea and ploughing through the waves in a Galway hooker.[1] That love of the sea remained with him until the day of his death.

There is nobody yet born who hasn't some element of self-pride in them; my father's greatest 'claim-to-fame' was that his grandfather had fought in the Year of the French.[2] A captain who was one of leaders of the O'Donnell clan arrived in Connemara to encourage and organise the people for revolt. Also, it was at the Brinane's in Joyce Country where the people gathered in large numbers.[3] There was such a huge crowd in attendance at that gathering that when the many thousands had left the area and headed off to join the French, the leftover food and meat-skins (beef and mutton) they left behind formed big piles – like reeks of turf – along the hillside.

The people of that time were unique in many ways. They were very hardy and were used to walking great distances; my father's mother once walked a full sixty miles across hill and bog from Roskeeda to Recess to take the pledge against alcohol from Fr Mathew.[4] Not a drop of alcohol passed her lips from that day onwards.

Another unique achievement that occurred in my family was that my father learned to read and write while sitting at the hearth of our house, a travelling teacher who went from house to house teaching him everything he needed to learn. There was no talk of the Irish language being taught in Ireland at that time. Having said that, it was in Irish that my father made his confirmation, Archbishop MacHale performing the ceremony.[5] While they might have had no formal education in Gaelic history or language, this didn't mean that many people of the time, my father included, didn't have a good knowledge of their own language and cultural history as transmitted orally between the generations. My father, for example, could recite the sagas of the Fianna and much of the poetry from the Bardic schools, all of which had been handed down from father to son.[6] They would barely be warmed up in their storytelling and recitation on a winter's night when they would have to put a stop to it to ensure that they got enough rest before the next day.

I was always fonder of my mother than of my father, truth to tell. I'm not sure exactly why this was, but I suspect it was because she was a bit more lenient on me as a child than my father was. Not a day went by – from my first day at school until my last – when I did not kiss her upon leaving for a day in the classroom. In fact, I was always more worried about leaving her behind for the day than I was about any of the tasks that I was assigned during the course of the day in the classroom. What my father and I had in common was a love of walking and endless tramping through the hills and across the bogs. That said, I think I always had more of my mother's nature in me than my father's. The story goes that her people settled in the west of Ireland not long after the defeat of O'Sullivan Beare and the flight of the Gaels to the north. I often remember my mother saying that her side of the family were descended from a man who fell along the wayside on the march back to the north, yet survived and made it as far as the Connemara foothills.

My mother was a strong-limbed woman, devout and religious in equal measure. She had hair as black as a berry and eyebrows as dark as pitch. She had as fine a set of teeth as anyone and she had the same teeth going into the grave as she had when she was a young stripling of twenty – the same was true of my father. My mother was a quiet-spoken woman, but if she had to discipline us children she never shirked from her duty. She was kindly with the neighbours and she wore her nature on her sleeve in a way that wasn't as obvious with my father who was a much more private person. I remember my mother's tears of emotion on the nights that they were singing around the fire and especially when she began to recite songs as tragic as *Caoineadh Muire*[7] and *Mailí*

Ní Mhaoileoin.[8] You had to be there to appreciate the manner whereby she put her very heart and soul into the singing of such songs.

We survived somehow on twelve acres of scutch grass and stone, land that my father began to cultivate after he was married. A strip of mountainous land that wouldn't have fed a bird was all that my father had to work with in reality, and no sooner did he take over responsibility for the land than he was paying £16 rent for the privilege. This price included neither the turf nor the seaweed that one needed to grow anything in that barren soil.

My earliest memory is of the time when my mother first brought me to Mass. The church at this time had very few seats and the parish's two shopkeepers occupied the front two. Behind them sat the schoolmasters and behind them again were the guards. There were no seats for the cold-feet like ourselves and you wouldn't believe how much I upset my mother when, while clinging to her skirt on the way home, I asked her whether our experience in the church would be much the same when we got to Heaven. I compounded her misery when I told her that if that was the case then such-and-such a shopkeeper whom I had spotted in one of the seats, wouldn't let us within a stone's throw of Heaven's gates. I had a grudge against the same man as he had refused my father a bag of flour a while before this. He had refused my father to spite him as my father had refused to sell him a goat that he had taken a shine to as he went around collecting his debts.

I was only four years of age when the poor of the area suffered a difficult year. People were put digging the roads as a form of poor relief, a shilling apiece as their daily wage. The men in charge of these roadworks were members of the British army.

The second earliest memory I have is of a red-coated soldier who was responsible for the roadworks near where I lived. I remember seeing him going around supervising matters on his horse and there wasn't any occasion that I saw him that I didn't feel terrified of him. I spent the day under the bed hiding from him, I was that scared of that soldier.

Not a day went by that the Gael didn't detest the English soldier. The Gael looked down on the Saxon considering them a degraded and contemptible people, a rabble who were the dregs of humanity. When one spoke of the Saxon, it was with a sense of aversion and repugnance. It wasn't this attitude that frightened me, however. What made me quake with fear as a child was listening to my mother describing the war. Her stories about the war were horrifying, so frightening that they froze the blood in our veins. I exaggerate slightly of course. Not all of her stories were horror tales. She had a story about two neighbours of ours who lived in Turlough, for instance. These people lived in that era when everyone was expecting military assistance from France. One day they heard a sound like deafening thunder and they became frightened. 'May my heart and soul evade the devil's clutches,' said one man to the other. 'The French must be here! We better rush home and kill our best stock to prepare for the trials that lie ahead.' They killed their best animals and waited for the war that was coming. But nothing happened. Day after day they waited, expecting the war to begin but the time passed and the day of rebellion never came any closer.

When my mother was young, there were still Irish people alive who had an excellent recollection of the Year of the French. In my grandmother's generation the nearest priest was either in Oughterard or Carraroe. Oughterard was eighteen miles away and Carraroe was fourteen miles from them. Oughterard,

Lettermullen and Rosmuc were all part of the one parish back then. When my mother's grandfather was preparing himself for death, his son had to travel as far as Carraroe to summon the priest. When he reached Carraroe there was no priest available and he had to travel on to Oughterard. As he travelled through the mountains he actually found the body of a man who had died. The priest also had to make his journey by foot then, as there was no road in that area except for the New Road that was ten miles from Rosmuc. As it happens, the man who went in search of the priest died within the week, while the sick man actually survived and lived on for a good few years afterwards.

The man who was sick on that occasion was the person who in his day managed to put to an end the payment of 'contributions' or tithes by the families in Rosmuc. Before this each family in the parish had to pay the O'Malley clan a tax of sorts. Every Easter Saturday one of the O'Malleys went from townland to townland collecting this tax, a creel on his back. Each house paid a fee that took the form of a certain number of eggs or a portion of butter. One Saturday my mother's grandfather came in from work to eat his dinner. When there were no eggs for the dinner he asked his mother what had happened and she told him that O'Malley had been there and taken all of their eggs. My great-grandfather grabbed his fighting stick and went after O'Malley. When he caught up with him, he destroyed everything O'Malley had gathered, smashing his creel and all its contents into smithereens. The fat was in the fire. The following Sunday the O'Malleys and their extended family gathered and the Keanes – my grandmother's people – joined forces with the Connerys. The O'Malleys were routed and there was no family tax gathered from that day onwards.

My mother's grandfather was considered one of the best

stick fighters of his era, a type of combat which had been passed down from the time of the Clans. Every man had been educated in sword-fighting during the era when the Clan system was still in place, but when the Irish were oppressed the law forbade fighting with swords. In spite of this, sword-drill survived in many areas until very recently. The transfer to stick-fighting was a variant of this drilling tradition and stick-fighting survives to this very day in some parts of Ireland.

The law of the O'Malleys was greatly resented while they held sway in Rosmuc. There was a chapel built in Kilbrickan and the O'Malleys decided who they would permit to lay out their dead in that church. This custom survived for a long time after that battle which put an end to their rule.

The area where I grew up was surrounded by hills. The hills formed a type of fence around us; one that was breached only by a small gap formed by the sea. This opening was Kilkerrin Bay, which ran south-south-west of us. The Twelve Pins formed our protective fence and on a cloudy day you could have sworn that the peaks of these mountains were burrowing their way into the clouds and tunnelling their way into the sky. This view, as encompassed within those fenced-in fields that skirted the horizon, was my first hint of the vastness that is this world. As my childhood understanding of the world developed, I imagined that all somebody had to do was cross the hill that backed onto the schoolhouse and they would be in America. I thought, too, that all one had to do was stand on the peak of the same hill to poke one's head right into the sky. I had cut my teeth twice before I came to the realisation that the peaks of those hills were a good deal wider than the width of a knife blade.

The day that I managed to escape our field and explore a piece of common that bordered it was a momentous one for me and for a full week afterwards I let nobody rest easy. I badgered them instead, boasting of the great journey I had undertaken. I imagined then that I had already circled and explored a significant portion of the world. I got a right fright the same day when a hare jumped out in front of me from his bed of reed-grass. He took about nine or ten hops and stood up on his hind-legs. He pricked his ears and made another dash. Then he got on his hunkers and pricked his ears again. I turned away and didn't stay to see the rest of his antics.

I heard my mother-in-law say that her father's house and three others were the only houses in the village that had wooden doors when she was a young girl. It was a rare house that had more than one door back then. They made straw mats and placed them in the doorways at night; they had to make do with these mats instead of the half-door and there were hardly any houses that had a chimney in them that was constructed from the ground up. When my father was a young man he attended a Carraroe meeting, one of the few gatherings or assemblies organised in Connemara that continues to remain uppermost in people's memories. The Land League was in full swing then and the landlords were doing their best to oppress the people. There was only one law then and that was the law of the landlord.

Carraroe is on a headland between Casla Bay and Greatman's Bay. It is a wonder how people manage to eke out a living there at all. The bits of land there are really just streaks of marsh growing between the casts of rock in terrain that is no deeper than the length of a spade. Whatever mountain was there has been cut away to the core now in the search for turf. That same mountain which today is a spent resource, was completely untouched back then as the landlord's law forbade cutting the turf.

One of the tenant's sons got married in the parish and

suddenly the rent on that particular landholding was increased from £5 to £10. The same trick happened in relation to a number of other landholdings and, to make matters worse, it was a difficult year for the harvest and the tenants weren't able to pay their rent. The landlord served processes on these tenants. These processes had to be served on a particular day. When the day came, the bailiffs arrived in tandem with the man who issues the processes and a whole town full of police. The people of Carraroe were not at home. Instead they had prepared well and placed every possible barrier and obstacle in the way of the law to prevent them from getting their way. There was not a hut or a cabin that the landlords might visit that had not prepared ditches full of bushes to impede their progress. The roads were broken up, trenches were cut into them and any cabins that had doors were shut and bolted. Inside the cabins, the hearths were still warm with their fires, the pots still bubbling away. Every woman worth her salt was on edge, waiting expectantly for what might happen. The men were equally agitated, the blood coursing in their veins in readiness for battle. The people were hiding behind their windows, saucepans of boiling water in hand. Every kettle and container was ready for action.

The first house the process men tried to enter was MacHale's. It was there that the fight started. The people grabbed a hold of the process man and dragged him into the house where they gave him a good hiding. The police came to his aid and a police officer got a saucepan-full of boiling water into the face for his trouble. The two sides tore into one another after that, the police charging at the locals with their bayonets. The men came to the aid of the women who were in the house and drove the police back. The people grew in confidence then and next thing the police were running away. They fled back to their barracks, the locals in pursuit. Men and boys were beaten up and women and children were stabbed during the violence, but the people held their own in spite of these injuries and drove the authorities back from their property. These incidents took place on Friday, the Feast of the Epiphany, 1880.

The landlords sought further reinforcements but no back-up was available until the following Monday. The police found themselves trapped in their barracks, confined without food or drink, a threatening crowd just waiting for them to go outside once more. None of the locals would offer them a bite for love nor money and after only a short while the police were weak with the hunger. The process man, one of the Fintans, nicknamed 'Thunder bags', also found himself trapped and under siege, the same as the policemen. By the time the reinforcements arrived – on the Monday – these policemen were unhappy and weak with the hunger. This group of reinforcements comprised 300 men, all of whom were uniformed and armed. All of these reinforcements didn't make a blind bit of difference, however, because, by now, the locals from every parish in the region had joined the 'resistance' and there were at least 2,000 cottiers in Carraroe ready to fight to the death. The law dictated that the processes be served no later than that Monday. By sunset of that day, however, the police and the gentry had made no progress. The locals got the better of them and the landlords and their lackeys decided to give up. They retreated again.

I often remember my father recounting the brutality and the violence that occurred on that infamous weekend. People on both sides of the conflict suffered severe injuries in the fighting. Horses trampled three elderly men and two children and those same horses were attacked with swords. Some local people claimed afterwards to have seen a vision of the Glorious Virgin who was their protector in the battle. The name of one man who was involved in the struggle that weekend became famous in later years all over Ireland. This was Michael Davitt, the well-known Fenian.[9]

While I only heard tell of these stories, I did see evidence of the cruelty of the landlord class myself when I was just a child. I remember seeing two households being evicted in the village of Ballinturly while the police, the sheriff and the landlord's bailiffs surrounded the house in a circle. I remember watching the head officer as he walked up to the door of the house and shouted in at the top of his voice, asking the people inside whether or not they were ready to leave. I remember the landlord's lackey standing outside the house like a bigwig and fiddling with the eviction papers as if he couldn't wait for the moment when the people were actually thrown out. I'll never forget the cruel look that was in that man's eyes that day, the venomous rasp of his voice and the chilling smile he gave as he went about his brutal business. No sooner was the last person out of the house, than the bailiffs set about their dirty work. They didn't leave a scrap of furniture in the house but threw everything outside before the crowbar brigade set to destroying the place. The woman of the house covered her eyes with her hands and let out a haunting wail. The children then gave out some piercing screams and the man of the house looked on in horror as these dregs of society got into a sweat knocking the roof and the walls of his house to the ground. With every crushing blow that hit the house he had grown up in, the poor man visibly winced. It was a terrible sight to see. That same night when the bailiffs were gone, I watched the young men of the village gather together and re-build the house that had been knocked to the ground only hours earlier. My own brothers Micil and Tomás were involved in this communal effort and by morning the men had the house built again with just the thatch left to be added.

There have been some big changes in our lives since I was a child. In truth, we were quite isolated where we lived and it would take a while for the latest news to reach us. Many's the fight or argument we local children had about the truth or not of the latest rumour or piece of news that was then circulating. As a child when I listened to the local people discuss the length of time this or that took to come from Galway I often assumed that they were referring to the length of time it took to transport whatever food that we didn't have locally – i.e. flour and other cooking materials. These items were often transported by boat back then – a journey my own father made from time to time. Nearly everything was home-produced at that time. The locals made all of their own clothes, for example. The men wore drawers, *báinín* (white wool) pullovers and soft black boatmen's hats while the women wore flannel or woollen shawls and hoods that were multicoloured and oily. If my memory serves me correctly, there were only three slate-roofed houses in this townland in those days. The opposite is true today, of course. If you were to go and stand on the highest hill in the parish now, you could look down across the landscape and see houses dotted everywhere, like beetles that have sprung up in the bog.

In those days the country was full of beggars and travellers of one kind or another. Not a week went by that two or three of them didn't call to us to get lodgings. It always amazed me how they had such an uncanny sense of where their other fellow-travellers were or whose house they were headed for in search of lodgings! It was as if they had some kind of invisible radar – so that they always knew where they could find one another and secure a night's lodgings in the process. Many of these travellers were great fun, although there were always a couple who were a bit cranky. This latter few used to act as if they were doing you a favour when they were lodging with you – rather than the other way around! The travellers who were strongest amongst them did not beg for food or other provisions from house to house. They just relied on the local people for sustenance and got food wherever the people were kind enough to give it to them. The older or weaker wanderers generally carried a provisions bag with them and they went around from place to place begging for whatever they could get.

At one stage, one of these beggars stayed with us for a week and we could never get rid of him afterwards! He kept calling to the house every afternoon. They say that 'familiarity breeds contempt' and this was certainly the case in relation to this man. In the end, my father came up with a plan. He told my mother to make this man a big breakfast and to give him a lunch into the bargain. His hope was that the beggar would be so far from home when he got hungry that he would be too far from our house to make his way back. Whether that is what happened or not, I'm not sure, but we didn't see that beggar again that afternoon – or for a while afterwards. He was a big, strong, wild-looking man and he used to sell razors from house to house as he went through the country. I think myself that he chose razors as his sales item so that he could frighten people into buying them from him. He was a stubborn and insistent individual, especially if he found somebody at home alone when he called to the door. He was the beggar that everybody in this area was most afraid of when I was young.

A beggar named Tuohy used to call to us regularly as well. One night we gave him a big feed of fish that my father had brought home that same day from Galway. Later that night

Tuohy was very thirsty and started drinking lots of water. The salty fish had made him so thirsty that you could hear him swearing and cursing in between big gulps of water. 'May whoever bought that fish smother and drown!' My mother overheard him saying this and he didn't get it too easy after that. Every time Tuohy cursed, she would counter him with the phrase – 'I send an angel against your wish.'

I was particularly fond of one of these strollers. This was the pedlar with the bag, a man whom I would never have put in the same category as the other beggars at all. This man travelled around selling pins and needles and other such items. He was better-travelled than the other strollers and consequently better known. He used to sell ballads as well and you could buy a big bunch of papers, including seven ballads from him for a penny. These ballads included many nationalist songs and rebel songs and that ballad-seller did a great deal to foster a spirit of resistance in the Irish people.

Back then, people had small tin lamps in their houses, lamps that can no longer be seen today. They had a very poor wick in them, so that the light they gave out was very weak. The slightest gust of wind and the flame would go out. Sometimes it was necessary to replenish these lamps with oil near the front door or outside the door altogether, for fear that something in the house might catch fire.

A man named Egan from Oughterard was the first man in this part of the country to get a bicycle. He was a land-rates collector and anybody who saw him arriving on his bicycle – made of one big wheel and one smaller one – would head for the hills straight away!

When grass for pasturage became increasingly scarce for cattle around the beginning of May, the cattle would be sent off to a particular area to graze. Usually what happened was that a couple of households would come together with their animals and the cattle would be sent to a hill where the land was commonage. The people would construct a small hut or lean-to and whoever's turn it was to watch over the cattle would stay there during the night. These watchers would return home again having milked all of the dairy cattle early the following morning, while another couple of people would start herding the cattle during the day, and it was up to these people to source the best pasturage in the hills and to find those hidden meadows where the grass and foliage was at its richest and most luxurious. The cattle would spend a month like this and only when they were fattened enough would they be brought home by their owners again. I remember I spent a month that year booleying.[10]

When I was a young child the small bumps in the bog seemed as big as hills while the hills looked big enough to be mountains. The flowers in the heather were like perfume then and the lily-flowers in the ponds were wondrous and beautiful in a way that isn't the same when you reach adulthood. There was no hill or crag that didn't have a hidden hive of bees somewhere. The man with his scythe had to be quick on his feet or he would have been stung to death with all of the bee-nests that were hidden in the grass and the undergrowth.

St Ciarán's feastday was the biggest fair in this vicinity then.[11] Scores of women would travel to the fair from Joyce Country to sell clothes and yarn. You wouldn't see any clothes sold there today but back then people would spin yarn at home by the light of their fires. We have seen a lot of progress in recent decades but many skills have been lost as well. There are very few people today who would know how to use a spinning wheel, never mind make clothes with one.

Back then, there were two healing women living in Erris. One woman was based in Ardmore and the other was in Loughaconeera. Those of us who lived closest to them didn't pay much heed to them, but they were inundated with people from other parishes and counties who came to see them in search of various cures. Not a week went by that you didn't see men and women, walking and travelling by horse, making their way to see the healers. The Ardmore woman's reputation as a healer was well-known throughout the length and breadth of Connemara and West Connacht, while the other woman's fame was more locally based. One of the reasons why the Ardmore woman was so well-known was because her house was actually located on one of the main roads going through Connemara at the time. Her house backed onto a neighbouring house that skirted the edge of the road. Many people would call into this neighbouring house before actually visiting the healer and while they were sitting there – or so the story goes – they would tell the people of the house what ailment or affliction had brought them to that place. The 'man of the house' then passed on this information to the 'witch' beforehand or at least that was the rumour anyway. Later, when the healing woman made her 'diagnosis', it was so incredibly accurate that the gullible customers were amazed at her wisdom and foresight.

We hated to see the people travelling past our house in the direction of the healers because we were superstitious too and we always feared that on their return, the people who had sought the services of the herbalists might drop some of their healing herbs near us, herbs which would bring us sickness and bad luck for the coming year. You don't hear anything about such healing women today.

Women rarely wore shoes in those days and going to Sunday

Mass, they generally carried their shoes under their arms until they were close to the chapel when they would put them on. It was the same when they were going to a market, a fair, a wedding or a wake.

November was the month for fishing and groups of neigh-bouring men would gather in a 'meitheal' and harpoon the red fish in every river and bog-lake.[12] These men often stayed out fishing all night and they brought their food with them so they wouldn't get hungry. I remember seeing a very large group of men going out one night, one man carrying a large bag of boxty cakes so that the whole crowd would be fed when the time came.[13] As luck would have it, the game-keepers on the estates surprised the fishermen that night and a right battle ensued on the edge of a lake. You weren't allowed to fish the lakes at that time without having a special licence and without paying an appropriate fee to the gentry, and when the two sides came upon one another there would be a clash that usually involved stick-fighting. The man who was carrying the huge bag of boxty on the particular night that I am recalling here was also a highly rated stick-fighter and it wasn't long before he threw down his sack of food and tore into the fray. His intervention helped them rout the game-keepers that night and when he was finished swinging his stick he went back to the bag and picked it up again as if nothing had happened. Ever afterwards that man went by the nickname of *Bacstaí* (boxty).

I once knew two men from Ballinturly who walked from Dublin to Rosmuc. One man was a big-boned 'power' of a man while the other was small, sprightly and slight. What happened was that they were working as labourers on a farm in England one day, when there was an accident. The farmer's son was supervising the work and the bigger of the two Irishmen was awkward in his movements and spiked the farmer's son in the eye accidentally as they were piking hay onto a cart. Naturally, the two Irishmen thought that they were in big trouble and decided to make a run for it. Despite the fact that they had very little money, they somehow made it back to Ireland.

One of the biggest difficulties they faced, unbelievably, was finding their way home to Galway. If one of them hadn't remembered the name of the town of Mullingar, the men would have had a real problem getting directions from anybody concerning the road between Dublin and Galway. Once they mentioned the word 'Mullingar', however, scores of people were able to put them in the right direction. The difficulty lay in the fact that the men could not speak any English and very few of the locals in that part of the world would have understood their Irish. Adding to their communication difficulties was the fact that the two men were absolutely starved with the hunger. Luckily for them, they overheard a travelling man requesting alms and having memorised the word 'charity', the men were able to use this English word to beg enough food to get them home to the Irish-speaking districts again. Their conflicting descriptions of that journey would be the source of many an argument between the pair for years afterwards as the smaller of the men had no qualms about describing the hardships they'd faced on that long walk. The bigger man was a very proud individual and hated any mention of the 'charity' that they had been forced to survive on during their journey.

The first trade that I considered as a possibility was tailoring. In those days the tailor would come to a person's house where they would make clothes for the entire family, particularly if that same family was a large one. A tailor who once stayed with us for a week put this possibility in my mind, the first day ever. This man, known as Philip the Tailor, was a well-known character throughout Connemara, and not just for his tailoring skills. In fact he was nearly as reputed for his chatty nature and the eloquence of his speech as he was for his clothes. Philip had only one leg but his disability was no hindrance to him and there was no corner of Connemara that he did not visit. He had a big wide face, I remember, with long bushy eyebrows that hid his small beady eyes. He also had the strange ability to contort his face so that when he pulled back his mouth, his facial features were nearly parallel with his ear on that side. I have never seen anybody since who could distort his features in such a manner. Although I was still just a child then, these contortions of his features didn't frighten me in any way. Funnily enough, his tricks made me happier than ever to see him arriving at our house and on those occasions when I imitated the limping movements of his crutches and his strange grimaces, my parents gave me a good slap for my troubles.

Philip Conroy was this tailor's real name and he was from the village of Ahasla originally. In those days it was customary to keep the tailor well supplied with drink while he was working in your house, and Philip was the first person I ever saw drinking a concoction of cold eggs and poitín.[14] I have a vivid memory of Philip working one day and he sitting on the half-door that was stretched flat on the floor. He had obviously had a good deal to drink already. You could always tell this by the noise that he made as he ran his iron across the cloth he was preparing. He was singing the song *Bean an Leanna* but he stopped suddenly in mid-flow and glanced over in the direction of the dresser.[15]

'Where's that again?' he asked my father. 'There's nothing better to help arrange the seams on this devil than a hen's egg and a drop of the good stuff.'

The bottle of poitín was handed over to him, as was a cup and an egg. I watched in amazement at the speed and dexterity with which he emptied the contents of the egg into the cup. All it took was the very slightest of taps on the rim of the cup and in the blink of an eye he had the egg drained into the cup, its yoke still intact. A second later and he had the mixture thrown back and swallowed, all in one gulp.

'It's the heart's nectar, that is,' Philip announced, screwing up his face.

I must have been sent out for a few minutes on an errand of some sort then, because when I returned the tailor was 'out-for-the-count'. He was stretched out flat on the floor, lying across the half-door. He was like a demon when he eventually woke up, he was so badly hung-over, and nobody would go anywhere near him for fear that he would hit us a skelp.

Boat-building was the next trade that I thought I might take up for a living. It was an accomplished boat-builder named Páidín Mhánais, the first man I ever saw wearing a knitted jersey – believe it or not – who persuaded me to consider that trade as a possibility. I remember well that first day I saw him sporting the blue knitted sailor's jersey. He was sanding down my father's boat at the time and I had the poor man tormented with requests to borrow his jersey – if only for a while. Just to annoy me one night – and to gauge my reaction – Páidín pretended to be very sick. He claimed to have terrible pain in his side and he told me that he was dying. The fact that he was on his 'last legs' made me re-double my prayers to God that I could 'inherit' the sailor's jersey and I implored God that evening to take the boat-maker with him up to Heaven. Ironic as it may seem, and despite the fact that I beseeched God to take Páidín with him into the next world that night, I was always very sensitive about doing any harm to either people or animals. Even as a child I would steer clear of a spider's web while walking along the path, rather than wilfully destroying it. The same if I came across a bird's nest with eggs or young chicks in it. I would keep an eye on it every day for fear that another animal would attack the nest and I wouldn't rest easy until the young birds had grown up and flown away.

2

My First Day at School

I can't remember anything now about my first day at school although I've been told since that I was a right wild buck that day. I suppose that I had more in common with a wild and untamed bird then, than anything else. I threw myself in under one of the seats in the classroom and I refused to come out, come hell or high water. Anybody who reached in and attempted to pull me out was met with the screeching of a wild and strange bird that had had the misfortune to be captured. In the end, the schoolmaster decided to go and get my sister Máire from the building that was the girls' school to see could she persuade me to come out from my hiding place. On the face of it, this seemed a clever strategy as Máire used to bring me to school every day and look after me generally in those first few months when I was getting used to my existence as a scholar. After a good deal of prompting, Máire managed to persuade me to come out – although I spent the rest of the day with my hands over my face out of shyness. My poor sister was mortified but what could she do?

At home that night it was explained at length to me that hiding or covering my face at school wasn't appropriate. Slowly but surely, I got used to the school and the other pupils. Although it would be easy to find fault with them, I don't blame the schoolmaster or the educational officers of the day when they pronounced me dull or 'backward' as regards my intellectual abilities. There was a reason for the fact that they came to this conclusion. Before that first day at school, and as with every other pupil in the school, I had only ever spoken Irish. Indeed, the schoolmaster himself had only known Irish as a child since it was what was spoken in his family. Now, however, we are all thrown into this bizarre environment where we were expected to forget all about our native language for the best part of each day when we were in school. This rule was so strictly adhered to that I never heard a word of Irish – spoken or taught – for the six years that I spent inside the walls of that school.

In this period of our history, neither the Irish language nor Irish culture was considered deserving of the slightest respect. The prevailing view amongst the older generation was that our culture was something useless and embarrassing that we had been saddled with and the sooner we left it all behind us the better. This was the dominant view of the 'powers-that-be' in those days also. The clergy, the state, the legal profession, the political and intellectual classes, none of them had the slightest interest in preserving or reinforcing our native culture. Worse than this, however, the intellectual class all despised everything to do with Ireland or Irishness and were hell-bent on Anglicising us as quickly as they could. What a disaster! Everybody had such an inferiority complex then that they were doing their best to promote the English language and culture everywhere and at all times.

This anecdote will explain the mindset of those days better than any other. It was one of those incidents that occur in your life that you can never forget, no matter what. I was in sixth class at the time and in addition to the many other subjects that we had to study, we were also obliged to learn off a set number of poems in the English language for the purpose of the exams. One day the schoolmaster asked me to recite one of these poems for him. His practice at that time was to stop you about halfway through any lengthy poem and leave it at that. He would go through the second half of the poem then and in this way we learned the poem off in sections and were able to memorise the words more easily. I started reciting the poem anyway – a poem called *The Raven* – as I had been instructed to do. I was sure that the master would stop me when I came to the eighth or ninth verse but what happened instead? For some strange reason – and that day was a complete exception – the master didn't tell me to stop at verse eight or nine. Instead, he motioned me to keep on going – and I lost my way in the middle of verse twenty-two. I just couldn't remember any more of that poem – hardly surprising, given that I didn't understand the meaning of any of the material that I had learned off by heart!

I learned the poem by heart after that day and I never once forgot a verse of any poem – no matter how long – after that. The ridiculous nature of this entire system was not lost on me, however. There we all were, pupils of the Irish educational system – pupils who could parrot off scores of poems in English for exam purposes, and yet we did not understand the meaning of even one of these poems. Looking back on it now, that part of the educational system was a complete sham. It was the same when it came to the learning of the catechism and the various questions that you were required to know for your confirmation. Rather than recite the catechism as it had been passed onto us at home by our parents – in the Irish language – we were obliged to undergo our questioning by the bishop in English and had to learn off a stream of questions and answers as with the English poetry.

I remember well the two questions that the bishop asked

me on my Confirmation day. They were – 'What's meant by an Act of Contrition?' and 'Say the Act of Contrition'. I had the two answers ready and on the tip of my tongue and I passed the 'examination' without any difficulty. If that same bishop had asked me the meaning of any of the words that I recited to him that day, however, I would have been in big trouble. I hadn't the foggiest idea of their meaning. I just knew how to memorise them and spout them off at the right time.

There's no doubt about it – the people of my generation received a very strange and unnatural education as regards anything linguistic or cultural. I never missed a day's school during all of the years that I attended national school. It wasn't that I wouldn't have loved to take a day off every now and then; it was just that I was too afraid of my father to do so. I used to run out the door to school every day of the year – as conscientious a pupil as you have ever seen – right up to third class. From third class to fifth class, my awe of school eased off and I never showed any interest in any aspect of my schooling or spoke about it to anyone from then on, if I didn't have to.

The same schoolmaster taught the classes in the school right up the way along. I had him for each year that I was there and he would continue teaching at that school many years after my age-group had passed through. He was a very dedicated teacher, a hardy man who never, ever missed a day's work. Fair-haired and of medium height, he was slightly stooped and sported a big wild blond-coloured moustache. The tone of his voice never changed and he was an easy-going person, an individual who rarely lost his temper. While he was a good teacher, he had no voice for singing or music which was one of the subjects we regularly covered in school. He also had one unusual physical trait, a mannerism which I never saw in anyone else throughout the years. When he was laughing he would give his head a shake and the skin and hair on his forehead seemed to recede back even further on his head. He had another strange physical quirk. He was always sneezing as well, I remember. Once he caught a fit of sneezing he couldn't stop for a good half-hour. Secretly we loved it when he got a fit of sneezing in the middle of a particular lesson and sometimes we even brought on a fit by playing a trick on him. He had a habit sometimes of leaving his pocket handkerchief on his desk and when he wasn't looking we sometimes placed the smallest piece of tobacco-ash on this handkerchief in an attempt to make him start sneezing. His sneezing probably wasn't helped by the fact that he had a good many long nose-hairs sprouting down out of his nostrils; hairs which he spent a good deal of time trying to remove. We were always coming up with new ways of tricking the master and while our tricks proved successful on occasion, more often than not we were caught out!

There were five other boys in my class and each one was a bigger rascal than the next when it came to playing tricks – all except for one lad who was so clever and circumspect that he always went by the nickname of 'Solomon'. No sooner had the master disappeared out of the class but we were up to some devilment or other. One game that we had was called 'the splits' and it involved lying back on the floor, splaying out our legs, and seeing who could stretch their feet up highest on the wall-map. One boy had much longer toes than the rest of us and he always made his mark a couple of inches higher. One day when all of us were stretched upwards and straining our feet the highest that they could go, who should suddenly arrive back into the class but the master himself. Poor 'Long-Toe' got such a fright that his toenails tore the map by accident and he pulled a couple of counties down with him!

Huge preparations went into our religious instruction for the visit of the bishop and for our confirmation. Rumours abounded and we were all 'on edge' waiting for his visit to the parish and the school as a prelude to the day of the Confirmation. If the bishop did get around to visiting us, we were very well prepared as the schoolmaster had made certain that we knew every protocol and the answer to every possible question that we might be asked. Our school was situated not far from the road on which the bishop would have to travel to reach us – so, it was possible for us to keep a close watch out for his arrival at all times. The master had taught us how to genuflect on our right knee if we were presented to the bishop and the special way that we had to kiss his episcopal ring.

We then got word that he was to visit us on a particular day and all our plans and preparations were put into action. The slightest hint or sound of a horse and car out on the road and the whole school went silent. It was so quiet that you could have heard a pin drop. Eventually, towards midday, the sound of a horse and coach was heard out on the road. The bishop was at the school gates. Our hearts were in our mouths – some of us already scouting out a patch of the classroom floor in front of us where we could genuflect when the time came. We heard the latch of the gate being lifted on the outside of the school and each one of us whispered quietly in our minds – 'He's here now!' The master went down to open the door leading off the school hall to bring the bishop in. Our master was dressed very smartly for the occasion and stepped correctly forward, his left foot in front of his right. He placed his left hand on the door-latch ready to raise it, his right hand free to kiss the bishop's ring.

He had just reached the door when it swung open quickly from the outside. One of our class fell to his knees and we all followed suit. The master bent solemnly to his knees in readiness – but who should walk in the door only Páraic Bhairbre Shaidhbhe – the master's neighbour. You never heard such an explosion of laughter as came from the whole class then. In his confusion, poor Páraic thought that everybody was laughing at him – so that he didn't notice the schoolmaster jumping to his feet like a shot – and covering up for the fact that he had been down on one knee!

'Hello there master,' announced the bemused Páraic. 'Just wanted to let you know that Máilleach na Muc is outside at the gate and he wants to speak to you for a minute.'[1]

Another huge roar of laughter went up but the master's blushes were further spared.

Another day that none of us in that class ever forgot was the day of the exams. The examiner would arrive at our school on the back of a horse and car, travelling from Cashel where he stayed in a small hotel. As with the bishop's visit we would be at 'high-doh' and readying ourselves for this visit for a good month beforehand. The day that the examiner arrived we all had to look our best. We had to wear our best clothes and look as neat as possible. We also had to make sure that we had the answers to any questions he might ask us at the ready. The examiner would be carrying three or four bags and it was the job of the schoolmaster to carry them in from the car and into the school. On this particular day, I was in fourth class and as part of his examination, the examiner told us all to write a piece of prose about sheep. When we were all finished writing in our copybooks, they were collected up and put in the examiner's bag for him to look at later. The examiner was having a quick scan of the various copies as they were being put into his bag and I remember him suddenly grabbing one of them to have a closer read. I remember the change that came over his features when he read this piece. His mouth slammed shut and his eyes narrowed. He ground his teeth in anger and let out a big roar, shouting my name in the process.

'Are you the man that shaves the sheeps?' he asked, mocking me.

Although I had no idea that I had made a serious mistake in my English, I could sense the sarcastic tone in his voice.

'Yes Sir!' I answered him, my voice shaking nervously.

I had the feeling that same inspector had it in for me somehow. The year before this he had asked me to spell the English word 'shepherd' for him and having done this to his satisfaction, he asked me the exact meaning of that word. I answered him immediately, explaining that the word 'shepherd' referred to our dog at home. After that mistake, I think that inspector had found a weakness in me, one which he was eager to exploit at any opportunity afterwards.

I remember those particular years at school as difficult ones. I was constantly hoping that the schoolmaster would forgive my very 'public' mistakes but he never said anything at all afterwards. Worse than this was the embarrassment and shame I felt at being so publicly made a fool of in this way. I didn't care one way or other about the slagging I got from the others about my mistakes. It was when I recalled my mistakes later in the privacy of my thoughts that I felt humiliated. Despite such occasional incidents or humiliations, I would never have dreamed of answering back or giving cheek to our schoolmaster. In all of the years that we were in school, I never, ever, answered him back and any time that I met him my attitude alternated somewhere between embarrassment and fear.

There was a rascal in our school at that time whose name was Donncha. He was one of those boys who had stayed on in national school for a long time and he must have been sixteen or seventeen years of age by then. His pockets were always full of buttons that he used for our games. It always amazed me how he seemed to have such ready access to so many buttons and how he would give them away with such apparent ease if he lost some of them during a game. No sooner was the schoolmaster out the door but Donncha was on his feet and shouting out the word 'Fuist' in a loud whisper.[2] He'd flick a button into the air and a mad scramble would ensue in pursuit of the button. The rush for the button would be so intense that we often didn't hear the schoolmaster's steps returning to the room. Everybody, except Donncha would be so engrossed in the scramble for the button that they wouldn't hear the master coming back into the class again and they'd get caught red-handed. Funnily enough, Donncha was never caught!

One day I managed to win the battle for the button and I felt very pleased with myself. Strangely enough, it wasn't too long before Donncha came to me asking whether he could have the button back again. That's the day that I finally realised that Donncha didn't actually have as many buttons as we all thought he did. It was all a bit of pretence on his part.

I'll never forget the day that I lost twenty-one buttons in a game with Seán Ó Máille. It was one of the worst days of my childhood. When he was playing buttons he never threw them any higher than knee-height and he used to give them a little spin with the tip of his fingers as well. There was hardly a piece of clothing at home that night that didn't have a piece cut out of it in the search for buttons. Coats, trousers, even my mother's own shawl! It was the same old story – as encapsulated in that saying 'The hope of recompense is the bane of the gambler'.[3]

I was kept at school for two years longer than any of my classmates. I was nearly a half-grown boy by then and if it hadn't been for the setting-up of the night schools at this time I would probably have been kept at school even longer, I think. I couldn't wait for my parents to give me permission to leave school but I never let on of course. If I had given any indication that I was eager to finish school, I'm convinced that my father would have probably made me stay on another year again. He was an eccentric and awkward man when it came to education matters. Many was the prayer I said to God, begging him to release me from school. It paid off in the end and I found myself attending the night school instead.

I was exactly eleven years of age when the war between America and Spain began.[4] The reason that the beginning of this war is so engrained on my mind is because the prices of some local goods rocketed at this time. The local merchants and shopkeepers decided to raise the price of flour for example, and this caused a lot of hardship for the poor people of the parish. As far as I could see there was no reason for this sudden price-hike other than that the local merchant had got together with his supplier and they had decided to hike the prices up so that the price of flour went sky-high. Flour went from eighteen pence a stone – to three and sixpence a stone – all within the space of a week.[5] You heard the older people saying then that if the shortages caused by these price-hikes went on much longer, things would get even more difficult than they had been during the days of the Famine. It was at this juncture that the first ever branch of the Society of United Irishmen was formed in our parish, an association that met after Sunday Mass at the sites of various memorials to the martyrs of the past – up at the monument stones.

My father never became a member of the association although I was too young then to understand fully why he did not do so. In political terms he was a strong Fenian, one of the older stock who had never held any truck with the agreement that had been made shortly before this between the Fenians and Parnell. In fact, it was my father who was the template for the character of Old Matthew in Pearse's *Íosagán* but that's a story for another day.[6] That this United Irishmen's association was not very radical in nature seems clear from the fact that it was in cahoots with the local police and judicial authorities. All of us who were still at school then have a good recollection of one particular meeting of the association which was held at the church after Mass one Sunday. The association had only recently been formed and it was due to be addressed by Lord Dudley who was the king of England's representative in Ireland at this time, and a man who used to rent a summer house in Rosmuc back then.

This meeting was announced about a week beforehand and the story was that it would be a great day out. We schoolchildren had to be dressed to the nines for the occasion and there were many preparations that we had to see to. We were instructed to cheer and clap when his 'eminence', Lord Dudley arrived at the church at the invitation of the United Irishmen's association and the local parish priest. The association was being officially dedicated to Lord Dudley and the dedication, on which a group of people had spent a week working, was to be read out publicly in his presence. The honour of reading out this official dedication had been bestowed on our schoolmaster and as his pupils we were required to do the necessary in terms of supporting him and directing the other local people as regards the etiquette required for such an auspicious occasion. Of course the master had already spent some time teaching us the etiquette and ritual that went with such an important occasion and all the social graces that we needed to exhibit in the presence of such an important social figure. We had to be prepared for every possible eventuality based on the behaviour and mannerisms of Lord Dudley. It made no difference whether his eminence sat down or stood up, turned this way or that, or did this particular trick or the other – it was all the same to us. We had to know the appropriate response in each situation – i.e. whether to clap or to cheer; whether to shout out our agreement or our approval – depending on the appropriateness of the circumstances.

Eventually the big day arrived and the people of the parish were all on tenterhooks. The priest was in charge of the gathering and the local shopkeepers and merchants were vying with one another to see who could sit closest to his lordship. People who considered themselves important members of the community were watching one another to see who his lordship would pay most heed to amongst the locals. The dedication was read out and the parish priest said a few words of welcome on behalf of the people of the parish. The priest announced that Lord Dudley was one of the mainstays of Home Rule and a seminal force in the campaign for Irish freedom. There was nothing that this lord wasn't capable of if the same priest was to be believed. The lord said a few brief words in response and spoke to one or two people who had pushed their way forward to stand closest to him. Then he hopped into his coach and left again. That was the sum total of what that man did for the cause of Irish freedom that day.

Shortly after this gathering, we set up the first branch of the Gaelic League in the parish.[7] I was chosen to be secretary of this new branch and its members comprised the handful of us who were attending the night school in Gortmore and the local parish priest who was the president of the branch. This branch went from strength to strength in the years following this and some of its members went on to fight for Irish independence also. It is worth noting that our members were 'mixed' in terms of political 'affiliation' and there were a few members of our branch who favoured maintaining Ireland's connection with England, including one member who was one of the last people ever to accept the title of JP (Justice of the Peace) in Connemara. Immediately after setting up our Gaelic League branch we decided to get a hall built; a hall in which to hold our local activities. We issued a call throughout the region in an effort to collect the necessary money and we managed to raise a good deal of money in this way. There had been very little progress on the construction of the hall, however, since I had begun training to be a teacher. All the money which was collected went to the Gaelic League.

I remember one particular autumn afternoon when I found myself in the post office. I was cycling home having posted my various packages and letters when I noticed a man walking in the near distance. This man was a stranger who was walking at a steady pace at one moment and then slowing down again the next – like somebody who was debating some big question in his mind. As I cycled past him, we began to chat and I told him about the fund-raising efforts we were involved in for the hall. He promptly gave me a gold sovereign as a donation towards the hall. That man was none other than Patrick Pearse. I already had an idea of what he looked like and recognised him immediately once I saw him. It took a while for it to sink in that I had been speaking to the great man. Normally, we had an idea before his visits to the Rosmuc area that he was on the way. On this occasion, he must have decided on a spontaneous visit, however, as nobody had been expecting his arrival in the area.

Other than my father and mother, the man who was the biggest influence on me during this period of my life was a former British soldier, a pensioner who had spent twenty-one years in the British army. He lived in the next village to us – Derryrush. He was a character and the difficult times he had seen during his military service in foreign countries had done nothing to diminish his spirit or his zest for life. He had spent a full eighteen years in the West Indies. He would buy the newspaper, the *Weekly Freeman* every single week and, apart from the priest, this soldier was the only person in the parish who would read the news on a regular basis. My father and I would go to visit the soldier every week where we would chat with him and listen to him read out the newspaper. We never missed a week and the soldier had a plethora of stories about the injustices and rapacity the British inflicted on so many foreign countries as part of their colonial enterprise. He had so many stories that he could have filled a book with them. The soldier received a pension of £21 a year from the British army and he would have to travel to Oughterard – a distance of more than twenty-two miles – every three months to sign for it. It was rare for him to visit Oughterard and not have a run-in with the local police who didn't like the old soldier or his political views. There was usually a brawl and the poor old soldier always came off the worst.

I was twelve years of age when the Boer War began. Nearly everyone in this part of Ireland (the west) was in favour of the Boers in that war including the old soldier who, in spite of (or perhaps, because of) the years he had spent in the British army hated the English more than the devil hates holy water. Although I was still young then, many of the major historical events of that era made a big impression on me. That was the first time that I heard mention of Major MacBride who was supporting the Boers in that war.[8] There was much talk too of a military leader named Colonel Arthur Lynch who was on the same side as the major.[9] Little did I realise then that, one day, I would find myself imprisoned in the same cell in Kilmainham Jail that had once held the major – the cell that held him before his execution in 1916. By another strange coincidence I would also find myself incarcerated only two cells away from the cell that had held Lynch in Lewes prison in England, a man who was sentenced to death by hanging. Life is strange!

In between times Lynch had spent time in France – subsequent to the Boer War – and as a political representative in Galway. After his stint in Irish politics, he was arrested and brought to England where he was sentenced to death. Lynch received a reprieve from the gallows at the very last minute. This reprieve, instigated by the English government, proved a wise move for the English in the long run as the same man travelled the four corners of Ireland enlisting men in the British army for the Great War of 1914.

It was in my last two years at school that I began for the first time to study my own native language, Irish. The Gaelic League had set up a scheme whereby prizes were allocated to the schools that agreed to teach some Irish. These grants were an incentive for the schools to promote Irish even in a small way and the main prize was awarded to the student who spoke Irish the most, both at home and at school. One notable thing about these prizes was the fact that it was the young people in the school who judged the competition and had a big influence in terms of choosing the prize-winner. The first year that the prize was allocated, the political wheeling-and-dealing and skulduggery going on was worse than anything ever seen in a general election! A boy who was very well-known amongst the local people and I were the sole contenders for the prize that year.

The week before the election, the other candidate and I canvassed as strongly as we could amongst the other pupils of the school. There was nothing that we two candidates didn't promise the other pupils if they agreed to vote for us. Whether it was the black-horned buttons that were popular back then or the 'worn-out' items that we agreed to sell at a loss – there was nothing that we didn't promise our 'constituents'. Any type of a knife was 'guaranteed' as a present to those who agreed to vote for us. A twin-bladed knife or a half-bladed one. A knife that folded and closed at either side or a knife that didn't close at all. Every type of 'bribe' was offered as an incentive to the potential voters. When it came to sweets or sweet sticks (rock) we promised them the earth and the sun. To those voters who were literate I guaranteed to let them read the books that were assigned as prizes if they agreed to vote for me and I was successful in the election. I also let on to them that they would have no opportunity of reading these same books if my rival was voted in, as the boy's father would keep the books under lock-and-key in their book cabinet which was in the village. What a range of promises and assurances were given by the candidates during that particular election! The day of the vote finally arrived. To give him his due the master made certain that the vote was conducted in a manner that was fair-and-square – by ensuring the presence of a policeman at the polling station. The schoolmaster was a conscientious man in that way. He would not like to have been seen as favouring one side over the other.

3

The Teaching Certificate

We focused more on the Irish language than on any other subject in the first year of that newly inaugurated night school. We received copies of *An Claidheamh Soluis* regularly and we tried to read them as a way of practising our written Irish.[1] That newspaper used to have advertisements for jobs as Irish teachers in it, advertisements where they were looking for Irish-speakers in particular. A good number of us who were attending the school applied for these posts but we never managed to secure a job, mainly because we did not yet have the required teaching certificates. With the help of the head of the night school, we decided to improve this situation so that we would be better positioned to secure these jobs. *An Claidheamh Soluis* always included an advertisement where the annual exam for new Irish teachers seeking to secure their appropriate certificates was publicly announced. Those entrants who were successful in the exam received the Gaelic League's certificate which qualified them as Irish-language teachers. By sitting this exam, we cleared the final hurdle in our plan to make a living as Irish teachers. Twelve of us paid the requisite half-crown that would fund the examiner who had to travel from Dublin to Rosmuc and back. The main texts on the exam syllabus at this time were the books of Fr Eugene O'Growney and the book *Tadhg Gabha*.[2] We focused carefully on these books in the month before the exam. We knew those books backwards by the end of the month – so much so that there was hardly a boy or girl in the area who didn't know the story of *Tadhg Gabha* inside-out as well.

The day of the exam was a beautiful sunny Saturday in 1903. It was the first time I ever officially laid eyes on Patrick Pearse. Aptly, Pearse turned out to be our examiner. They say that there is no memory as good as a child's memory and that was the way it turned out for me. I still remember my first sight of Pearse as if it was only yesterday. He was a young, dapper and handsome man, pale-faced and studious, with a high forehead and a thick head of black hair. He was a very timid person with that shyness that is the preserve of the loner. A silent, reserved type, he preferred listening to speaking, and he had a squint in one eye, which only seemed to add to his dapper appearance. Whether it was because I wasn't used to Irish-speakers from outside my own region, or not, I realise now that I had problems understanding a few words of Pearse's Irish. For instance, during the oral Irish exam, I thought Pearse was saying the word *portán* (crab) when he was actually saying *portach* (bog). Mind you, it may have been my nerves on that exam day that led me to mishear what he was saying. The truth of the matter is that being examined by a person as renowned as Pearse left me in a bit of a daze, that day. I was so much in awe of this man.

It must have been around the time that this exam took place that Pearse fell in love with the village of Rosmuc in particular. Instead of going back to Dublin once the exams were over, Pearse stayed that evening and the next day. He was at Mass that Sunday in Rosmuc when the priest announced that there was a scandal in the parish, one which he was too ashamed to discuss that day given that there was a stranger of high standing in the congregation.

The idea for Pearse's short story *An Dearg Daol* came from the priest's sermon that Sunday in the church. On the Monday, Pearse headed back to Dublin, travelling to Galway first by horse and cart. Not a year passed subsequent to this (i.e. between that weekend and the historic week of Easter 1916) that Pearse did not spend some time in Rosmuc. In fact, he loved Rosmuc and its people so much that he would come to live in a small cottage there from time to time. Whenever he had any holidays, he would head straight for Rosmuc for a break. When Pearse stayed in Rosmuc, he didn't hold himself aloof from the people. You would always find him down in the cabins of the poor people, speaking Irish and learning the history and lore of the Irish-speaking areas at their firesides. More often than not, he'd be recording whatever folklore and oral history he could from the older people in the community.

The local gentry and their flunkeys thought Pearse an eccentric. Why an educated man such as him was more interested in the needs and culture of the rustic poor rather than spending his time with the 'higher-ups' of society was a mystery to them. This was an era when the twin forces of Anglicisation and imperialism were pressing in on the Gaelic culture of Rosmuc, a pressure that was probably more intense in Connemara then, as compared with any other part of Ireland at this juncture. The signs of this 'aping of the English' are still there in the local landscape, even decades later in the form of 'bricks-and-mortar'. The then representative of the English king bought himself a big house in the vicinity – a place where he and all the other gentry passed both the summer and autumn seasons. It was here that the gentry entertained any 'social climbers' and made them feel that they were important while secretly mocking them behind their backs. These pretend 'gentry' would imitate the English aristocrats and spread their ways and customs throughout the countryside. There is no group that doesn't have its fawning lackeys and its hangers-on, I suppose.

The English gentry did their best to ingratiate themselves with the local people too, by inviting all of the schoolchildren of the area to big parties that they used to hold on the front lawn of their estates. The local schoolmaster had no option but to send the schoolchildren along, as he wasn't given any choice in the matter. It wasn't politically helpful either to insult the king's local representative and the schoolmasters feared the potential repercussions if they 'stood up to' the English. Once the children were 'fed and watered' at these parties, they would have a man who came over from London show them moving pictures. There was no party if the man with the moving pictures wasn't available and his arrival in the vicinity would always coincide with the announcement of an upcoming party.

The films he showed always depicted British military heroes, people who had come from poor backgrounds (such as the children watching the films had) and 'made good' or become famous by performing heroic deeds in the service of the British army. We didn't really realise the harmful influence that such propaganda was having at this time.

Patrick Pearse did see the insidious nature of what was going on, however, and he soon put a plan in place to counteract what the gentry were doing. News soon spread through the countryside that all of the locals, both young and old, were invited to a night of entertainment in the school at Turloughbeg organised by Pearse. It was a great night of poetry, storytelling, song and speeches, at the end of which Pearse had organised for a man from Dublin to show us a film about the rich history and culture of our own country and people – Ireland and the Irish. Pearse was an animated figure that night and his speech was the best that I ever heard from him, his oration at the grave of O'Donovan Rossa notwithstanding.[3] People had walked ten miles and more to this celebration of their own culture and to listen to a man who told them that their culture and history were worthy of support and enormous respect. Pearse's speech that night and, indeed, that whole event, left a lasting impression on those who attended. Pearse had struck an important blow for Irish cultural 'freedom' that night, one as important as any blow he would later strike as part of the armed struggle. Interestingly, the English gentry never held another party for the locals on their estates after that, a fact which really irritated their lackeys and hangers-on. That Pearse himself was very happy with the success of that cultural evening is clear from his short story *Na Bóithre*, a story that he wrote shortly afterwards. He also asked me to write an account of that night's events for *An Claidheamh Soluis*, a request that I duly complied with. There isn't a square foot of earth in Rosmuc that doesn't appear somewhere in Patrick Pearse's writings. While many of the local people and places which are mentioned in his work have passed on or have become part of our cultural memory, there are others still with us.

Pearse heard the plot of what became his short story *Ábhar an tSagairt* only half a mile down the road from where he stayed himself in Rosmuc. What sorrow! It is many years now since news of that priest's death came to us from America. And Brídín – whose character is described beautifully in that story *Bairbre* – was a nun who was doing God's work far away on the missions. Pearse's cottage, where the great man wrote a good deal of his literature, is actually situated in the place known as Allmore, the place where Eoghainín na nÉan waited for the swallows to arrive. Dearg Daol is long gone from this place and so too is An Gadaí, the great crime which he committed as a young man now long-forgotten. Nóra Chóil Labhráis is in a faraway country where the roads are scarce – a place where, on occasion, she recalls the verses composed in her honour at the party of Turloughbeg.

Pearse was actually staying in Rosmuc when the body of O'Donovan Rossa was brought home from America. It was in Rosmuc that he put his famous speech for the graveside oration together. It was from Rosmuc, too, that he set out to collect the weapons that were secretly smuggled into Ireland in 1914. Pearse had also brought Liam Mellows (God's grace to both men's souls) to Rosmuc a long time before the IRA Volunteers were set up in that vicinity. Liam Mellows was actually working as a travelling teacher for Fianna Éireann at the time and between them, they had set up a branch of the Fianna in Rosmuc.[4] In fact, it was from poor Liam Mellows' mouth that we locals first heard the song *Óró, 'Sé do Bheatha Abhaile*.

Once the structures were in place for organising the Volunteers in the vicinity, Pearse did not rest until he had set up Volunteer battalions not only in Rosmuc, but also in Carraroe and in Garmna Island. Not only did Pearse undertake the work of travelling teacher in relation to these groups, but he was also the commanding officer for all three areas.

Looking back now, those were truly wonderful days! We raw recruits lined up in our new and spruce uniforms, some of us unclear as to which was our left foot and which was our right – our battalion leader patient and yet firm in his instructions. At the end of each night's drilling routines, Pearse made a point of speaking to all of us before we went home and I will never forget the fiery idealism and enthusiasm that was written in his features. In addition to our various drilling and weapons routines, Pearse also oversaw three hours of athletics for us each week. We were all intensely loyal to him and gave it our all, irrespective of what tasks he assigned to us. Proof of this was the fact that only three members of our company went to the other side when the IRA split during the Civil War.

Mayoman Michael Timoney was the thirteenth man in our group to take the Gaelic League exams in Gortmore that day. He was a few years older than the rest of us. A thick-set man with a sunburnt face, he sported a big red bushy beard. He had actually arrived into the area sooner than Pearse. Given his age, the schoolmaster assumed that he was the visiting examiner and didn't ask any questions. He just collected Michael from the train station and brought him to his house. When the 'real' examiner arrived into the village, he had to find lodgings somewhere else as Michael had already taken his bed. Michael Timoney did huge work on behalf of the Irish language throughout his life. There was nowhere in County Mayo that he didn't walk or cycle to note down and preserve the cultural jewels of the Mayo dialect of Irish and a great deal of the material he recorded would have been lost forever otherwise. He wrote like a demon even as the Irish language was dying in certain parts of Mayo and he published the results of his researches in such valuable works as *Amhráin an Iarthair* and *Tairngaireacht Bhriain Ruaidh*. He also spent a long period of his life living in Australia – both in the years before that Irish exam and afterwards – and was one of the first students of Coláiste Chonnacht in Tourmakeady. It was Michael, too, who collected the money to erect the memorial stone in Lahardan to Fr Ó Conaire, a priest who was hanged by the English in Castlebar during the Year of the French (1798).

It was around the same time as the Irish exam that the first motor car visited my home place. It was a Sunday when this car hove into view and it frightened the living daylights out of both people and animals for miles around. A bunch of us (men and boys) were playing a game of rounders on Curraninver when we heard this strange noise making its way towards us. We stopped the game and scanned the horizon to see where the noise was coming from. The engine of the car slowed as it reached the top of the hill but the noise of this strange creature – that was without head or legs – increased again as it made its way in our direction. It came down through some trees and made as if straight for us where we were playing on the road, and you never saw a bunch of fellows run for cover as quickly as we did that day. We dived into ditches and ran into the shelter of the rocks. The cattle and sheep were already sprinting towards the hills in shock and they were soon only black dots on the horizon. We didn't come out from our hiding places until this fast-moving machine had put a good distance between us. Later, we heard that this motor car belonged to a representative of the king of England, a member of the British gentry who was touring the area.

Oysters were very plentiful when I was young and they were eaten as food or bartered for export. By law, we locals were not allowed to collect any of these oysters as the English landlords held claim to all of the beaches and shore-lines and had wardens employed whose duty it was to prevent any local people from collecting oysters or other types of shellfish. These wardens would patrol the shorelines around the clock in the summer and worked at the oyster-dredging during the winter months. Oyster-dredging was paid by the day and the wardens received additional payments, depending on how many hundredweight of oysters they managed to collect daily for the landlord. Anybody caught illegally taking oysters could expect a heavy fine or a period of imprisonment, if caught. The wardens were very loyal to their masters, more loyal even than the policemen of that era and many a starving person found himself nabbed while trying to gather a few oysters under cover of night.

One night a man who was starving went out under cover of darkness to see could he get a few hundred oysters and secretly sell them in Oughterard. Somehow the unfortunate man was caught out in the changing of the tide and he drowned. The next morning his body was found on the shore, his small bag of oysters beside him. One of the oyster-wardens found the body and instead of commiserating with the man's widow and children, he actually served her with court papers – in order to fine her for the oysters her dead husband had 'taken' from the sea. The widow, whose case was tried in English – so that she couldn't understand a word of what was taking place – was duly given a heavy fine. Worse again was the fact that the warden never informed the court that the woman's husband had drowned. Instead he said that 'the man has left the area a while ago and his whereabouts are unclear'.

Despite these hazards and attendant tragedies, there were always people who had no option but to go poaching – and who sometimes managed to get away with a few hundred oysters that they could subsequently sell. If they were successful in their poaching, they would have to walk about eighteen miles to Oughterard – often cross-country in darkness and carrying the bags of oysters on their backs – where it was possible to sell them without being caught. Even then, they would be lucky to get a crown for a hundredweight of the oysters. Life was difficult in those days, that is for sure!

One night a neighbour of ours, Neda, had a couple of hundred oysters to sell. He was due to leave our village at nightfall but he was a nervous type of person, a person who was afraid of the dark. He wouldn't even go down the road from his house to ours at night unless he had someone with him for company. For the trip to sell the oysters, he had arranged to go with my brother Micil, because Micil was going to Oughterard anyway. In order to get from his own house to ours in the dark, Neda had asked my mother earlier that same day if she would send me down to his house as company for him. We regularly had people from neighbouring houses over to our house at night for singing and storytelling and this night was one of those nights. Neda and I walked from his house to mine as soon as darkness fell and we made a plan for later as we walked – one which would ensure that none of the neighbours knew what his plan was with regard to the oysters and Oughterard. He would go into our house and join in the talk and the singing for a while and when he gave me the nod I was to go out of the house and wait for him outside. He would come out later and give a little whistle and then we would pick up the oysters and walk down to where he would meet Micil. Micil and he would then go on to Oughterard while I went home – it was a long journey to Oughterard after all, even for a grown man who was used to walking long distances.

Initially, everything went according to plan. Neda gave me the signal and I went outside. Instead of waiting for him on the road as we had arranged, however, I decided to play a trick on him and hid myself in the bog nearby. Neda came out after a short while and whistled but I didn't stir from my hiding place. He whistled again and again and I could hear him stepping impatiently up and down the road. He went back into the house then and told my mother that there was no sign of me outside. When my mother heard that I was missing, she became hysterical. She began to scream blue murder and told everybody in the house to get out quickly and go searching for me. Neda meanwhile, was trying to calm my mother down – although he wasn't doing a very good job. 'Don't worry. Dead or alive, we'll find him in no time Máire Ní Shúilleabháin,' I could hear him saying to my poor mother.

'You're a fine one Neidín boy, aren't you? What sort of a comfort is that to me – that my young boy might be found dead with your rotten oysters.'

'Hey, hey. There's no need to tell the whole world what I was doing with those oysters Máire!'

I watched Neda emerge from the house and come down the path shouting out my name as my mother gave out stink to him. My poor mother was now keening at the top of her voice and slapping her hands together – 'My poor little son! My poor little son that I will never see again!' I decided it was time to appear from out of the undergrowth then. The whole crowd who were looking for me seconds earlier now wanted to lynch me – and my mother, who moments before had been crazy with grief, was now trying to hit me!

The original arrangement made between Neda and I had involved a good deal of negotiation. In fact, that same night when we went in search of the oysters was the night when we were due to discuss what my payment would be for accompanying Neda in the darkness. We agreed that my payment should be a penny and so I asked Neda to bring me a handball (which was valued at a penny) back from Oughterard with him. I had seen the schoolmaster's son with a handball shortly before this and I wanted to have one also. 'If I was in your shoes,' Neda advised me, 'I wouldn't bother with a handball. You'd be much better off getting a half-ounce of tobacco. There would be more demand for a payment like that whereas with a handball; what use would that be to anyone? The first time it is hit against the wall it'll puncture and then it'll be no good to anyone.'

Once he saw that he was getting nowhere with this line of argument, Neda changed tack. 'It'll probably be cheaper for me to bring back the ball, I suppose. The ball only costs a penny whereas the tobacco costs a penny and a half. I'd have to make up the half-penny difference out of my own pocket. Mind you, that wouldn't bother me so much really, since the tobacco would be more useful to everybody all-around.' He was only wasting his time, of course. It was the handball that I was interested in getting and nothing else. When he returned from Oughterard, believe it or not, Neda had bought neither the handball nor the tobacco. It was a while before I forgave him for that, I can tell you!

4

How I Began Writing in Irish

When I was young, I was a real home-bird. I preferred to stay at home, doing odd jobs in and around the house. I was never asked to do any heavy work around the place. I remember well the day that I earned my first ever shilling. I went with my father on his *púcán* to the Aran Islands where we were delivering turf.[1] I was promised a shilling for my work, which was a lot of money at that time. *Amhráin Choilm a Bhailís* had just been published as a book and I had promised myself that I would buy it with my first ever wage. It was a beautiful day as we sailed out to Aran, one of the finest summer days that you would ever see in this part of the world. As it happens, it was my first time to be out sailing with my father. The tidal currents carried us as far as Golam Head. The sea was incredibly calm, not a whisper of a breeze in the air. Then all of a sudden, the wind picked up and the sails began to flap. The colour of the sky changed and the surface of the sea darkened. It was incredible how quickly everything had changed, the waves now chopping around us. 'The weather's turning a bit rough, there's a dash of rain on the way,' I said to my father.

'Don't worry son, we'll have the worst of it ridden out before the storm gets anywhere near us,' my father answered and I noticed him glance back hopefully in the direction from which the gusts of wind were flying. We reached Portmurvy by midday but since this port was not particularly suitable for sailing ships – especially in changeable weather – we did not beach her there. We waited there for a half-tide but there was no sign of anybody who wished to buy turf. In the afternoon we headed to Kilronan where we spent the night. The following morning 'Seán Bán, an báiceara' bought the turf from us for ten shillings.[2] My father emptied the full load of turf out against the quay wall and we headed for home again. I insisted on getting my pay of a shilling from my father before we left Aran. We made good time on the way back and were home again on the mainland early that afternoon. The next day was the feast day of Peter and Paul when there was always a pattern on Droim a' Báire in Kilbrickan. After Mass that day, myself and a group of other young lads waited back at the pattern. I was so tempted by the goods available at the various stalls that I spent three pence from my shilling on apples. Apples were actually a rare enough commodity in our part of the world at that time. Of course there was nobody more sorry than me the day after the pattern when I realised that I had spent so much on the apples that I didn't have enough to buy the book *Amhráin Choilm a Bhailís*. It was quite a while after this before I again managed to saved enough money to buy a book and once I had the requisite amount saved, I kept a tight rein on the money, I can tell you.

Another way in which I earned some money at this juncture was working on a road construction job. A shilling a day was the pay on this job and I spent many days that spring carrying a basket of sand on my back from one section of road to another. We had a well-organised group for this work, hauling sand. Some of us were filling the baskets while others lifted them onto the backs of the other men; there was a line of us standing equidistant from one another. If we didn't follow the system correctly the ganger who was in charge of us, and who never missed a trick, would let a roar out of him that could be heard for miles around. We weren't allowed to speak to the others with whom we were working, despite the fact that we would only have been consulting about the work itself anyway. You had to speak to the ganger or keep your mouth shut. I never worked in a job that was so demanding and many is the time that I thought back on those days when years later I found myself incarcerated in an English prison. To tell you the truth there was not such a big difference between this road work and prison – particularly with regard to the necessity of remaining silent. We worked twelve hours a day on that road job and we were lucky the weather was so beautiful that year; from the time that we started the work until the time that the job finished on St John's Eve we only had one half-day of bad weather.

There was one man there who always took it easy when we were working, a man by the name of Briain. This man had spent some time working in America and he knew how to pace himself on a day's work. For every three baskets of sand the rest of us carried, he only brought one. There was scarcely a walk up and back that he didn't stop to tie one of his shoelaces or open one of them. If he wasn't messing with his shoes, he was rearranging his clothes or sorting out the strap on his basket. If he took off his shoe to empty out some sand once, he must have taken it off ten times. One day I was silly enough to try to imitate his tricks. I had hardly carried my second basket of the day when the foreman came over to me to give me a warning. If I didn't desist from my antics I would get what was coming to me. I never could understand why that foreman didn't challenge Briain whom everybody knew was taking it easy whenever possible.

That winter I began trying to write fiction and poetry in the Irish language for the first time. The old stories that the people told to one another around their fires at night were a form of literature, in my view. To be able to write in the Irish language and get my writings published in a journal such as *An Claidheamh Soluis* seemed like the greatest thing on earth to me, especially as Pearse used to send us on free copies of *An Claidheamh* on a regular basis. Once, shortly after this, Pearse was in Rosmuc for a short period and I called up to him to show him some of my Irish-language essays. I found him very encouraging in relation to the stories. He advised me to forward some of the traditional stories which I had transcribed from the older locals in the area so that he could see about getting them published. The first one that I decided to send on to Pearse was actually *Scolb Glas Mac Rí in Éirinn*, a story I had actually transcribed from my own father. A while later Pearse published it in *An Claidheamh Soluis* and you never saw a happier man than me the day I picked up the newspaper and saw my story in print. That first story was quite a long one and it appeared in sections in the *An Claidheamh* over a period of seven or eight weeks.

From that time onwards I continued collecting stories and poems that were in the oral tradition of the various western townlands roundabout. When I had written down a good selection of stories, Pearse advised me to send them onto the *Coiste na Leabhar* that was then run by the Gaelic League. I did as he advised and this collection was eventually published as *An Fíbín*. When I first started writing up these stories, everybody in the locality was quite derisory about it. I suppose they probably thought that I was just wasting my time. *An Fíbín* wasn't long in print, however, when I was sent a royalty of £5. I wasn't long letting everybody know about this large sum of money, I can tell you. Back then, if somebody had earned a seventh of that price for a cow at the fair or any other successful transition – they would have been over the moon. And to earn money for writing down ancient stories and poems; most people would have found that difficult to credit. If it wasn't for the fact that the postmaster had cashed the cheque for me, nobody would have believed that I had earned this sum of money at all. The postman was an honest man, a man who wasn't given to exaggeration and so the locals had no option but to believe him! Those who had been teasing me earlier were laughing on the other side of their faces now. Before you knew it, every Tom, Dick and Harry who had even a smattering of written knowledge in relation to Irish, was travelling the local villages trying to record folklore and poetry. Whether their efforts ever came to anything, I haven't heard.

It was around this time that I first heard talk of the phenomenon known as 'provincialism'. I didn't understand then what the basis of this provincialism was, but I was certainly aware of it from then onwards as the Gaelic League itself was rife with it. Right down to the organisation's newspaper, *An Claidheamh Soluis*, this provincialism ruled the roost. The newspaper's editor had to be careful not to include more of one Irish province's dialect than another. I even have in my possession a letter from Pearse where he discusses the scourge that this provincialism was for the Irish language movement at this juncture. It is important to give a sense of the pervasive nature of this problem – as it related to the Gaelic League, in this case – for the younger people who might be reading this book and who may not have experienced such a phenomenon. Jealousy, rivalry, competition and the insistence on one group's rights over another, were all at the source of this problem. One province vied with the other in relation to which had the purest or richest Irish. Loyalty to your own province and the Irish language was the motive for this provincialist outlook, but it still caused huge problems for the Irish language movement in its early years. One province wanted their dialect of Irish and their Irish-language writers promoted more than another's. If the Irish-language groups in one province brought in a new or positive development, for instance, another province would be very slow to bring in a similar measure in their region, even if that same development would have bolstered the Irish language in their area. There was hardly any aspect of the Gaelic League at the time that wasn't infected with this 'provincialist' disease and the annual ard-fheis would see it all come out into the open.[3]

It is no exaggeration to say that this provincialism nearly destroyed the Gaelic League. There was one particular Munster writer who wrote for the *Freeman's Journal* at this time.[4] Some of the more senior members of the Gaelic League lobbied for at least one Connacht man to be appointed to the committee which produced this newspaper. Their lobbying eventually paid off and a writer from Connacht was appointed instead of the writer from Munster. The Munster contingent weren't happy, however, and a special national convention was held to discuss this issue and deal with their complaints. The Gaelic League nearly split over it and the bitterness of the controversy ensured that the Gaelic League was severely weakened as an organisation for many years afterwards.

Tea was not as commonly available a commodity then as it is now. Back then you might have one cup of tea a day, but that was it. Irish people continued to have potatoes every morning for their breakfast in many villages also and it was only at nightfall that they might drink their cup of tea. The thought occurred to me one day that I should travel beyond the boundaries of my own parish in order to gather folklore from the older people in the neighbouring villages. One Monday, I took the road for Erris in Mayo, with the intention of spending the week there collecting folklore. My people were very surprised then to see me back home again on the following night. When they enquired what had brought me back I told them I would be unable to put pen to paper without a drop of tea in the morning. I realise now that tea would put people in a good mood back then. It was like a minor drug and there was no end to the amount of stories and poetry the people I was taking down the material from would recount, once they had a cup of tea. It gave them a lift and boosted their confidence when it came to reciting the stories. Tea had nearly the same effect on people then as a drop of alcohol does today.

It was the feast day of Peter and Paul 1907.[5] It was a day to make the lint blow, it was that warm.[6] The sun was already high in the sky as I climbed out of bed early that morning. It slanted halfway across the peak of Knockadaff from where I looked up over the gable-end of the house. The sun was an early riser on this particular morning, just as I was myself. The morning air was still a little chilly but as the sun climbed higher its heat filled the air and covered the earth, and the cold wasn't long lifting. Shortly before this, I had decided that 'today was the day of decision'. Before this, I had never travelled more than a day's distance from home. Now I was going to spend a full month away from home and such a change was going to be a shock to the system. Tourmakeady, County Mayo was my destination; the recently founded Irish college there to be precise. There were very few cars in our parish back then and the few that existed would never have undertaken a journey that long anyway. There was no such thing as a coach service either. It was shank's mare or nothing. I hit the road in my bare feet, my leather satchel on my back. My mother, my sister Sorcha and a neighbouring girl by the name of Máire Bheairtlín had climbed to the top of the tallest hill in the area where they stood weeping. The three women stayed there and showered me with blessings until I had walked out of sight.

Tourmakeady is fifty miles from home. I was strong and fit then and as we had experienced a drought for some time before this I cut across the mountains to shorten the road. I paused on the shoulder of Shannavara hill and looked down at the village. Once I passed the top of the hill my home place would be out of sight. I felt a loneliness come over me and with a heavy heart I sat down on the crest of the hill and sobbed a little. My mother's sensitive nature had broken through in me again. The morning sky was warm and clear but just at that very moment a cloud passed across the sun. The sunlight turned a darker combination of purple-black as the clouds chased one another across Shana-conroy hill. I took this as a bad omen.

Then I spotted a herd of newly shorn sheep relaxing close to a small pool of water nearby. Grazing quietly in the cool shade of the water, the sheep were the picture of relaxation as they munched away on the scutch grass, their jaws working like quiet little engines. The quiet calm of the sheep infused the air and I felt happy that they were there at that particular moment, given the anxiety and sorrow that was running through my thoughts. Weren't they lucky, these sheep – grazing away there without a care in the world? If I could have swapped places with them there and then, I would readily have done so.

Just then I heard a loud shout from behind me and my reverie was broken. A tall, wild-looking man was making his way towards me. He was big and lanky and he had two big bunches of hair sprouting from his nostrils! From the look of him, I could tell that this strange-looking man was not a local. He sported a beard shaved in the shape of a horseshoe and he was wearing a battered-looking tweed suit and cap – all shop-manufactured.[7] There was nobody local that I wouldn't have recognised either, of course.

'Listen up,' was the first thing he said to me. 'You didn't come across any sheep on your travels, did you?'

'Look, there's a herd of sheep below,' I answered, nervously, pointing in the direction of the water pool.

The man didn't register any interest in my response and asked me another question instead.

'Do you speak English?'

'I have a couple of words, or so they tell me anyway.'

'You can bet you don't have as much English as I do,' the man said and before I could utter another word, he launched into the following ditty:

Hoky poky, penny a lump,
The more you ate, the more you jump!

I stared at him transfixed as he went on to recite the following:

I am the air
I am the clouds
I am the sun
I am the moon
I am …

I was rooted to the spot and tried to avert my eyes from his. I did manage to steal a quick sideways glance in his direction once or twice and the thought crossed my mind that this strange man had the look of somebody whose heart and mind were somewhere else, in some place that was beyond this sphere of existence. He was the most unusual and otherworldly person that I had ever come across. With every line he recited, he struck a grassy mound in front of him with his stick, as if in emphasis. He showed no sign of slowing down but continued with his rhyming rant until I decided to make a run for it. He let a roar out of him as I sprinted away across the heather but I didn't look behind me again until I had put a good distance between him and me.

I kept running until I made my way out onto the main road, a road that was known as New Road, which was a good mile and a half away. I didn't dare look behind me during this run for fear the strange man was following me and would give me a belt of the stick across the head. 'Caught or not, I have to stop,' I said to myself, after I had got as far as the road – as I was completely out of breath. I had a good look around and there was no sign whatsoever of the English-speaking man. I was mightily relieved and sat down to have a rest. The one good thing about the whole incident was the fact that the fright I'd got had made me forget all about my sadness at leaving home. From that moment on, I never felt the same loneliness or home-sickness again.

I never did find out anything about the strange man I encountered on the mountain that day, either. Despite many enquiries over the years, I never heard who he was, or anything else about him. Over the years since, I've often thought that I owe a debt of gratitude to that eccentric individual in a strange sort of way. Before my encounter with him that day there had been a part of me that was still undecided as to whether to continue with my journey or return to the safety of home.

Unknown to him, that man had forced me to make my decision and to break out into the big world that lay beyond my home village.

After I was well-rested, I hit the road again. I made my way through Killbeg and Shanadooley until I came to the crossroads at Maumwee, a place that skirted the railway line. I'd always been told to be wary of a road like this because if you went too close to the train, its power could suck you in under its wheels as it roared past. The main road that I was following actually crosses the railway line at the intersection in Maumwee. Reluctantly enough, I made my way towards the gates of the railway crossing and had a quick look up and down the line. There was no sign of any train and with my heart pounding I ran through the level crossing. As before I didn't stop running until I had left the danger well behind.

Near Sruthán na Samhlachán, I came upon two carters who were transporting barrels of beer to Leenane. As the peak of Maumwee was closer now, I slowed down the pace of my walking. I was glad of some company because it is well-known – since the day when Páidín an Roisín came across the witch late at night there – that Maumwee is a tough and lonely uphill climb.[8] The carters started chatting to me and when I told them where I was headed one of the men said he felt sorry for me. 'You'll never walk all of that way,' he said. 'You've no idea how many mountain passes, glens, hills and plains you still have ahead of you. It's unusual country up there, full of strangers and desolate woodland.'

The carter gave me a wink and tipped the horse with his whip. The poor horse was already struggling against the incline with the weight of the barrels it was dragging behind it. The carter said nothing for a moment. He was a clever man of course and he was giving it a few minutes for his words to sink in. At that moment, I thought to myself that 'this man is a kindly person who is trying to give me some useful advice for the journey ahead'. For some reason, I changed my mind about him a moment later, however, and became suspicious of him. I just got the sense that there was something suspect or dishonest about him. He was the first to break the silence.

'You'd need a car for a journey as long as that,' the carter said, and I got the feeling that it irritated him how little notice I was taking of his advice.

'Walk on ahead of me until you get to Leenane tonight. As tomorrow is Sunday I'll travel on further with you at around midday.'

I thanked the man for his kindness and his advice but told him that as I had already travelled a good distance, I didn't want to break my journey. As he had pointed out, tomorrow was Sunday and I, too, could use the day to complete my journey. I wasn't as sure of this man now and wanted to make a clean break with him. The carter didn't seem too pleased as I said goodbye to him and speeded up in my walking.

'Mind yourself on Maumtrasna' were the last words he said to me as I disappeared out of earshot. The carter's mention of Maumtrasna mountain was supposed to frighten the life out of me, I think. The further I walked into the mountains, the more I noticed the land becoming less rocky and craggy. The mountains were smoother and grassier here than back home and the gaps between the mountains were wider. Everything was bigger here; the rocks were huge and the dried-out chasms between the hills were huge and gaping. I took out the lunch that my mother had made for me before leaving home and ate it at the top of Guigeallach Road. Once I'd eaten some food and rested a bit, I was as lively again as a kid goat. I made my way along the lonely Benwee road without meeting a soul on the way. I arrived at an tEas Dubh from where I could see the sun radiating on the hill across from me, the bright sunlight like an enormous white hand. The waterfall at Alduff is nestled in a hidden mountain glen. It is here that Diarmaid Ua Duibhne is supposed to have rested on his journey around Ireland; the place still carries his name.[9] While I have had the privilege of seeing such famous waterfalls as Niagara, the historic waterfall of Red Hugh and the waterfall known as Torannbridge in West Connacht, none of these sites hold a candle to the Alduff waterfall in my view.[10] The beautiful clear waters of Maamturk thunder down onto this waterfall and when the water finally hits the bottom, it shoots in a spray that can be felt up to 100 feet away. There was a unique sense of solitude to be felt in that place. A lonelier and more isolated glen one has never seen. Hills on all sides, the valleys and glens were green and fresh with vegetation. The hills which were closest to me were lush and green while those furthest away appeared as a hundred shades of blue.

As the evening light fell back into the earth once more, the sun formed dark shapes and shadows, statuesque silhouettes on the hills far away. The retreating shapes and shadows reminded me of the movements of the tide. I watched the changing landscape with a sense of wonder and awe from the very bottom of the glen. It got dark quickly in the depths of the glen as the sun faded. Far away on the peak of Maumtrasna, however, the sun held out stubbornly for as long as it could.

My path eventually took me into a small village that I didn't know the name of. A couple of scattered houses faced one another on either side of the street and one or two people passed me as I walked up the village. I ran into an old man near the edge of a wood. As night was about to fall I decided it was a good time to find some shelter for the night.

'Come with me,' the old man said. 'My hearth is nothing worth talking about but you're welcome to stay there if you wish.'

I accepted this offer gratefully. This man was elderly and weather-beaten-looking but he surprised me how quickly he could walk. The two of us headed down a boreen in the direction of his house. The road was decorated with wildflowers on both sides. It was the same all around the house itself, front and back, where the air was pungent with a hundred different perfumes. If the old man was generous and welcoming, his wife was even more so. She was kindness personified. Their house was cosy, warm, and very neatly kept. They gave me a fine dinner and then we pulled into the fire for a chat. I told them everything about my travels, everything I had seen and heard.

'You're able to read and write Irish then?' the old man asked.

'I'm supposed to be,' I said.

Next thing, the man opened a small cupboard that was off to a corner of the hearth, from where he pulled out a big heavy book.

'Would you be able to read any of this, I wonder?' the old man said handing me the book.

The book was a Bible written in the Irish language, the script in the old Gaelic print. I began reading the book but found myself confused by certain letters in the older Gaelic alphabet that I had never come across before. I don't think I made a great job of reading it. I didn't get the impression that the old man was too impressed with my efforts, to be honest. That was the first time I had ever seen the old Gaelic alphabet. The woman of the house noticed that I was having real difficulties reading the Bible and she put me out of my misery.

'Leave the book aside now, let you, and let the stranger go to sleep,' she said to her husband.

The woman was only trying to distract her husband, of course. There was no question of us heading off to bed. We stayed awake and chatted happily for many hours after this. At one point, she mentioned that women from Erris who went from place to place peddling dulse had visited their townland some years before and the herbal remedies they sold had not come cheap.

It was well past dawn by the time that I gave in and felt the softness of the bed sheets beneath me. The old woman was as lively and sociable a person as you could ever meet but she was crippled with rheumatism. She thought that if she was living closer to the sea, she'd never suffer any real sickness or pain. She was convinced that anybody who lived near the sea would not suffer from rheumatism or arthritis. What wouldn't she give for a couple of bottles of sea water that she could use as a balm for her ills? When I saw how much a bottle of sea water would mean to this woman, I promised her that when I came that way again, I would be sure to call into her with a bottle of sea water. Even better than this, I would also make sure to bring her a concoction made of seal oil, the best remedy ever for rheumatism.

For a long period subsequent to that evening, I intended to call but my good intentions faded over the course of time. I never did get back to visit that couple and bring the remedy with me, I am ashamed to admit. Perhaps I would have done so one day – although I heard that the old woman died just a short time afterwards. God called her home to himself, that woman who was the very soul of generosity and kindness. No sooner did my head hit the pillow that night but I was fast asleep. I travelled every corner of Connacht at different times and yet I can honestly say that I was never treated with such kindness and hospitality as I experienced that night in Tomás Ó Cadhain's in Dooletter on the banks of Loch na Fuaidhe.

I must have been very tired that night because the woman of the house didn't disturb me in the morning and I slept in much later than I would normally sleep. When I had eaten breakfast the old woman even made me a packed lunch for the day ahead. I expressed my deep gratitude to the couple and said goodbye. The couple's son accompanied me for the first mile of my journey.

Not so far away from where this couple was living was Maumtrasna. This part of the country was as isolated an area as you could find, a place where an entire family was murdered in the year 1882. These killings were particularly brutal and their import was felt throughout that part of Connemara for many years afterwards. From childhood onwards, I had heard about these killings and the way in which they had impinged upon subsequent relationships amongst the local community. Unsurprisingly, I felt a sense of dread as I walked in the direction of where this crime had taken place. I felt a cold sweat on my back and it was as if the presence of those dead people could still be felt in that place. Circling the upper edges of the mountain, I could see down into the dark valley where the killings had taken place so many years before. The bare ruins of the cottage where the murders occurred were still visible and I increased my pace of walking to put as much distance as possible between myself and that place. I didn't rest until I had reached the houses in Derrypark, a townland where some of the brakes constructed by the police during the era of the Land War were still standing.[11] There were still a few elderly people living in that parish who had once worked for the English king's representatives and it was they who made sure that all of these lean-tos were not completely gone to rack and ruin. An assassination attempt on Old Robinson, once the landlord's rent-collector and lackey in Ballinahinch, had taken place here years before. Some of the locals had shot at him while he was sitting in a horse and car, two policemen on either side of him. Unfortunately for the local country-people who were evicted at his hands, Robinson had been wearing a secret suit of body armour under his clothes, a thick metal plate which covered him from the top of his shoulders downwards. If they had only known this, the shooters would have realised that aiming their shots at his heart was a waste of time. The fact that Robinson's two bodyguards were extremely drunk and unable to get their guns out to fire back only rendered this missed opportunity more frustrating for the would-be assassins.

The last slivers of sun were disappearing from view when I reached Tourmakeady. The next day was 1 July 1907. It was the first day of term and the day that I met Mícheál Breathnach, the headmaster of Coláiste Chonnacht for the first time. Mícheál was a tall thin man with a tan moustache and black curly hair. He had small hawk-like eyes that were green and piercing and you knew by the look of him that he was an intelligent man. He was an excellent conversationalist and a good mimic in addition to being talented at both singing and writing. A highly educated man, he was a brilliant teacher.

My God! Little did we realise on that first sunny day of class in Coláiste Chonnacht that poor Mícheál was not long for this earth. By year's end, he had passed on to his eternal reward.

There were about twelve of us in the class that year, each of us aware of how privileged we were to have Mícheál and Seán

Ó Ruadháin, another talented writer, as our teachers. It was about this time that the monthly newspaper *An Connachtach* was founded. Dr Tomás Breathnach was the newspaper's editor at the very beginning and Seán Mac Giollarnátha quickly followed him in the post. Mícheál Breathnach was a regular contributor of both prose and poetry to this newspaper; he wrote essays and poems with fluency and style. Unfortunately, as with many Irish-language newspapers, both before and after this period, *An Connachtach* didn't survive for very long. In fact, the newspaper had closed down within the year. The fact that I too was a contributor to newspapers and wrote occasional pieces for *An Claidheamh Soluis* meant that a close friendship soon developed between Mícheál Breathnach and I. Many was the afternoon that we spent walking across the hills and plains near Ballybanaun. Mícheál taught me a great deal about the history and culture of the people of Switzerland, the country where he spent the winter of that year. Mícheál died in October 1908.

5

Working as a Teacher

The Gaelic League became much stronger during this period. Every county and province in Ireland had its own travelling teachers at this stage. I duly received the certificate which qualified me as an Irish-language teacher and began to seek work straight away. While the League was going from strength to strength at this juncture, it wasn't clear whether this new enthusiasm would be a short-lived phase or whether it would prove a longer-lasting phenomenon. I wrote to the head language organiser for that area introducing myself and asking him to consider me for a job as an Irish teacher as soon as one became available. I reminded him of the sacrifices I had made in order to attend Coláiste Chonnacht in Tourmakeady and the fact that I was determined to see my studies bear fruit by securing a job as quickly as possible.

The head language organiser replied to me with a pleasant letter where he requested that I refrain from sending him any more letters. He assured me that I shouldn't worry and that a job would present itself in due course. He would make sure to remember that I was in the running for a job when the time came. What he said proved true and I managed to find a job a few months later. I lived at home in Rosmuc between August and November of that year and there was hardly a day that went by that I didn't write a letter to somebody in search of a job

– based on job adverts that I often spotted in *An Claidheamh Soluis*.

Unfortunately, I didn't receive even one reply to all of the application letters which I sent off. The fact that week after week went by without any hint of a job on the horizon was a great blow to my confidence. As one letter after another disappeared into a 'black hole' somewhere, I began to worry that I would never get a job and that I would have to spend my days doing odd jobs and moping around my parents' house. It wasn't too long either before the odd person in the villages nearby began to snigger at me – referring to me sarcastically as the unemployed 'little Irish-language master'. They used to get so bad with the ribbing and mocking that they whispered the three worst deaths of all – in the following order: the death of an old white colt, the death of an old sailor and the death of an old schoolmaster! Any time I visited somebody's house for a nightly singing session, the slagging would soon begin. It became so bad in the end that I eventually gave up calling to people's houses in the evenings completely.

They say that every cloud has a silver lining and that's the way it turned out for me that year. One afternoon in November, I had just returned from driving the cattle up rocky Creggan Hill when my sister Anna – peace to her soul – came out to tell me the good news. The parish priest had called to the house earlier looking for me. I had received a job offer from the head language organiser in Erris, County Mayo. The priest asked my parents to make sure that I called into him at the parochial house before the post went the next morning.

I was so edgy that night that I could barely sleep. I must have heard every crow of the cock that was down in our shed and every call our neighbour's cock made too. The priest was still in bed when I was knocking at his door the following morning, it was that early. His housekeeper let me in and I spent a nervous hour waiting for him to appear. When I heard the details of the letter he'd received and the job offer it contained, I thanked my lucky stars. I thought I had it made and that I would never see a day's hardship for the rest of my life.

'You'll have to be ready to leave for Erris, on such-and-such a day,' said the priest. 'You'll also need a bicycle. Have you got a bicycle already?' he asked.

'I don't have a bicycle father,' I said.

'You're in luck so,' the priest said, 'because I have a bicycle here that I don't use much during the winter at all. I can sell it to you cheaply.'

Nine pounds was the price the priest asked me for. No matter what price he wanted for that bicycle, he would have got it and welcome. It would have been the height of rudeness to have bargained with anyone who had helped me to get a job, as he had done. He was welcome to any amount of money. And it wasn't as if I would have had the cheek to start bargaining with my own parish priest either.

'You can pay me half now and half when you start earning a regular wage and you're able to support yourself without any difficulty.'

I thanked the priest for his kindness and for all he had done for me with regard to securing the job. When I got home and told everybody the details, I was a bit put out to see that they were not as ecstatic as I was about this turn of events. The reason for this, as I soon found out, was that my parents thought the priest had been a bit greedy with the price he'd asked for the bicycle. After a while, of course, this irritation about the priest's asking price was forgotten about and the subject was never raised again.

Everything was set in motion for the day of my departure. My brother Micil went to Galway city where he bought a new suit of clothes for me. This included a jacket with collar and a fashionable tie to go with that same suit. I'll never forget the evening before he left for Galway. There was never as much time spent on discussing the merits and attributes of jacket collars as there was in our house that evening. The only collar that would do me was the low-cut collar of the same type that I'd seen Pearse wearing when he was staying in Rosmuc. There were very few people in our place back then who had ever worn a collar.

In the meantime, the priest sent another message to the house saying that I wasn't to leave for Erris on the appointed day but that I should wait on at home for another while until I received another update on the situation. I waited and waited and as the days went by I began to get suspicious that there was some sort of trickery or corruption going on 'behind the scenes' in relation to the Erris job. I was down to the priest practically every morning to see had he received any news in relation to the job. One morning as I was making my way to his house who did I meet on the road but Patrick Pearse himself. He was on a horse and cart and had just left the parochial house where he had visited the same priest that I was about to call on. Pearse had given a lecture to the Irish language society in Westport the previous day and he was going on a quick visit to Rosmuc. We started chatting and I told him all about the job in Erris and my suspicions that the Gaelic League weren't treating me fairly in relation to this job. Of course I didn't have any evidence with which to back up my suspicions other than that the date for my commencement in the new job kept being put back.

'You won't be waiting too much longer for news about this job,' Pearse assured me. 'Your appointment was ratified at the last meeting of the committee of the Irish language organisers so I don't know why all the details haven't been finalised a long time before this. I'll sort that out with the relevant officials the minute I get back to Dublin.'

Pearse was as good as his word. He returned to Dublin the next day and I had the job as a travelling teacher for the Erris region within the week. My brother Micil and I had to leave the house in the early dawn to ensure that I caught the early train from Maam Cross. We didn't go to bed at all that night but stayed awake until first cockcrow. It was still fairly dark when we hit the road and there were little puffs of a cooling breeze criss-crossing the air. My brother carried my bag with my clothes and other bits and pieces in it. I walked along wheeling the priest's bike in front of me and doing my best to keep it in a straight line. I had never ridden a bicycle before unfortunately, although it wouldn't be long before I was covering miles and miles of countryside on that same bicycle.

My brother and I walked along chatting quietly to one another, when, all of a sudden, we heard a low whistle coming from somewhere nearby. We both heard it and went quiet but funnily enough we didn't say anything to one another. The whistle had come from very close by and it was as if both of us were too afraid to say anything. Then, just as we were going around a corner in the road, we heard it again, a low weak whistle on the early-morning air. We both stood stock still in the road. The dawn air went quiet again. No sooner had we walked on again but the whistle came again.

We stopped again and, once more, everything was as quiet as the grave. We quickened our pace again and the whistling started one more time. The quicker we walked, the more this strange whistle increased, but as soon as we came to a standstill the whistle disappeared. We came to a halt and had a quick look at the bicycle. A few minutes fiddling around and we had located the source of the strange sound. There was actually an empty valve underneath the saddle and every time we moved, the sound of air rushing through it made a low whistle.

I was absolutely frozen by the time the train arrived at the station. This was only my second time ever on a train and to make matters worse it was the feast of St John in Oughterard, when the ghosts are around. It felt spooky getting on an empty train in the murky dawn. There wasn't another soul in the carriage as I boarded the train and sat down. A few moments later and the train gave a sudden lurch forward, startling me so that I fell forward and grabbed the seat in front of me. Lurching forward slowly, the train picked up speed and we were chugging our way along through the early-morning gloom. It took a little while for my body, my feet in particular, to adapt to the strange movements of this giant monster of a machine, but after half an hour on the train I was beginning to feel like a seasoned traveller. The design of the trains has come a long way in the years since I went on that childhood journey. All that lay between you and the tracks below was a series of wooden boards and the steam swirled about you like a fog.

There was no such thing as being able to move between the carriages either, as one can today. Each carriage on that train between Clifden and Galway was like a separate and disconnected world unto itself. It wasn't for the child who was faint-hearted. When the train came into Galway city there were men working on the roof of the station there. I was so anxious to make sure that I didn't miss the next train that I must have asked about seven different people what platform the train for Claremorris was leaving from. I was that nervous that I think I asked the same station porter that very question three times in a row without realising that he was the same man I had already spoken to. The man eventually became a bit irritated with me and brought me to my senses with an abrupt question of his own. 'Do you think I have nothing better to be doing than standing here answering your questions? That's not even my job,' he said to me, stomping away in a huff.

I reached Claremorris about midday. As soon as I stepped off the train, a hotel porter who had been sent by the head language organiser was waiting for me. The man was a porter in the hotel where the organiser was staying but he had been sent to meet me because the organiser was gone to Ballinrobe on business and wouldn't be back until later that evening. Given that I was still only a child, my experience of life outside of my family's home place was still very limited at this juncture and I wasn't too sure whether I should follow this porter's instructions or not. How could I be certain that the man was who he said he was? After all, he was wearing a uniform that was not too dissimilar to a policeman's. I had also heard that it was very expensive to stay in a hotel. And so, having thought it over for a few minutes, I told the man in the uniform that I did not wish to have any more dealings with him or his affairs.

Having safely deposited my bicycle and my luggage in the baggage room of the train station, I decided to strike out on my own in search of lodgings for the night. I walked down the main street of the town where I spotted a thatched building that had black and white puddings hanging in the windows. I went a bit closer to the front of the building and realised that this must be one of those eateries where people prepared and sold food for a living, much as they do in a café or restaurant today. I went in and ordered some puddings for dinner. Whether it was the fact that I was already very hungry or not, I thought they were the tastiest puddings I had ever eaten. I asked the people in the restaurant where I could find the nearest lodging house and they gave me directions. I found the place without any difficulty and when I had settled the price for a night's lodgings, I went back to the train station to collect my stuff, accompanied by the son of the people who owned the lodging house. There was no way I was letting my bag and bicycle out of sight for too long.

Later that evening, just as I was getting ready for bed, there was a knock on the door and who arrived in but the same man who had met me off the train earlier that day. 'The head language organiser sent me,' the hotel porter said. 'He told me to collect you here and bring you to stay in the hotel tonight.'

If I had been reluctant to follow this man's instructions earlier in the day, I was doubly so now.

'It's a bit strange that he didn't give you a note to that effect,' I said to the man. 'Unless I see the man himself, or get a note of some description from him, I'm not budging from this lodging house tonight, I can guarantee you that.'

The porter left again, his face furrowed in anger. He was no sooner gone than he was back again. This time he had a note signed by the head language organiser. I was to leave for the hotel immediately – under pain of death!

I said my goodbyes to the people who owned the lodging house but there was no refund of the 'three-and-six' I had paid for my room. In my naivety I thought that was a bit churlish of them. After all, I had neither stayed the night, nor eaten a bite. The only thing they had given me was a single cup of tea. When I saw the language organiser's face, I knew I was in trouble. He proceeded to read the riot act with me. He lectured me about my 'strange behaviour' since arriving in Claremorris but, to tell you the truth, I didn't fully understand everything he said. 'There was neither rhyme nor reason to my antics' since arriving to the Clare, he told me. 'Not everyone is a criminal or a robber, you know.' His tone softened as he saw that his words had sunk in.

I was intimidated by his presence, of course. I had been wondering what the boss in my first job would be like and now, on my first encounter with him, he had asserted his authority in no uncertain terms. To my child's mind, this man was as important a figure as the king of England was to the English. From now on he was my master and I had to show him the utmost humility and respect. When he had fully explained to me the nature of my 'childish antics', I understood that this was how he viewed my behaviour and the fault was entirely with me. My new employer was a very tall and stocky man with the pale complexion of a studious and intelligent individual. He had the slightly rotund girth of the man who is approaching middle-age, and wore a black suit and one of those bone-shaped collars fastened tight just below the chin. He had more of the air of a priest than a countryman about him and he walked along with the measured steps of a soldier or a businessman. Even his speech had an air of dignity about it. He spoke slowly and clearly like somebody who has considered his words carefully before uttering them.

We went for a bite to eat before going to our rooms for the night. I asked for a cup of tea because that's what I was used to drinking before going to bed at home. We were alone in the dining-room and whether through nerves or habit, I must have made a bit too much noise with my teaspoon. At home, we liked to lash plenty of sugar into our tea and give it a good stir with the teaspoon. Unfortunately, this habit of mine irritated the head language organiser and it now instigated another lecture on his part. 'The likes of you who is taking his first steps into the world. You'd want to smarten up your act. The racket you're making with your teaspoon there would wake a herd of deaf cows out in the woods! Stirring your tea-cup to death won't get your tea to taste any better than it already does. And can you not sip your tea without making that loud slobbering noise every time?'

'We've a lot to put up with in this life,' I thought to myself just then. If it wasn't for the fact that I had a huge respect for this man, I might have said something I shouldn't have. Instead, I kept my thoughts to myself. In fact, I didn't utter a word during the course of that entire conversation. There was a part of me that felt some sympathy for the head language organiser also. I got the impression that he wasn't a healthy man and that he was suffering from some sort of physical ailment. He would give a short cough on his every second word, as if he had a heavy cold or was having problems with his chest.

We left the dining-room and made our way to the bedrooms. 'Now, make sure to leave your shoes outside the door when you're going to sleep. Do you know why you do this?'

This question of his caught me by surprise. When I didn't answer him quickly enough, he answered for me. 'To your mind, I suppose it would be a tiresome adornment, getting your shoes polished, wouldn't it?' That was the first time I had ever heard someone use the Irish word *fadálach* (i.e. tiresome, tedious). He explained then that the reason that you left out your shoes was that they would be polished clean for you in the morning.

Half-asleep at this stage, I turned and asked the head language organiser worriedly – 'Suppose a robber comes around and steals them or somebody misplaces them, I'd be in right serious trouble then – without a pair of shoes.'

'Every mother and son of you lot in Connemara must be a robber!' said the organiser, getting angry again. 'Since you arrived here in Claremorris, you've been paranoid about every single person you've come across.' He launched into another lecture. Once again, I couldn't say what was on the tip of my tongue – 'It's better to be safe than sorry.' When he had finished lecturing me again the organiser gave me one of those funny looks. It was one of those looks that said – 'well, give me an answer, will you?' I was so tired by then that I couldn't think straight any longer, never mind provide an interesting response. The only phrase that came to me at that moment was the old stock Irish phrase which we've often heard – i.e. 'It is better to sit near it than to sit in its place.'

The head language organiser ignored this comment on my part. 'We'll have to be up with the first chirping of the birds in the morning. And we'll have to sort some more of the wheat from the chaff while we're on the train.' He walked off to his bedroom and the last thing that came to mind was – 'It's just that I've never slept in a room on my own before.' The head language organiser turned to me and gave me a look that would break the heart of a stone. His parting shot was the following: 'You were brought up as a right pet; I'll say that much for you. Into your room there and get shut of your sheltered childhood. Switch off the light before you go to sleep. Sleep well.' He turned, went into his room and shut the door.

He was gone before I could think what was the best thing to do. I stood there for a moment and considered this latest dilemma I found myself in. Given that I was used to sleeping surrounded by other people, I was loath to spend the night alone in a strange place. It looked like I had absolutely no choice in the matter, however. I spent the night worrying about how naive and unprepared my 'misguided' childhood had left me for life in this new and 'modern' Ireland. The lectures I'd received from the head language organiser that evening were the first indication that I still had a lot to learn about etiquette and the modes of behaviour practised by the people in the 'professional' classes. 'Dear Christ,' I said to myself, as I tossed and turned from side to side in the bed that night, 'I'm only at the beginning of this whole process now! Today was only the first few shots across the bow. Imagine all the different issues I'll be pulled up on tomorrow!'

Instead of sleeping, I spent that night in a torment of anxiety. I lay there in the dark, worrying about both the living and the dead. Nobody needed to call me in the morning. I was up and dressed before anybody else in the hotel. I looked outside the door for my shoes but there was no sign of them. I wasn't sure then whether to go off in search of the shoes or whether to stay where I was. If I went off, I mightn't be able to find my hotel room again, given that they all looked the same. I decided to stay put and sat there worrying about the fate of my now-missing shoes. I had heard a light knocking sound on one of the bedroom doors earlier and after about an hour a loud rap came on my own door too. I heard somebody walking quickly away from the door, then I summoned up the courage to look out the door again. To my surprise, my shoes were there now and I grabbed them and pulled them into the room before shutting the door again. I checked them up and down in case a mistake had been made and they weren't actually my shoes. The shoes were like new, they were so beautifully polished. You could see yourself in their reflection, they were so shiny. Even the underneath of the shoes had been scrubbed clean and somebody had marked the figures 12/1 on each shoe with chalk. I put the shoes on me and agonised over whether to leave the room or not. As I say, I was worried whether I would be able to find the room again or not.

Eventually the porter made up my mind for me. He arrived hurriedly up to the room and told me to accompany him to where the organiser was already waiting for me. I said 'good morning' to the organiser and he told me to sit down at the table quickly.

'Time's slipping by and we haven't done any work yet.' He gave me a glare and pulled his watch from his pocket. 'I've been waiting for you this long,' he said, jabbing at the watch.

'To be honest, I was just waiting for you to call me sir,' I said to him. 'I'm awake since the break of day but I didn't want to leave the hotel room in case I had difficulty finding it again.'

The organiser didn't pay any attention to my explanation. He was rummaging through a bag of papers at his side searching for some form or other. The porter arrived then and placed two glasses of warm milk and sandwiches in front of us on the table. I missed the cup of tea that was the usual wake-up drink we had at home but I certainly wasn't going to make any comments that might get me into any more trouble. Then we headed off to the train station, the porter accompanying us. Although I would have preferred to have wheeled the bicycle and carried the bag myself, the organiser insisted that the porter do this. Every now and then I had an anxious look behind me to check that he was still following us. I was still afraid that my bag and bicycle might do a disappearing act. The organiser must have noticed me looking behind me and eventually he enquired: 'What are you looking at?'

'You wouldn't know where that porter might go or what corner he might disappear around,' I responded in a concerned voice.

'I give up,' said the organiser angrily. 'Only God can sort someone like you out.'

No sooner had we sat into the train, but he began grilling me. We were the only two in this particular carriage.

'All right, let's get down to business. How much English have you got?'

'I wouldn't like to comment on the level of my own English,' I answered him.

'Well! Well! Well!' the organiser said, emitting a small cough after each 'Well'. 'Isn't that lovely Irish coming from someone like yourself, someone who intends teaching Irish to others? – *a'm, a't, a'inn*. Why don't you pronounce the words "correctly" as follows: *agam, agat, againn?*'[1]

'But I would never pronounce those words like that. *A'm, a't, a'inn* – that's how we pronounce these words back home in Connemara.'

'*A'inn,*' he said again, imitating me. 'You need to be more careful about these small issues relating to pronunciation.'

He started commenting on my English then. It seems that he hadn't been impressed by my Irish or my English, this despite the fact that the only English words I had spoken to him were 'Yes sir' and 'No sir'! Eventually, just as the train was pulling into the station at Balla, the organiser announced: 'I want you to be ready to make a speech in English to me about "The State of the Irish Language" just as soon as the train moves away from Balla.'

My stomach began churning again with anxiety. The organiser gave a few small coughs and a sly smile crossed his face as he took note of my discomfort. The train came to a halt at Balla and a big crowd got on. I barely noticed them as my mind was elsewhere. I was rigid with fear at the prospect of having to give this speech.

Two men sat into the same carriage as us and placed themselves in the corner opposite to where the organiser and I were sitting. One man was a small, thin rake of a fellow, while the other was a big, huge block of a man. The pair of them were dressed in big tweed coats and their boots and trousers were plastered with muck. Red-cheeked from the outdoors life, the men each carried ash-plants in their hands and sported hats that were so squashed and misshapen-looking that they might as well have been used as pillows. As the train picked up speed I threw an occasional sidelong glance in the direction of the organiser – in case he asked me to begin on the speech in English. As it turned out, he made no further mention of the speech at all, a fact that was even more surprising given his apparent enthusiasm for the idea earlier. He adopted a different 'tack' now, instead.

'Wouldn't you think somebody like yourself would wear Irish-made clothes instead of that tacky English stuff you have on?'

He looked me up and down for a second, a look of disdain on his face.

'Even your shoes aren't Irish-made! Look at those two fine men across the way and how well-protected they are against the elements in their thick tweed clothes. And another thing. Why didn't you get one of those fixed collars for your suit instead of what you have on your lapel there? That way, all you'd need is your towel and your water every morning and you'd have your shave over and done with in no time. That fancy collar that you have on looks like a withered old stump of a thing!'

Naturally, I was very embarrassed by his constant 'put-downs'. I was willing to put up with anything at that particular moment, however, as long as he didn't tell me to make that speech. I tried to 'stand up' for myself in a small way by saying in a quiet voice that the clothes I had on were then fashionable and that the people back in my village wouldn't have considered the countrymen's frieze to be very 'à la mode'.

Hearing this, the organiser went quiet and he stayed that way for a good while after that. I said a secret prayer to myself that the two farmers would stay where they were until we came to the end of the journey. Luckily, that is exactly what happened – the two men were on their way back from Balla fair. Another travelling teacher, a man by the name of Pádraig Ó Maoilchiaráin, was waiting for me there in Westport. A loyal Gael, he was a very friendly man, a man who would always be very good to me.

We went to a lodging house on the Railway Road where the three of us had our breakfast and a quick meeting. We had to prepare for a big meeting that was due that night in the local town hall. The arrangement that we made was that the travelling teacher would 'show me the ropes' in the new job and that when my period of training was over he would 'deliver' me up to my new job in Erris. The first task which I was given that day was to write my weekly activity diary detailing the various meetings and classes I would be tasked with. Given that my job would involve a good deal of independence and working on my own for the most part, I would be required to send an outline of my work to the head language organiser on a weekly basis.

The meeting in the local hall that night was very well attended and the organiser gave a speech about the aims and progress of the Irish language movement. It was obvious from the way that the organiser spoke that he had presented this same speech on more than a few occasions before this. I got to know Páraic Dóras that evening. He also spoke at the meeting and little did we know that we would find ourselves sharing the same prison cells in the future while incarcerated after Easter Week 1916 as republican prisoners. If there was anybody other than John MacBride who kept the spirit of nationalism alive in that part of the country, it was Páraic Dóras. His brother Liam was a parliamentary representative in John Redmond's party, albeit that they often disagreed on questions relating to Ireland, nationalism and the quest for Irish freedom. Liam's newspaper *The Mayo News* was a great support to the nationalist movement at this juncture.[2]

The head language organiser left us the following day. Despite the fact that I had got off to a 'shaky' start with him, the organiser's bark proved worse than his bite. He was certainly a hard taskmaster, a man whose word was law, and a person who was able to strike fear and loyalty into the men who were under his supervision. He was a good man too, however. He cared for the men he had responsibility for and advised them well both in terms of their lives and their health. He was also a man who did trojan work on behalf of the Irish language, often receiving nothing but sarcasm and rejection as his reward. There were countless villages and townlands who didn't want to hear about the work of the Gaelic League then and who weren't shy about telling him as much. In general, people still had a very negative attitude towards the idea of reviving and strengthening the Irish language in those days and many people found it easier to mock somebody who was working towards its revival than to give them any support. Worse than this again was the fact that many of the 'leaders' of the day, intellectuals both lay and clerical, were also afflicted with the same cynicism and negativity.

Despite all of these obstacles, the head language organiser never lost hope and he had great heart even when the situation was at its bleakest. His hard work certainly paid off and the Gaelic League found it enormously difficult to replace him when he retired years later. This man spent a full fourteen years of his life travelling the length and breadth of Ireland by bicycle while working as a travelling teacher. There isn't a true Gael either in Ireland or abroad who hasn't heard of that head language organiser – the man known as Tomás Bán Ó Conceanainn.[3]

When the first day of nice weather came along, the travelling teacher, Pádraig Ó Maoilchiaráin, and I intended making our way to Erris from Westport. It was Christmas time, however, and it wasn't easy to get a day that was good enough for travelling. One night we decided to take our chances and made plans to set out the following morning. We were ready to get up at dawn to catch a train for the first stage of the journey. As any Irish person will tell you, however, the weather can be very changeable in this country of ours. During the night I was awakened by the cold. The temperature had dropped well below freezing and it was so cold that it was impossible to go back to sleep. Morning found the countryside buried under a mantle of snow, snow that was still falling in heavy sheets. The snow fell continuously until about midday and then the winter sun came out high above the blanket of white. The snow kept us 'confined to base' in Westport for another while and we busied ourselves with work at various locally based Gaelic League branches. I myself attended League meetings in villages such as Newport, Ballyfeechan and Kilmeena every night of that week and it was at one of these that I met Páraic Ó Dónaill, a shopkeeper in Newport and another diligent Gael who did a power of work on behalf of the Irish language.

Christmas night of that year was a sad one for me. I had to remain in Westport for the Christmas period and it was the first

time that I had ever found myself away from home at that time
of the year. I felt particularly lonely that night and missed the
company of my family. Although the house I was staying in –
Páraic Uí Chonnacháin's house – was very nice, I still couldn't get
the sense of loneliness and loss out of my mind. That holy night
my thoughts kept drifting back to home and what my family
would be doing. It was as if the memories of every Christmas I
had lived through up until then had come together in a stream of
images, one after another. The holly tree that was at the back of
the house came to mind as clear as day. I knew that tree so well
that I could actually remember each and every branch which had
been cut annually to supply holly for our home. In fact, I had
already prepared some large boughs of holly – pruning the tree
on the feast of St Michael – for this same Christmas night that
I now found myself absent from. I could imagine the big red
candle lighting up the darkness, flickering brightly in the shelter
of our kitchen window. I pictured too one of the doors left open
– as was the custom – so the Glorious Virgin and her Child
could enter in search of lodgings. Neither could I ever forget the
special joy and excitement that coursed through us as we left our
house at the darkness of midnight – to attend Christmas night
Mass.[4]

Isn't it always memories such as these which stir the
loneliest and most poignant of emotions in the person who finds
themselves far away from home at Christmas? This was also the
first time I had spent the festive season in a town rather than
out in the silence of the countryside and I remember hearing the
racket of the wrenboys heralding the early dawn of St Stephen's
Day. The rig-outs and the antics of these performers appeared
strange to me and when I made a few enquiries the people of the
house explained to me that these entertainers were referred to as

mummers. These performers wore masks and strange clothes and they had changed their voices so that the people wouldn't know who they were. They all looked like scarecrows to me. They carried musical instruments which they played, and bucklepped to every tune. The hopping and jumping wasn't real dancing if the truth be told. They worked their way along the street, stopping at four or five different places to put on this short performance.

I didn't really understand what the locals found funny or enjoyable in this strange display. The only thing it reminded me of were the pictures you saw in the books back then – of these strange tribes who lived in the jungles of Africa, or the strollers and vagabonds who would traditionally appear at weddings in places like Erris. The 'get-up' of these mummers was quite different from that of the groups of wrenboys who used to go around in the villages back home on St Stephen's Day. The groups back in Connemara did not disguise themselves with such strange outfits. You were still able to tell who the wrenboys were and they didn't frighten old women or children with their bizarre movements and antics. Instead, they went around from house to house in a steady and civilised fashion, the wren kept in a glass container which was decorated with holly or green ribbons. In that sense they functioned as an amalgam of both Christian and nationalist symbolism. These wrenboys would be delighted if you gave them a penny or even a sandwich in the houses where the people were too poor to afford anything else as an offering. The wrenboys were a good example of the generosity and religious belief that were important markers of that era.

The day finally arrived when the travelling teacher and I were able to set out for Erris. We took the train as far as Mulrany and cycled the rest of the way. It was a dry frosty day without any sun. Given that I had never ridden a bicycle before this, I fell off more than once and every time I came off I had to prop myself on a small mound of grass or some other raised thing so as to climb back on to the saddle again. The frost meant that we had to go slowly anyway but the travelling teacher was more than patient with me as I got used to the bicycle. Every couple of miles, he had to stop and wait for me to catch up with him. Initially, I felt embarrassed at the fact that I was so 'green' in the ways of the world, but I soon realised that there was only one way to learn a new skill such as riding a bicycle, and that was to throw oneself into it fully.

We passed that night in a small townland in the lonely hills of Bangor Erris. The countryside around about was quite barren and uninhabited and although I had grown up in hilly country, I soon realised that the poor land of my home-patch was still positively 'rich' in comparison with the barren and uninhabited countryside here. If you weren't full of enthusiasm for your new job, as I was, the place could have served to depress you somewhat.

It was noticeable that there were actually more shops in Bangor Erris than there were houses that still had inhabitants. As with other poorer areas in the west of Ireland, the place had been decimated by emigration. There were so few young families living in the area, in fact, that it was a wonder how all of these shops survived. We reached our final destination – Gweesalia – the following day, a day of heavy frost that left our hands and feet numb with the cold. As we made our way along the roads the travelling teacher would stop and greet anybody who came our way with a hearty 'God bless you'. We were coming to the end of our journey – somewhere on the road between Knockanlogey and Gweesalia – when an untidy-looking man in his fifties came in our direction. The travelling teacher was slightly ahead of me on the road and he had barely uttered his 'God bless you' when the man shot back with this hostile response: 'May God and Mary bless you and may bad luck strike you down you dirty old Protestant.' When I expressed my surprise at this incident to the people of the house where I was lodging that same evening, the family explained to me that the 'strange' man on the road had probably suspected that we were soupers.

'Why would he have thought that?' I asked them.

'Because the soupers would never pass anybody without making sure to greet them before the others could utter a word.' The reason for this was that they were afraid of saying the word *Muire* (Mary) in the Irish response *go mbeannaí Dia is Muire duit*.

Between them, the travelling teacher and the local priest – a young man by the name of Antaine Ó Toimlín – arranged lodgings for me and a weekly timetable of classes and meetings. Once this was all organised, the travelling teacher said his farewells and headed back to Westport again. Fifty pounds a year was my agreed salary, £40 of which was to come directly from the finance committee of the Gaelic League. Each of the two parishes I was 'working' in would have to pay £5 to 'top up' this £40. The two parishes agreed enthusiastically to this arrangement. They didn't fulfil their promises, however, and I didn't receive a penny from either parish at the end of the first year – other than a small amount of extra money that Father Ó Toimlín kindly gave me from his pocket. I just earned the bare £40 that year. It was the hardest-earned £40 anybody ever slaved for, I can assure you. Despite this shortfall, I still considered myself relatively lucky.

There were many other teachers who were promised nice salaries in those days only to find that these commitments were not met at all, and they barely had enough to eat despite long months of work. One teacher I knew was promised £80 a year. He was worked to the bone and required to set up new branches and committees of the Gaelic League all over the place. The poor man was given so much work that you'd swear he was being paid £1,000 and not £80! The worst of it was that the poor man didn't see one penny of his wages, come the end of the year. He had been hired based on a series of false promises. Believe it or not, on first arriving in the area, the travelling teacher – an incredibly hard-working individual – had been brought up to the top of a hill which overlooked the surrounding villages by the man who was organising the new job for him. Stretching out his hands, as if encircling the landscape beneath them, he had said to his enthusiastic new 'recruit': 'Now, look out over that fine countryside! A richer or more beautiful land you will never see! The people in the villages below are the kindest and the most honest people anywhere in Ireland. Remain here permanently, and it will be the crags and the meadows below that will ensure you are always provided for – both in financial and material terms.'

Newport and Bleachyard were the two areas assigned to me for teaching purposes. I was completely unaware of it at this point – but I couldn't have been assigned to a more difficult or (indeed) physically dangerous posting as that one. Thinking back now, maybe I had been physically selected for this job because I was young and physically fit. The narrow stretch of water known as Tullaghaun flows between the two parishes, i.e. Newport and Bleachyard. A perilous channel of water at the best of times, I had to cross it twice a week to get to my Irish classes. I arranged with a local boatman and paid him a shilling a week to get over and back. There were many occasions, however, when the wind was so strong and the sea so rough that we weren't able to get the boat into the water at all. The boatman's sister always accompanied us on these journeys and she was as powerful a rower as I have ever seen. Not only was drowning in the sea a big danger in this place, so too were the sands on the shoreline, sands that were constantly shifting. Like quicksand, the shoreline here could pull you under and swallow you up in a matter of seconds if you weren't careful.

There was one spring morning just shortly after my arrival in Erris when I came as close to death as I had ever come at any time in my young life, before this. I had been rowed across the water and left out on the beach at Bleachyard, just within sight of the castle at Doona. Unfortunately, the friendly boatman who had rowed me across had neglected to warn me of the dangers posed by the shifting sands in that area. He probably thought I was aware of such dangers, given that I had grown up near the sea myself. How wrong he was! I was making my way across the shore when the sand suddenly began to give way beneath my feet. Within seconds, I was up to my knees in sand. Thank God, I managed to use the bicycle that I had with me to lever myself out of the swallowing sand. By sinking the bicycle's wheels into the sand, I was able to move forward slowly, gripping my way across the sand while using the bicycle as a sort of a climbing frame. Eventually I managed to extricate myself from danger but it was undoubtedly the closest I'd ever come to dying.

While these beaches could be very dangerous during the winter, they had a more pleasant aspect to them later in the year. Come autumn, for example, these same beaches would be crowded with young people fishing for sand-eels or sand-herring as we used to call them back in Connemara. It's hard to beat these fish for taste when they are in season and both young and old were very fond of them. Of course, there is no tribe in the world that doesn't also have its 'outsiders' and that's the way it was with the fishing for sand-eels too. There was often rivalry and fighting in relation to the sand-eel fishing and sometimes the 'outsiders' had to be 'driven away' to avoid conflict.

The land in Erris is poor and wild. If you walked in a straight line from Mulrany to Belderg you would be traversing a black and infertile mountain, where only the odd secluded nook is cultivated. It's a place where snipe or woodcock can survive but no humans or animals could live up there. This means that the majority of the people in that part of the world survived by subsistence farming, a hand-to-mouth existence which was precarious at the best of times. I was only a short while in Erris when I noticed the differences between it and Connemara. In Connemara, those small fields which were cultivated and manured had the look of life about them. In Erris, similar-type fields would absorb large amounts of manure and still look arid and infertile. With few exceptions, the fields looked craggy and encrusted with stone. Another thing about Erris was that there were few rocks or trees, whereas in Connemara there were rocks everywhere but you didn't have to travel too far at all to come across the small copses of trees that dotted the landscape at regular intervals.

In Erris the land's natural boundaries were formed by the clay, the sod that was a dead, impenetrable barrier between one piece of land and the next. There wasn't really enough rock there to form a clear boundary between one place and the next. In contrast with this, the land in Connemara was criss-crossed and partitioned everywhere by a patchwork of stone walls. There, the land was all narrow ridges with small fissures of fertile soil between them. In Erris, the opposite was the case. You had wide ridges, separated by ditches that were deep and in which it was only sometimes possible to grow something. In Connemara, the corn was harvested with a reaping-hook and then tied in large fistfuls. The system was different again in Erris. Here the corn would be cut with a scythe and then tied into sheaves. Another difference was that in Connemara they fed the animals from the cocks of hay and corn that they had built during the harvest, whereas in Erris they put these materials into their thatched roofs instead. These same roofs tended to be made with sedge-grass back in Connemara.

The majority of the Erris people migrated to England and Scotland where they worked as migratory labourers on the large farms there during the summer and autumn months, returning home again for the winter. I often saw the steamship that travelled between Ireland and Britain for this purpose pulling into Erris to fill up with passengers. The ship would always sound its horn as it came into Blacksod Bay. As soon as that horn sounded, you saw people appearing from all the houses and running towards the quay. Young and old, men and women, it made no difference. The people were mad to get onto that boat to earn the money that would tide them over for the rest of the year. On the arrival of this steamship, the only people left behind were the old, the infirm, or those children who were too young to work. The sight of that steamship or the blast of that horn saw a new energy infuse the local people. If there's the same enthusiastic rush on the last day when the angel sounds the trumpet, then there'll be no necessity to round up all the living and the dead.

Most Connemara people went to America where they usually settled for the rest of their lives. Again, in contrast with this, the people of Erris tended to go to Britain from where they returned speaking English, following English customs and speaking with English accents. When I saw this happening, I realised that it was often our own people who were Anglicising the Irish-speaking regions of Connemara. The same people would often imitate the non-Irish speakers who visited Erris on their holidays, while at the same time pretending to teach Irish to these visitors, who were sometimes native speakers themselves.

There was no village in Erris then that did not have a céilí and a lottery every Sunday or feast day. The slightest pretext was enough to generate the bit of excitement that a lottery would bring. I often saw a lottery organised on foot of as small a prize as a quarter pound of tobacco – a piece of tobacco which fetched just over a shilling back then. Various dancing masters travelled around Erris in those days also, and they organised classes in all of the small villages and townlands they visited on their travels. This was different to the part of Connemara I was from where we didn't have either céilís or dancing masters during this period.

The main source of entertainment we had in my home place then was on those occasions when a travelling musician came that way and even then it was only a few houses that would give him lodgings. The reason for this was simple. The clergy in West Connemara at this point were very hostile to the musicians and entertainers who travelled from place to place and they severely reproved those houses that provided them with hospitality.

The differences which existed between Connemara and this part of Mayo can be best exemplified in this short anecdote. I remember quite a poor man – who had never been outside Erris in his life – who began a career as a shopkeeper just based on the seven or eight pence he made from one Sunday céilí. He used this money to set up a service whereby he walked from Erris to Claremorris and back on a regular basis, transporting his newly bought provisions on his back. Within a couple of years, he had set up a thriving grocery business.

Contrast this with a man from Rosmuc who had done well in America and came home to set up a shop. Within two years, he was broke. It seemed to me that the Erris people were more go-ahead and more clued-in to the ways of the world than the Connemara people were then.

Storytellers and writers were plentiful in Erris at this time. There weren't so many poets amongst them, however. One of the most talented poets of that era was Máirtín Ó Calghaoille who lived in Gweesalia, and who composed 'Father Páraic Ó Maoileoin' – a piece which I included in the publication *Sidheog na Rann* (1911). Ó Calghaoille was a schoolmaster by profession and he taught Christian doctrine through Irish in his school for a full thirty years, at a time when very few subjects were taught through the medium of Irish. In addition to his job as a schoolmaster, Ó Calghaoille was also a shoemaker and many was the morning that he travelled all the way from Doohoma to Belmullet to collect a new batch of leather only to be back at his desk for the beginning of school early the same day. That was a journey of eighteen miles but Ó Calghaoille would still have the energy to do a full day's teaching after that. In the village of Belmullet itself was where Seán Ó Monacháin – the poet of Erris – lived. He was still a young man then, recently married, and he had just begun composing poetry. He was a self-taught man, having spent very little time at school, but he had the older learning of the poets who'd come before him. I came to know him well while I was living in Erris. He could compose a song in three seconds and he left many songs after him when he passed on a few years ago. Eternal rest to both Máirtín Ó Calghaoille and Seán Ó Monacháin.

I taught my first ever Irish class in Clery's Hotel in Bleach-yard. I'll never forget that first class, held in the evening. I had just crossed over Tullaghaun Bay where I got soaked to the skin, the sea being a bit rough. I was so eager to start teaching, however, that I got cracking straight away. The class was waiting for me and I went in to them looking like a drowned rat! The class consisted of the local parish priest, the local Protestant minister, the local hoteliers and one or two other people. It struck me as odd and unnatural somehow that the Catholic priest and the Protestant minister were in the same room. The other thing that was off-putting was the fact that the people in the class were not the pupils whom I'd expected to be there. These people were all the 'big-wigs', whereas I had hoped that the locals would be my main attendees. 'This is going to be a "posh class",' I said to myself.

Back then, schoolbooks weren't used as much as they are today. There was good reason for this. Very few books were printed and even when they were, we travelling teachers were often unable to afford them. The odd time that a teacher would buy some copies of a particular book, he might find himself 'stuck' with them because the pupils were reluctant to splash out their hard-earned money on them. So it was the 'direct method' of teaching that we employed. That first night I spent a good two hours covering the basics: *Céard é seo?* (What is this?). *Is fear é* (He is a man). *Is sagart é an fear* (The priest is a man) or *Is fear é an minister* (The minister is a man). I kept repeating these different phrases and their various meanings and mixing up the order of their usage over and over again for the duration of the class and it was then that it came home to me the difficulties of teaching in the absence of any books, notes or a blackboard. By the end of the night, even I was beginning to get confused. I finished the class with some words of praise and encouragement for the group. 'If you keep learning as well as you did tonight, you'll all have a good grasp of Irish in no time.' Funnily enough, neither the priest nor the minister attended the class again!

Any evening that I was doing the class there, the people of the hotel always insisted that I stay there for the night rather than go home at a late hour. They were the most kind-hearted and generous people I ever met. They wouldn't accept payment for anything – either food or lodgings. To tell you the truth, their unstinting welcome and generosity caused me to cancel that evening class in the end. A shyness overcame me and I felt beholden to those kind people, so much so that I was embarrassed to hold the class there any more. A house in Doona, close to where Granuaile's castle had once been, was my main regular lodgings at this time as it happens.

Sean-Shéamas Mac Giontaigh was the best storyteller then living in that parish.[5] I had heard tell of him already from Páraic Ó Dónaill in Newport, the latter a man who always demonstrated a great interest in Ireland's folklore and the struggle for Irish freedom. In fact Páraic had already had the foresight to transcribe a great deal of Fianna-related lore from Mac Giontaigh before this and he made me promise that while I was working in the vicinity, I would note down whatever material he had not had the opportunity to record. Like many other promises I made during my lifetime, I never fulfilled this pledge of mine. At the time, many storytellers expected some form of a payment – you couldn't blame them I suppose – and, given that I was just starting out in my working life, I couldn't afford to pay for the chance to record someone. Another reason why I didn't want to pay them was that I didn't want the word going out amongst other storytellers that I was a 'soft touch' in this regard. I knew that both Páraic Ó Dónaill and Mícheál Ó Tiománaí had both paid other storytellers and I was sure that the same seanchaís probably expected me to do the same. It put me off transcribing material from many of these storytellers as I would have been too embarrassed to tell them that I couldn't pay them. These storytellers – and I don't want to be too harsh here – didn't really understand that the folklore-collecting was part of a national project of cultural reclamation, particularly for someone like me, a person who made their living from the Irish language.

One 'disadvantage' of being a travelling language teacher at this time was the fact that everybody would be constantly asking you to translate phrases into Irish. You never got a break from it – 'How would you translate the two ends of a stick?' Another one they had was – 'How would you say "leg of mutton" in Irish?' They'd often put me 'on the spot' with a difficult question or try to get me to translate something inappropriate into Irish.

A few days after my arrival in Erris the Irish speakers in Doolough produced the play *Casadh an tSúgáin*. Seán Ó Ruadhain was the play's director and I attended the performance. Once the play was finished, Seán introduced me to the local audience. He gave a speech praising me and the great work I was undertaking in the area. He invited me to come on stage and say a few words but I had already slunk down into my seat by then. I was shaking with nerves and by the time that I got up there, I actually couldn't say a word. I was mortified.

I wasn't long in Erris when I realised that the Irish language spoken in Bleachyard and Achill was very similar to the dialect spoken in Ulster whereas that spoken in the part of Erris that was closest to Northern Ireland seemed more like Munster Irish to me. Everybody in that part of Mayo could speak Irish at this juncture. The problem was that nobody had the slightest respect for the Irish language or felt that it was worth preserving. The majority of people there spoke English both inside their homes and in public. They spoke English at weddings and céilís, on the playing fields and everywhere people gathered to meet. Even the local schoolteachers were against the Irish language, this despite the fact that most of them were native speakers. The consequence of this was that I had to teach Irish in six schools in that area. All of the credit for the work I did in these schools always went to the schoolmasters, believe it or not, this despite the fact that most of them didn't want me there at all.

6

In Erris

Belmullet was as Anglicised a town as any big town in Ireland then. It was also the main business centre for the people of the Erris region since a market was held there every week in addition to a once-monthly fair. Irish was spoken by the people coming into Belmullet from the country areas around about, but it was primarily English that the Belmullet locals spoke to the country people. This served to weaken the Irish language. Other factors which worked to diminish Irish further include the fact that all of the administrative functions of the Erris region were located in Belmullet. The poorhouse was in the town, as was the local hospital.

Belmullet was the focal point for all of the local councillors and politicians and anybody seeking employment had to go to the town, given that all of the 'big-shots' lived there. It was in and around Belmullet, too, that I saw the last vestiges of the landlord class. Although this 'elite' was in decline by then, it was surprising how much power it still held. I remember one individual, in particular, a member of the gentry who carried himself with all of the pomp and swagger of the 'older' upper-class. It came as no surprise then that 'shoneenism' and attempts to imitate the gentry were still common amongst those locals who had an 'inferiority complex' or who wished to ape the manners of the gentry.[1] Ironically, despite its status as an Anglicised town, Belmullet was where I first came across a copy of the *Sinn Féin* newspaper.[2] The woman who ran the post office, Lasairfhíona Ní Shamhráin was the person who showed me a copy of the newspaper. She was a staunch Gael (nationalist), and contributed to the newspaper herself from time to time. She was also the secretary of the *Cumann na nDéantús Gaelach* right up to her death, just a few years ago.[3] Her death came as a big blow to the other nationalists of the area, including myself.

I spent two years working between Gweesalia, Bleachyard and Bangor Erris where I had to visit six schools each week and teach twice a week in each school. I also taught Irish to two different branches of the Gaelic League every night of the week. On top of this, I taught Irish to the headmasters of the local schools every Saturday and had a class every Sunday after Mass. The travelling teachers worked a huge number of hours in those days. After Sunday Mass I would be expected to give out the rosary and teach a class that same night to the local branch of the Gaelic League depending on what part of Erris I was at Mass in that morning. The work schedule we travelling teachers had to follow in those days was too much. It was up to ourselves to travel the long distances between one place and the next, whether on foot or by bicycle. While we supposedly got a holiday during the summer, we were actually sent off to teach in one of the Irish colleges.[4] By the time our living expenses were covered, there was none of our salary left over. In fact, travelling teachers such as me were the closest thing to the archetypal 'Wandering Jew', that travelling pedlar who was always just beginning his journey, a man whose work was never done. Nobody born worked as hard as we travelling teachers did and that's the truth.

Unbelievably, it wasn't that unusual for us to be assigned

extra duties in addition to those I have previously mentioned. One day, for example, the head language organiser instructed me to survey every school east of Ballina and to enquire into the state of the Irish language in that entire area. Once I was finished with that survey, my instructions were to do the same on Achill Island. It took me quite a while to get this work done and there was no talk of any extra money to help cover any of the extra expenses that were involved, travel expenses and the cost of lodgings included. My annual salary of £40 wouldn't be long disappearing at this rate, I thought.

Despite all of this work, this was the period of my life when I was most broke! It was summertime and I had been wearing the same suit since the previous winter. It was well-worn at this stage and covered in patches. The inspector's instructions were clear however. I always had to appear professional and dressed in a formal manner any time that I entered a school. A new suit would cost a fortune and I needed one sooner rather than later. I could have asked my parents at home for the price of a suit but I was loath to do this having already spent the best part of nine months working. Éamann Ó Gacháin, a shopkeeper in Gweesalia would have looked after me and sourced a new suit for me too if I had only had the temerity to ask him. I was rightly stuck and I had to come up with a plan quickly. It was then that I thought of the man whose family I was lodging with. He had a nice suit that he only wore on Sundays and when I explained my situation to him, he offered me his straight away. I was over the moon; having the use of that suit was a real weight off my mind. The man's family also arranged lodgings for me in Ballycastle, booking a room for me with a family they knew there.

I got my bits and pieces and hit the road the following

Monday morning, wearing my lovely 'new' black suit. My bicycle was well-weathered from the coastal wind and the rain but the fine sunny day soon raised my spirits. In the fields as I cycled past, I saw the cattle making for whatever streams or water-pools were in the area. The hills were beautiful, changing colour depending on which way the sun fell on them; the road alive with the soothing gurgles of the mountain streams. 'Isn't it awful that I have to travel across the freezing bay during the winter to teach some of my Irish classes, when being a teacher can be such bliss on a sunny summer's day like this?' I was thinking to myself, as I cycled along.

I got down to work immediately and surveyed a large number of schools on that first day. Some of the schoolteachers were very helpful while others obviously resented my presence and were not particularly helpful. The ones who weren't cooperative simply pointed to the school timetable and told me to take down whatever information I required from it. There were a few of them who were clearly lazy and who only put a stir under themselves as soon as I arrived at the school. That said, I wasn't too disheartened after my first day's work on the survey. Having visited each parochial house, I would call on the local parish priest. It wasn't that I was particularly keen on calling on them. If I'd had my own way, in fact, I wouldn't have bothered calling on them at all; I felt quite shy of some of the parish priests and somewhat intimidated by a few of them. It was just that I knew the head language organiser would give out to me if I didn't call in to each of the parish priests. Over time, I would become better at guessing each priest's likely outlook on the national 'question'. If I saw the *Leader* or the *Freeman* lying about when I arrived at the parochial house, I knew I was 'safe'. The chances were that the priest was a good nationalist in those cases. If, on the other hand, there was no sign of the *Freeman*, I would likely only find support there for the Irish Party.[5] If the *Irish Times* was the only newspaper that was visible, I had to be careful what I said and always keep my political opinions to myself.

I reached Ballycastle by Wednesday of that week having passed a pleasant evening on the way there, securing lodgings at the house of Liam Ó Dochartaigh, a loyal and true Gael. On arrival in Ballycastle, I got directions to the lodgings straight away, the people of the house giving me a great welcome. I had just headed off to bed when the woman of the house gave a quick rap on the bedroom door. A telegram had just arrived for me. She handed me the note but I had to read it twice before it registered with me what it was about.

'I hope it's not bad news?' the woman of the house asked.

'No, not at all,' I assured her. 'It's just that I have to go back to Gweesalia straight away.' The telegram was from the man of the house in my previous lodgings. It read as two short sentences – 'Come quickly with my suit. A wedding here tomorrow.' There was no way that I could let that man down and I set off for Doohoma immediately. I was young and fit in those days and it didn't knock much out of me to cycle that distance again. When I submitted my weekly work report to the head language organiser at the end of the week, he wasn't long coming back to me with a few queries. 'Had I bought a new suit?' was the first question on his list. I couldn't tell him that I had been forced to borrow a suit from somebody else because I couldn't afford a new one at that point so I made up some excuse or other to try to put him off. Whatever excuse I invented (I can't remember now, what I told him) obviously wasn't a very good one, as I received another letter from him, hot on the heels of the first one. He wouldn't accept any other excuses in relation to the suit, he warned me. The head language organiser put me on the spot that time but the people of Gweesalia went on getting married as they had always done!

I spent over four years in Erris altogether, more than half of which I spent on the Mullet Peninsula. I lodged in Binghamstown. I really loved the people – at least all of the Gaels amongst them – and the place. It was an area that still had traces of the old landlord or gentry class about it, the name of the townland known in Irish as *An Geata Mór* being a case in point. Many of the locals still referred to the area where they lived as Binghamstown because the Binghams had once owned every rock and field between Mullet Strait and Blacksod. When they had owned it, they allowed no cabins or houses to be built for miles. The countryside was completely devoid of people, the squires and landlords using every scrap of land for grazing their stock. Back then, the pride of Irishmen and women had simply emigrated to the four corners of the earth in search of a living rather than attempt to wrest the land back from the clutches of their colonial masters.

It was near Binghamstown that the celebrated Gaelic poet Riocard Bairéad had once lived. It was where he had died and where he was buried. There was still a good deal of oral history about Bairéad in the minds and on the tongues of the local people even when I came to live there. I wrote down as many notes as I could about it at this juncture but unfortunately these were destroyed when the Black and Tans burned down our house in April 1921.[6] One thing that surprised me was the fact that the nationalist spirit of his day was only a minor theme in Bairéad's poetry, this despite the fact that most of the folklore concerning Bairéad associated him with republicanism and rebellion. It was said, for example, that Bairéad had spent time in prison during the Year of the French (1798) because of his nationalist views. In fact, many of the stories concerning Bairéad had more of a resonance for the land agitators of a later era than they did for the rebels of an earlier generation. In these parts also lived 'Eoghan Coir' (Criminal John) the most malicious and tyrannical of any bailiff who ever lived in Erris.

The Irish language was an intrinsic element in the identity of the Erris people at this time. The influence of the 'pale' had never reached this corner of Ireland and back then you would never have heard a word of English spoken in this area. This struck me as amazing, given that just a few miles away in villages such as Blacksod and Teertraugh, the influence of Anglicisation was very evident. Maybe the more Anglicised atmosphere of these latter places was due to the fact that they had more regular contact in terms of international trade than did Erris. For example, a Norwegian company was based on the edge of the shore in Teertraugh where they skinned and processed whales and where the locals were able to get some work.

It was while I was based in Erris that I compiled the book *Sidheog na Rann*, which the Gaelic League published in 1911. One of the poets whose songs were included in this book was Seán Ó Monghaile or 'Seán an Chomhrá' who lived in Géidhe Island. He had died a long time before this and there wasn't a cove or port on the west coast – from Sligo to Galway city – where they didn't know his songs. The fact that he was a boatman meant that his poems and songs – which were typical of the west of Ireland style – spread quickly from one place to another. I regularly visited Géidhe Island at this time, an island whose inhabitants survived by fishing, and which is situated about three miles from the coast. A hundred years ago, when the closest priest to them was based in Belmullet, the island's inhabitants regularly had to brave storms and gales to get the priest in an emergency. The islanders had a rock hewn in the shape of a saint, a special rock that they referred to as the *naomhóg*.[7] If the storm was so violent that they were unable to put to sea, the islanders would immerse this statue in the sea as they had a strong belief that this would quell the storm.

It was also the tradition that each household on the island had to look after the currach for a year, a year during which they had to re-coat the frame of the boat. One day, the parish priest – a man who had a strong interest in Irish archaeology – managed to get his hands on the *naomhóg*. What did he do but fling the rock out into the sea. He threw it into a part of the bay that had always previously been as calm as a duck-pond. The transformation was incredible. From the day he threw the rock into the water, the depths erupted in that place. The bay next to the island became one of the roughest in that part of the country, the waves wild and furious. Ever since then, neither boat nor ship can get anywhere near the island in any safety.

The cemetery for the half-parish of Binghamstown was situated on Inishglora, another historic place that was no more than a mile from the mainland. The folklore relating to this island was still widespread at this time. Not only did the locals claim that it was on Inishglora that Clann Lir are buried, but they also claimed to be able to show you the exact spot where their graves are located.[8] They would also tell you that it was on this island that the devil appeared in the guise of a woman, in an effort to tempt St Brendan when he was engaged in his ascetic practices there. The holy well of St Brendan is on this island to this very day. Another piece of local lore is that it is only men who are permitted to remove water from this well. If a woman attempts to do so, the water is said to become disturbed and only returns to its normal state when the water that was removed is replaced in the well once more.

The Irish-language literature of this era was suffering from the absence of any published material relating to theatre. There were only a couple of plays in Irish then available in print and we were sick to death of producing the same few plays over and over again as part of our local drama festivals. There were so many productions of one particular play, *An Fómhar* by Fr Tomás Ó Ceallaigh – may he rest in peace – that the local people refused to come to see the play any more. Who could blame them? I'll never forget the last night that we had a production of this play in the town of Belmullet. It was on St Patrick's Day, the national feast day, when it was the custom for many of the Erris people to come into town for the day. They would play music, put on plays and carry the green flags of Ireland in procession through the streets. They would wet the shamrock, smoke plenty of tobacco and generally have an enjoyable day. Back then, the people didn't wear St Patrick's Day badges or medals; they wore every type of English medal instead.

In Belmullet courthouse was where the band would play and where the performance of *An Fómhar* was to take place. I had gone to a good deal of trouble the previous couple of weeks securing the permission of the local justices and clergy, both Protestant and Catholic, so that the event could be held in the courthouse. Any profits were to go to the kitty of the Gaelic League and yet all our efforts were in vain. The big night came around and the drama group, all of whom were native Irish speakers from Cross, were ready to go. A better group of singers and musicians you'd never have come across. The play began again and it was barely into the first act when three or four sturdy men – who'd obviously had a few drinks too many –

down at the back launched into song. They started singing 'The Wearing of the Green' and we had no option but to let the stage curtains fall. When everything seemed to have calmed down again, we gave the nod to Donnchadh Ó Monghaile, the best singer then living in Erris, to re-commence proceedings. No sooner were the first notes out of his mouth but the skittering and the laughing started all over again. There was nothing for it but to pack it in for the night.

The whole night was a big mess. The Gaelic League didn't make a bean and I ended up with a debt of one pound for my troubles. A pound back then was a lot of money, so you can imagine what a disaster that night turned out to be for both the League and for me. When God divided out men's talents, he was generous to all. The man who played the main role in the play, that is, the part of Seán na gCapall, was actually illiterate but he was a naturally gifted actor.[9] All he had to do was to have the lines read out to him a couple of times and the role briefly explained to him, and he was in business. He had a photographic memory and never made a mistake in his lines once he had first heard them. In fact, that man had one of the finest memories I ever came across. Only two other men were on a par with him memory-wise – both of whom were well-known public figures, i.e. Eoin MacNeill[10] and Piaras Béaslaí.[11]

A timely occurrence took place in Binghamstown at this juncture. It was as if Heaven had sent him when an Irish-speaking priest with nationalist leanings was assigned to the parish, a young man named Fr Pádraig MacAodha who had only just been ordained in Maynooth. This man's heart was with the Irish language movement. In addition to being a fluent Irish-speaker, he was also an accomplished writer of Irish. He wasn't too long in Binghamstown before he and I were in cahoots on a number of interesting Irish-language projects. Pádraig MacAodha soon came to our aid in relation to the dearth of dramatic scripts. He wrote a play, *An t-Ádh agus an Mí-Ádh,* which we produced in Binghamstown and in the poorhouse of Belmullet. A drama group from Pollatomish subsequently produced this play in that parish also. The play drew large crowds, no matter where it was produced. Apart from the fact that this was a well-written play, the fact that its author was a local priest and was involved in its production also ensured that everybody in Belmullet went to see it. The fact that the priest was also a playwright was a major boost for those of us who were involved in the promotion of Irish drama and culture. It garnered us a new respect as relating to that particular performance of Fr MacAodha's play, or that is what we initially assumed anyway.

The new priest's support didn't have as beneficial an effect in the long term as I had hoped it would, however – as I will explain shortly. The arrival of this young and energetic priest who was very favourable to the Irish language certainly gave me a big personal boost in my day-to-day work promoting the language. Fr MacAodha had an intuitive understanding of what the aims of the Irish language movement were and what the work of language activists, like myself, intended to achieve. His enthusiasm and energy gave all of us who were involved in Irish-language teaching and cultural renewal a new lease of life just when it was badly needed. His positive attitude and spirit even rubbed off on many of the locals and, after a long day's work, there was nothing I enjoyed more than to sit down and run through our plans to strengthen the Irish language movement in the area with him, the preservation of the spoken language in particular.

Our pleasant meetings were short-lived, however, and I

soon found myself on the move again. One night as the priest and I were chatting, we noticed an advertisement for a third teacher in the school at Binghamstown. This was a school in an area where every single pupil was a native Irish speaker and yet both of the teachers who were teaching there had no Irish. Neither were they interested in teaching or promoting Irish in any way. It would be an enormous shame and travesty if a third teacher was appointed to this school who was only interested in 'Anglicising' the people further and there was every likelihood that this could happen given that the advertisement for the new teaching job only mentioned the Irish language in terms: 'Irish a recommendation'.

That night I sat down and wrote a letter to the newspaper *An Claidheamh Soluis* publicising this case and outlining how shameful it was that this process of Anglicisation was still ongoing. My letter duly appeared in the paper. All hell broke loose then, however. Unfortunately, my letter had given the anti-Irish brigade in the teaching fraternity the opportunity to air their grievances against those individuals and organisations who wished to see Irish on an equal footing with all of the other school subjects. A meeting of the association of schoolteachers was called and a motion which was very hostile to the Gaelic League and its efforts in relation to the Irish language was put forward. Letters criticising my stance appeared in all of the national papers but the young priest stood his ground bravely. He countered the hostile motion that the association of schoolteachers had implemented and answered the letters criticising him with powerful arguments that undermined those who wished to continue the Anglicisation process.

That was when we both suffered, however. A number of priests and school managers warned me not to darken their doors again.

Various schoolteachers wrote to me warning me that I wasn't welcome in their schools ever again. There were even a number of shops in Belmullet who refused to serve me, all because they had a relative who was a teacher and who was hostile to the Irish language. The local people in Binghamstown were divided, some of them supporting the priest and me, others against us. I was impressed with how many of the locals supported us even when everybody else was trying to blacken our names. Rumours were spread that the priest and I were 'blow-ins' and trouble-makers from Galway, that we were misguided and leading people on the wrong path. There were the usual allegations to the effect that 'Everybody was happy before those two came to the locality and the sooner they leave here, the quicker everything will return to normal once more.'

Unfortunately, everything turned out much as we had predicted. A teacher who had no Irish was duly appointed. The public affairs committee of the Gaelic League organised a meeting to discuss the issue but instead of doing something constructive, they 'kicked for touch'. They appointed an irrelevant sub-committee to discuss the controversy in more detail and that was the last we ever heard about the issue. Rather than supporting us in our struggle against the establishment, the public affairs committee simply abandoned us to our fate! They did nothing and left us high and dry.

Shortly after this, I transferred to Clifden in Connemara and had extra work assigned to me. The same thing happened to the priest as he, too, found himself transferred somewhere else. Everything went back to normality once the two 'rebellious' Galwaymen had been removed from the scene. There is a saying that all good comes from friendship. They say too that patience always bears fruit. It seems that there was a strong element of truth in both of these assertions when you take into account how things panned out in the end. Fr MacAodha and I had the satisfaction of hearing that the government's education board actually removed that teacher from the school later. Why? Because he didn't have any Irish!

Fr MacAodha owned a gun that a relative of his had given to him as a present when he was ordained as a priest. It was a beautiful gun and the priest was no mean shot. Every variety of game was plentiful in the bogs and marshlands of Erris back then. Wild duck, snipe, lapwing, woodcock and plover. You couldn't move for the hundreds of rabbits throughout that countryside. In fact, there were many families in that region who would regularly have gone hungry had it not been for the rabbits they managed to catch with snares and traps. With just a few night's work, a man could easily catch well over 100 rabbits.

This was a period of time when I had less work than normal because of the boycott. The priest and I decided to spend a day out hunting then – partly in an effort to forget about the ridiculous scenario that was unfolding whereby we were likely to be 'fired' from our jobs. At least when you went out hunting you were guaranteed to forget your troubles with a day of pure sea-air and the soothing scent of the peat and the scrub. For one day you could set aside your worries and cares and forget that they ever existed. The first good day that came along Fr MacAodha and I headed off into the countryside, early in the morning. The priest and his hunting dog were slightly ahead of me, the dog running and sniffing the ground. I held slightly back with the bag for the game as we set out for that part of the countryside where we knew the game was plentiful. There wasn't a sound out of us as we worked our way quickly across the stretches of bog and plain, our eyes alert to the movements of the dog. We were walking like this for quite a while when the dog suddenly became animated. I saw the priest get down on his hunkers and I did the same. He gave a low whistle and began to move forward in a slow crouch. I followed slowly behind, bent double and low to the ground.

Crawling like this across the grass, my eyes were glued to the dog which was racing across the field. So focused was I on the antics of the dog that I fell into a dip in the ground where the surface was very rough. I dragged myself up out of the mud again as quickly as possible. By now the priest had caught up with the dog and had a hold of him by the collar. I cursed to myself and wiping the mud from my clothes, I heard the priest curse too – 'That bloody dog ruined everything on us there,' he whined. 'We could have had a dozen there,' the priest said, pointing his gun at the horizon where a line of curlew were disappearing against the light. 'He's only a young lad yet, this fella,' the priest added, pointing to the dog. 'Right now, he's too eager, but it won't be too long before he gets the hang of the hunting game.'

'That's always the way with the newcomer, isn't it?' I replied, grabbing a tuft of grass and wiping more muck off myself.

The priest looked over and noticed the state of my clothes then, and he began roaring with laughter as I smiled ruefully to myself.

We decided to head off in a different direction now and it wasn't long before the dog had raised some more game. This time the dog's body went into a silent crouch. He hunkered down, his tail rigid, as he sensed whatever was ahead of us in the grass. The priest stopped and got himself into position while I stretched myself flat on the grass. All I could see were the flicking motions of the dog's tail as it crept slowly and deliberately forwards towards its prey. Suddenly, a snipe burst skywards directly in front of us. I felt the rush of air as it passed my head and sped upwards, twisting and turning as the priest took aim. A shot rang out, the echo resounding all-round, and the bird dropped like a stone. The cats would be happy with their evening meal that day; there was no doubt about that.

Coming home, tired and foot-weary that evening, we raised another batch of game only a stone's throw from the village. The dog went rigid again and we came to a halt. 'Look out,' the priest whispered and raised his gun again, pointing it in the direction of the bush the dog was focused on. The priest let fly and the bush exploded. He fired again and then we trudged over to see how successful he'd been. He'd killed three ducks outright and another two were mortally injured. The dog slipped into the ditch to fish out the dead birds. The squawks of a lone duck came from the other side of the ditch and it was only then that we noticed something strange. Dusk was already falling, but up close these ducks were unmistakably different-looking from the wild ducks we had spent the afternoon shooting. Why so? They were domesticated fowl! The gloom of dusk had disguised their plumage somewhat but there was no doubting it. These fowl were farmyard stock as we would soon find out. They actually belonged to a local woman named Máire Ní Ghuibhir from Binghamstown. That day's hunting proved an expensive one by the time the priest had recompensed Mary for her loss. The loss of those farmyard birds was one thing. Worse, however, was the embarrassment of what had happened. The whole parish would have one hell of a good laugh at our expense! 'That untrained ignoramus of a dog of ours was the cause of this whole damned mess,' Fr MacAodha always said later, in explanation. Although he was right about this, it didn't take away from the fact that our day's hunting proved the butt of much joking and hilarity for years to come.

Mishaps aside, there's nothing more irritating in life than the person who attaches himself to you as if you were his long-lost 'best friend', simply because they have a son or a daughter who happens to be in the same line of work as yourself. I came across a particularly bad example of this during the period of time I spent in Erris. Unfortunately, I was the 'victim' of the attentions of one of these people. A man from Binghamstown – who shall remain nameless – had a son who was a schoolmaster in some other part of Ireland. Although the father had only spent a few short years at school himself – as was the norm for almost everybody of his generation – he latched onto me and I couldn't go anywhere that he didn't follow me. Whenever he met me, he constantly spouted out new phrases of Irish that he had recently learned – especially when there were others in the company. It was as if this man felt that the fact that his son was a schoolmaster somehow entitled him to be my new 'best friend' and intellectual 'sparring partner' – whether I liked it or not! The man became such a pain after a while I couldn't get away from him, no matter where I went. He became such a nuisance that I was often tempted to tell him to 'go to hell' and to leave me in peace – but I kept my thoughts to myself. One day, however, I just couldn't take it any more. He had me 'boxed in' at some social gathering or other – trying out his latest Irish-language phrases on me. What did I do but note down whatever phrase he was 'trying out' on me and hand the piece of paper to him with an accompanying translation of my own. 'Read that now and we'll see,' I said to him without a hint of sarcasm in my voice. Those others who were in the company burst out laughing and 'your man' wasn't long disappearing then I can tell you. As he slunk out the door, one of the others called out to him. 'Hey Séamas, if you turned the paper the other way up, you'd be able to read it!' I hadn't realised until then that Séamas had actually been holding the note upside-down. Believe me, that man didn't bother me any more after that!

You could say that that man with the 'upside-down' note was – in his own way – a 'unique' individual, albeit that he was an awful nuisance. Ireland's villages back then were full of 'characters', individuals whose eloquence and wit made them memorable long after they had passed on. An example of what I mean is outlined in the following anecdote. A dealer in kelp once lodged in the same house as me in Binghamstown. This man, who went by the name of 'The Kerryman', was a beautiful Irish-speaker. One day he was travelling down to Ballinard to buy kelp when he hailed a man who was breaking rocks on the side of the road.

'God bless the work,' said the Kerryman.

'Indeed! It'd be better if you blessed the workman, to be honest.'

'How do you mean?' said the Kerryman, worried that he had irritated the man in some way.

'You'd be better off if you blessed me,' said the workman again, 'because these rocks are so damn hard that I'd be better off hiding them under a few ricks of useless hay than spending my days trying to burst them.'

Sean-Donnchadh Ó Muinghile who was living in Cross then was one of the wittiest people I ever met. A short, intense little man with small twinkling eyes and swarthy skin, he was already an elderly man when I first got to know him. Once we became friends, I would regularly call around to him for an evening spent chatting by the fire. He'd travelled to America once by ship, a sailing that had to be abandoned twice before finally putting to sea from Galway docks. His journey took him three months in total and yet he only spent a very short time in America once he got there.

'Did America not suit you?' I asked him one evening.

'No, my dear friend. And even if it had suited me, I would never have suited America,' he answered.

Every time I called to Donnchadh's house I had to jump over a big wide ditch, a ditch which I only barely cleared sometimes. One night, when it was pitch-dark, I didn't make it, and I fell into the ditch. When I got to the house I told Donnchadh.

'I didn't make it over the ditch tonight, Donnchadh. I fell in.'

'By my soul, if you'd made it, you'd probably have hit something on the other side,' was his response, delivered as quick as a flash.

The last time I met Donnchadh he was over 100 years of age and confined to bed. He hadn't met me for a full fourteen years, and yet he recognised my voice the minute I spoke to him. Even then, aged and bedridden as he was, he could recall every one of the nights that we had spent chatting with one another years before – it was as if they had only happened yesterday.

7

Five Blissful Years in Clifden

The result of the stand taken on behalf of the Irish language by the young priest and myself was that both of us were transferred from Erris. I found myself transferred to Clifden. In the heel of the hunt, I was just glad to have held onto a teaching job to tell the truth. My new travelling teacher, Mícheál Ó Briain prepared the ground for my next post in Clifden, a job that I was both looking forward to and nervous about – in equal measure. I was very eager to begin work again, particularly given the fact that I was now nearer home and closer to people with whom I could share my hopes and worries. It was the middle of November and the weather was cold and severe. The postal service between Ballina and Belmullet was delivered then by two horses and a car. The two horses pulling that car were changed in both Bangor and Crossmolina on the journey out and back. This horse and car was owned by one of the Cearrbáin family, the head of which was closely related to Brian Rua the Mayo poet and mystic, a man whose memory was still very much alive amongst the people of Erris.

The man driving the horse and car was a huge monster of a man, a man who somehow looked out of place driving these horses and this long cart. The journey on that long cart was not an easy one given the freezing conditions. There wasn't a soul in sight that morning as we set off from Erris and for most of the road after that, something which left me with a more desolate image of Erris than I had ever had. Those people who knew in their hearts that I was being badly treated as a consequence of the 'controversy' over the teaching of Irish were too afraid of the 'establishment' to be seen saying goodbye to me as I left. That journey to Ballina was a full thirty-two miles and it was one of the loneliest journeys I ever made. It rained heavily, the showers swirling in from the hills and lashing down in a powerful stream on the road before us. There was nowhere to shelter because it was the bleakest and barest of landscapes. It was very late at night by the time we reached Ballina but there was no problem finding lodgings. Those people who specialised in putting up lodgers for the night were always out to meet whatever horse and car pulled into the town. It made no difference to them how late it was by the time the horses came to the end of their journey. In fact, there was always a bit of a scramble for lodgers in a bigger town like Ballina back then. You'd nearly be pulled asunder by the people vying with one another to persuade you to stay in their houses. I spent that night in a small hotel run by the Mac Giolla Easpag family.

Anxious that I might miss the following morning's train, my sleep that night was brief and fitful. The next morning the people of the hotel advised me to relax and take my time – because I was going to be much too early for the train. I didn't pay much heed to them, however, and barely ate the breakfast that they served before rushing off, bag in hand, in the direction of the train station. In the end, I was a good half an hour early for the train, which turned out to have very few passengers at that early hour of the morning. One other person got into the same carriage as me and no sooner had we started moving, but this man initiated a conversation. At first, I thought he was talking to himself as he had a bad squint in one eye and appeared to be looking out of the window of the train when he was actually looking at me. He spoke in English and we weren't long chatting before I understood from him that he was some sort of a travelling teacher in the Ancient Order of Hibernians.[1]

In fact, he was so enthusiastic about spreading the Gospel and strengthening Catholicism that the then pope wouldn't have held a candle to this man – Joseph Devlin.[2] There was hardly a country in the world which had Catholics in it that Ireland didn't have a special relationship with – and the maintenance of this relationship was in large part due to the diligence and hard work of Joseph Devlin – according to himself at any rate. Then he whispered to me conspiratorially about the dangerously irreligious and Socialist group known as the All for Ireland League, a group whom – as Devlin said – we all needed to be wary of.[3] 'Wait until you hear!' he was saying to me. He launched into a tirade about the All for Ireland League then and there was hardly a name under the sun (many of them 'complicated' English words that I didn't understand to be honest) that he didn't call them.

I was immediately suspicious of this man's approach. My natural inclination has always been to side with the minority and the fact that this man was so vehemently opposed to this group made me wary of his comments from the outset. Apart from anything else, I was actually quite friendly with a man named William O'Brien who was the then head of the All for Ireland League.[4] I knew for a fact that O'Brien, who was a staunch patriot, was both a dedicated cultural nationalist with a great interest in the Irish language and a religious man to boot. Every time I tried to get a word in edgeways during Devlin's rant, however, the man completely ignored me. Instead, he just raised his hands in the air as if forming an arc of the world. Then he dropped his hands into his lap, slamming his right fist into the palm of his left hand as if clinching his argument. He told me to remain patient for a couple of minutes until he finished speaking and continued to talk quickly without a break. Just as our train approached the County Galway town of Tuam, he told me that he was at his destination. He had a meeting to attend that night in the centre of town. When he left the train, I breathed a sigh of relief, I can tell you.

The closer we got to Connemara, the more my spirits were raised. This was only natural, I told myself. After all, I had spent four years living amongst strangers and now, finally, I was coming home. I was always a home-bird and there hadn't been once that I had returned home on a visit during those few years that I hadn't looked behind me three times before leaving the house once more. Some strangely dressed people with foreign accents got into the same train carriage as me in Galway station. They included two men and three women, all of whom were wearing black capes, the collars of which were made from some stiff-looking white material. The women wore bonnets sewn with the stiff-looking starch-like material. They were carrying two strange-looking musical instruments and as soon as the train set off, they began to sing and play their music, while reading from these thick black missals. Their hymns were solemn, their faces devout and humble-looking. In fact they were so intent on their singing that they wouldn't have noticed if anybody had come into their carriage. These religious people were members of the Salvation Army and they were practising their hymns before attending the fair of Oughterard, as I later found out.

As I had never heard its like before, I was very curious about their strange singing and the various books and leaflets they were carrying. I didn't feel like approaching them to ask them, but, my questions were answered only a few moments later when a man got onto the train at Maumwee and sat down beside them. This man was soon asking questions of them and leafing through their books and leaflets. The man glanced over at me a couple of times and I could see what was going through his mind. After a minute or so, the man threw the leaflets aside and his comments to me (in Irish) were none too complimentary. He clearly didn't like these proselytising types at all. As he spoke to me, I saw him glance downwards at my bag once or twice and I moved to reassure him.

'You needn't worry, I haven't gone anywhere near those leaflets or books.'

'I'm glad to hear it,' he answered, 'as less than two months ago, I was fined for being involved in a row with a group of people similar to this one. I thought that incident would have put them off coming this way again but obviously it didn't!'

'To tell you the truth I come from a parish where no "Jumper" or "Souper" was ever allowed to live amongst the people there,' I said to him.[5] 'Did you ever hear the story of how we drove them out?'

'If I did hear that story, I can't remember it rightly,' he answered.

'A few years after the Famine, a group of these proselytisers set up camp in Rosmuc, where I was born. When the locals heard about it, they came together and marched down to where this group was camped. They ordered them to leave the area and escorted them to the outskirts of the parish, whereupon they were warned that it would be dangerous for them if they ever dared return. They never did come back and it's probably just as well for them that they didn't do so.'

After I finished speaking, the man began. 'When I first spotted that crowd,' he said, throwing some leaflets out the window, 'I said to myself – if that man there is one of them, I'm going to give him a hiding, he'll never forget. I owe them that, as I have a score to settle with those people.' All this talk made the time pass quickly and before we knew it we had arrived in Clifden.

The travelling teacher was there to meet me off the train and we went straight to the hotel where he was staying. This same hotel, which was owned by Alistar Ó Dónaill, was later burned to the ground by the Black and Tans. We had barely eaten our food when the travelling teacher produced a detailed timetable of work for me that both he and the local priest had drawn up. The travelling teacher had already set up three branches of the Gaelic League in the area, each of which were ten miles apart. I would be teaching two nights a week at each of the three branches. There were ten schools in that entire area, none of which taught any Irish, and I would be teaching in two of these schools each day. In addition to this, I had two classes a week for schoolteachers and a weekly Saturday class for various groups of nuns, each of whose convents were as far apart from one another as the branches of the Gaelic League were.

Even Sundays weren't free from this crazy work schedule because it was also part of my duties to cycle eight miles to a local church to give out the rosary in Irish there, cycle back home again for dinner and then cycle on a further eight miles to teach drama to a branch of the Gaelic League in Aill Bhric. Somehow, I also had to find time each week to attend the committee meetings of the Gaelic League and ensure that the various branches came together on a weekly basis for an 'amalgamated' meeting of the three groups. Unbelievable as it may seem, any few hours that were left over had to be spent visiting houses in the area to speak Irish with the locals!

Unsurprisingly, the travelling teacher was only new to his job and filled with the fervour and energy of the novice. Just five weeks or so into the job, his over-riding mission was to transform the area's three branches of the Gaelic League into enthusiastic and vibrant organisations. Unfortunately he had failed to notice that such a crazy and demanding workload would kill a horse, never mind a travelling Irish-language teacher. I knew that there was no way that I could fulfil a weekly work schedule as punishing as the one that had been put together for me. Each time I felt like bringing up the issue with the travelling teacher, something prevented me from speaking my mind. Naturally enough, the work took its toll in the end.

Believe it or not, I actually managed to keep up this workload for a full two months before I collapsed with exhaustion. I was so badly run-down that I ended up spending five weeks in a Dublin hospital moving between the bed and the fire in an effort to recover. I was in a very bad way and an excellent doctor named Doctor Mac Giolla Choilligh was the man who helped me back to full health.

It was during my first week in Clifden that I met Dónal Ó Fatharta, the man who had published the book *Siamsa an Gheimhridh* many years previously. Ó Fatharta was an elderly man by then. An old Fenian, he was still a man who had a real presence about him. He had retired from teaching only a few years previously but still looked very young for his age. He wore a long beard, only some of which was flecked with grey. His appearance was very fresh and betrayed nothing of the tough times he had lived through. The only indicator of his advancing years was the fact that he was somewhat deaf and had a slight hesitancy in his voice when he spoke, as if he was afraid that his memory might let him down. If there was anything wrong with his memory, it certainly wasn't evident in any way. He possessed a rare store of folklore including stories, sayings and poems, all of which he could recite at the drop of a hat – and a good deal of which he had written down over the years. The day the travelling teacher and I called on him, Ó Fatharta made a prophecy of sorts. Both of us had travelled a long distance by bicycle that day in order to reach Ó Fatharta's house. The weather was very frosty and the two of us were sweating profusely by the time we arrived at his house. Greeting us at his door, Dónal stared at us momentarily, before announcing cryptically to the travelling teacher – 'I can tell by your countenance that you won't live to a good age.'

'What about this man here beside me?' the travelling teacher asked in a scoffing tone.

'Despite himself, that man will bury the both of us,' answered Dónal.

Strangely enough, what Ó Fatharta said that day came true. The travelling teacher did die a young man, passing away only a short time after this. Dónal also died just a few years later, may God be kind to the souls of both men. Such is life. Little did I realise that day, as I stood there exhausted and out on my feet – that I would outlive both men by many years. A thousand welcomes to God's grace! My earlier reference to Dónal Ó Fatharta as an old Fenian is not inappropriate. While he himself was too elderly to be involved in the struggle for independence, his only son Laoiseach fought alongside me in the War of Independence.

When my health was back to normal once more, I received my new schedule from the Gaelic League. Unbelievable as it may seem, it turned out to be the same as the last one. This time I refused point-blank. Unless they provided me with an assistant,

I warned them, I would not go back to Clifden again at all. They gave in to my request then and they assigned another young man to the Clifden area. This man was Séamas Ó Donalláin from Oughterard, a man who was young and full of energy. Rather than apportioning out the huge existing work schedule between the two of us, the League in its wisdom decided to increase our joint workloads instead. While the League had played a sly trick on us, neither Séamas nor I said anything about it.

Back then, it was almost considered a form of treachery to disagree with any decision the Gaelic League made. To do so was to act in a manner that was considered unpatriotic in some way. Unpatriotic or not, Séamas only stuck the workload a year before he decided that he had had enough and emigrated to America. It's a funny old world, because many years later Séamas and I worked together once more when we set up the New York Irish Language School, where both of us worked for a time.

In those years the Gaelic League's Oireachtas was the cultural highlight of the year.[6] I used to measure my annual calendar in accordance with when one year's Oireachtas came to an end and the date for the next year's festival was set. It was at the Oireachtas that you met all of the other Gaels and it was there too that you discussed the health or otherwise of the native language and culture. The Oireachtas was also an opportunity to see the newest dramas in Irish and to hear the latest traditional music. It was a great place to meet very attractive-looking girls too, young people who were full of fun of energy and who were deeply committed to the preservation and revival of Irish culture generally. It was one of the few annual events that I would never miss out on, no matter what the circumstances.

The Oireachtas was something you needed to plan for well in advance and I always used it as an incentive to save a few pounds during the course of the year. A few pennies here and there were set aside for the Oireachtas 'fund' during the year and you were guaranteed to enjoy yourself to the maximum. Although he had spent his youth in Rosmuc, it was at the Oireachtas a number of years later that I first met Sean-Pháraic Ó Conaire. The night that I met him was one where a play of his, *Na Gaiscithe*, was being performed. When the curtain came down on his play, the audience called out his name and Páraic came out onto the stage where he thanked the theatre-goers for supporting his play. Later that night a concert was held and I remember chatting to Páraic Ó Nia and Parthalán Ó Conaire. There were a pair of Scots-Gaelic singers performing at the concert and I remember Pearse, who understood some Scots Gaelic, explaining the words to myself and the other two men. *Óró na Mórbheanna* was the title of one of the songs and Pearse went into some detail explaining the meaning of each of the song's verses to us.

Pearse also delivered a lecture in the League's headquarters that week on the issue of bilingualism. He had researched this issue while visiting Belgium and a number of other European countries shortly before; countries where more than one language was spoken. He was a shy and nervous speaker in my view. Whether it was the hot day or his nervous demeanour, he was bathed in perspiration by the time he was finished speaking. At another Oireachtas, he asked me to help him share out copies of his book *An Scoil* amongst the attendees. He had written this book while headmaster of St Enda's.[7] It was also while attending the Oireachtas one year that a defining moment in my life occurred. It was where I first got to know a young nationalist named Seán MacDiarmada.[8] Although I had met him a couple of times before this, I had never really had a proper chat with MacDiarmada, who was a quiet, rugged, handsome man, whose nationalism and patriotism burned within him like a fire. Hard work and an over-exposure to harsh weather resulted in him contracting polio at a young age, a condition which left him debilitated for the rest of his life.

It was MacDiarmada who swore me in as a member of the Irish Republican Brotherhood one night during that Oireachtas festival, held in Galway.[9] He also gave me the authority to set up the brotherhood in the Connemara area. That night when I took the oath of the IRB was one of the most important nights of my life. Like hundreds of nameless Irishmen before me, I felt like I had come of age that evening. Now, I had the opportunity to strike a real blow for Irish freedom. The seeds of my republicanism were planted that night, seeds which will, with the help of God, bear fruit one day yet. Interestingly, that Oireachtas in Galway was a rallying point for many of the nationalists who later led the rebellion of Easter Week 1916.

Pearse was there, although, unusually for him, he had a slightly dishevelled look about him. Normally a snappy dresser, Pearse's dishevelled appearance was a reflection of the difficulties he was then experiencing in his personal life. He had set up St Enda's in Dublin shortly before this but now this new venture of his wasn't going so well. Setting up an all-Irish school, as Pearse had done, demonstrated a great level of idealism in an era when many Irish people, the middle classes in particular, were still in thrall to shoneenism and were very cynical of many aspects of Irish culture. The very people who would have been in a position to send their children to Pearse's school stayed away, even when Pearse set up a company so that the school could be self-sufficient.

Pearse and I were good friends by then. He was a neighbour

of ours back in Rosmuc every summer from 1908 onwards. When in Rosmuc, he and his brother Liam regularly went sailing in our boat, the *Naomh Pádraig*,[10] or *Púcán mór Rosmuc* as it was also then known.[11] Many of the discussions relating to nationalist issues would make their way as themes into Pearse's writings, including his dramas and short stories. I recall one conversation that took place concerning the political process of the day and its drawbacks, a conversation that occurred around this particular time and which is still firmly embedded in my memory. My father was with us and when we had finished discussing 'Home Rule' he exclaimed, 'There is no more frustrating process than the waiting process. The only thing that England ever gave for nothing was propaganda!' The conversation turned deadly serious then and we spent the rest of the night debating the Home Rule question. The consensus was that any acceptance of Home Rule would prove a 'sell-out' and a waste of time.

If anybody had eavesdropped on our 'insurrectionist' talk that night, we would have found ourselves in right trouble. Little did my father realise that every single one of us in the boat that night had already sworn the oath of loyalty to the IRB – just as he himself had sworn loyalty to the Fenians so many years earlier. The tide turned and we were able to go home in the end.

My sister Anna died in 1912. I never truly understood what sorrow meant until her death and it was a long time after she was gone before I got any enjoyment out of life again. Anna was the best-looking of all of us, and she and I were very close from the earliest days of our childhood. I was never somebody who was given to fortune-telling or premonitions but some of the events which unfolded around the death of my sister certainly heightened my awareness of the links between this world and the next. I was in Errismore the night before my sister died and the strange thing was that I actually dreamed of her that night. In my dream Anna was dressed in all her finery because she was getting married and it was a dream as vivid as any which I have ever had. It was only the following morning, when eating my breakfast that the message came through from home that Anna was dying. I rushed home to Rosmuc as quickly as I could, but poor Anna died that very night, only a very short while after I last saw her.

On another occasion, I was in Dublin when a strong intimation came over me that something terrible had happened to a good friend of mine. This man, whom I was very fond of, had never experienced a day's sickness in his life and yet when I bought a newspaper just a few moments later, I was shocked to discover that he had died. Another time when I was in America I had a dream about a boat-trip that I had taken to Inishbofin many years before. An old friend of mine, Liam Mac Fhlanncha, was a central figure in this dream. As before, the dream was so vivid that it was as if we were all really back there again, rolling across the waves and the churning foam of the sea. Imagine my sadness the next day when the news came from Ireland that Liam had died. A more loyal friend or better Irishman was never born in this country of ours than Liam. He was a great support to me when I was working in the Clifden area and I will never forget him for that.

Around the time Liam died the question of Irish nationalist self-determination was focused on one particular issue – 'If the people of Ulster considered it their right to set up a volunteer force to fight against any form of local government in Northern Ireland, then why shouldn't we in the south do the same in relation to the Home Rule issue? Home Rule seemed a strong possibility at this juncture and this branch of the Ulster Volunteers had banded together to prevent any move in that direction. This issue – as relating to the southern half of Ireland – was the main bone of contention when a small group of republicans, IRB members for the most part, came together at a meeting held in the Rotunda, in Dublin. The outcome of this meeting was that it was decided to set up units of Volunteers throughout southern Ireland. A Dublin branch of the Volunteers was set up and we followed suit in Galway soon afterwards when we held a meeting in the City Hall, a meeting which was addressed by Patrick Pearse and Roger Casement. I was so fit in those days that I didn't hesitate in the slightest about cycling fifty miles to attend this meeting, travelling from Errismore to Galway town. Roger Casement had a long association with both Galway and Connemara, of course. He had a great affinity with the people of Connemara and always demonstrated a strong empathy with the poor of the island areas, in particular.

8

Here and There in Connemara

Before the foundation of the Volunteers, it was the United Irish Association and the Ancient Order of Hibernians who were the two largest and most powerful 'indigenous' Irish political organisations with nationalist leanings. There was a large branch of the Ancient Order of Hibernians in the town of Clifden during this era, for example. This branch was so powerful in the area that I had to become a member of it in order to run any Gaelic League activities in the vicinity. A friend of mine was in the Clifden branch and he 'tipped me off' about the fact that they were discussing my request to run Gaelic League activities in the area at their meetings. The Ancient Order rented the local town hall and it was here that I eventually held my Irish classes and, as it happens, the vast majority of the people, whether clergy or lay people, who attended my classes were also members of the Ancient Order. For a time before receiving permission to hold the classes, I had been advised on a number of occasions that I should become a member of the Ancient Order and not be an 'oddball' by remaining outside it. After due deliberation, I decided that this was probably the best strategy. I therefore became a member of the order a couple of years before that Galway Oireachtas which I mentioned earlier. From that point onwards, there was no tension between the order and myself, although this isn't how matters would always remain afterwards – as I will now describe.

Given that I had actually been 'forced' to become a member of the group in order to promote the Irish language in the area, I was never going to be overly enamoured of the organisation anyway. Like many other people, I was always somebody who disliked something that is 'imposed' on them from the outside – and this was no exception. As I became better acquainted with the order, I found that there were aspects of their regulations and organisation that I wasn't particularly fond of. As a member of the order, for instance, you were obliged to come to the help of other members if instructed to do so – even if this other member happened to be a sworn enemy of yours. Similar regulations applied as relating to economic activities. If you needed to buy a suit or a pair of shoes – or anything else for that matter – it was a rule that you had to purchase them from a shop whose owner was in the order.

When my friend Páraic Óg Ó Conaire was getting married, he asked me to stand with him. I needed a decent suit for the occasion and with this in mind, I approached a shopkeeper in Clifden who was also a member of the Ancient Order and told him what I was looking for.[1] His best efforts notwithstanding, this man told me that there was no way that he would have a suit of clothes ready for me in time for the wedding. This was a big problem but there was no way that I could let down my good friend Páraic, who was living and working in another county at this juncture and who would have had no idea of the awkward situation I now found myself in with regard to the Ancient Order. I was left with no option but to buy the suit from a different shopkeeper in Clifden, a man who had no connection with the order. Sure enough, I was reported for this and called to account. I was ordered to pay a fine for my actions and my name was placed on a list of the order's 'black sheep'.

This didn't bother me unduly and I never did pay that fine. I left the order instead, having been a member for just one month.

About this time also, a huge gathering of people came together in Tully near Letterfrack. This meeting was organised by the United Irish Association and the Ancient Order of Hibernians, in response to tensions over land that had been building in that area for some time. The basis for these tensions was the fact that there were still significant estates of land in the area that were controlled by the landlord class and the local people drove the cattle off the land whenever they got the chance. The people who were caught doing this were put in prison, a fact which made the landlord class even more hated than they were already.

The old-time spirit of Davitt was alive and well in that part of Galway, a factor which was in no small part due to a man by the name of Páraic de Bhailís, an enthusiastic nationalist who had returned from a stint in America and who was inciting the locals to stand up for their rights. Joseph Devlin, the then head of the Ancient Order of Hibernians spoke at this meeting, as did a number of other people who, it was claimed, had been members of the Fenians in times gone by. The speakers at that meeting uttered not one word of Irish. The issue of Irish freedom wasn't even mentioned, and worse than this again was the fact that one speaker after the other praised the British government and their policies in relation to the Irish people. The speakers emphasised the need for the Irish people to exhibit patience with regard to political and social reform. Nothing could be gained from breaking the law or taking the law into one's own hands with regard to the 'Land Question'.[2] It was better to remain friendly with the British, the speakers maintained.

Before the meeting broke up that day, the speakers warned

the people against this Irish-American whom they claimed was leading them astray. This man who was agitating for land reform didn't have their interests at heart, the assembled crowd were told. He was only interested in himself, because it was his intention to seek election as a local representative. This was the ridiculous 'claptrap' that these various speakers spouted at this meeting. And there must have been some people who believed those speakers. It's a wonder that whatever sparks of nationalist fervour that remained burning in the hearts of people weren't completely extinguished at this meeting.

Séamas Ó Dónalláin and I had more reason than most to remember this meeting where anti-nationalist rhetoric was the order of the day. Why so? Because the pair of us were nearly beaten to a pulp on the same day, as I will now explain. The IRB had recently founded a newspaper, *Saoirse na hÉireann*, which was printed in Dublin. I used to write occasional articles for this newspaper and on the day of that meeting in Tully, Séamas Ó Dónalláin and I had only just arrived at the meeting when we noticed a couple of people monitoring our movements as we moved around the fair. These same people were obviously watching us as we made our way home that evening also, because a group of about twenty men attacked us at the crossroads in Letterfrack, all of whom were members of the Ancient Order of Hibernians. We would never have gotten out of there alive if it hadn't been for two members of the Clifden GAA club who saw what was happening and helped us to fight them off. Worse than anything was the fact that the local police noticed what was happening but did nothing and just watched while Ó Dónalláin and I received a terrible beating.

Despite our injuries that day, the fair proved very successful as regards sales of *Saoirse na hÉireann*. We sold over 200 copies of the newspaper that day, frequently explaining to the punters that this was a new publication that the Ancient Order of Hibernians had produced to boost the growth of their organisation. Afterwards, I sent that day's profits on to Seán MacDermott who was the newspaper's director, and informed him of the 'battle' that had taken place in Letterfrack that day. He sent me a congratulatory reply but warned us against putting ourselves in such a dangerous position again in the absence of adequate protection or support.

It was actually in Clifden also that I first spoke at a political rally, a speech that I had to give unknown to my superiors in the Gaelic League. Four people had only just been released from prison in Galway, having been arrested for driving four cattle from land which the landlords had fenced off, and which the poverty-stricken local people had no access to. When the four protestors arrived back from Galway Jail by train, not one person had the courage to meet them from the train or welcome them back into their community. The four men had essentially been boycotted. When my good friend Liam Mac Fhlanncha and I heard about this sorry state of affairs, we decided we had to do something to acknowledge the bravery of these four protestors. We got the bell-ringer from Galway to walk through the streets of Clifden announcing a public rally which would be held that evening near Clifden train station. We organised for the four recently released prisoners to be at the meeting where both Mac Fhlanncha and I praised the bravery and resistance of their actions.

Believe it or not, the following night saw another meeting organised in Clifden, where nationalists – the Ancient Order of Hibernians and the United Irish Association included – criticised the rally that Mac Fhlanncha and I had organised and accused us of fomenting tension in the area.

As outlined previously, there was hardly a parish in Conne-mara which hadn't set up its own company of IRB Volunteers by this point in time. All the indicators were that the political situation in Ireland was approaching a crisis point. The moment of truth arrived much more quickly than many of us had anticipated, however. When the Great War of 1914 occurred, nationalist leader John Redmond pledged the support of the Volunteers to the British cause. Not unnaturally this led to the Volunteers splitting into two camps. While a section of the Volunteers decided to pursue Parnell's 'constitutional politics' route as outlined years earlier, there were groups of men in every region who remained loyal to the philosophy of the senior council, the vast majority of whom were also members of the IRB. I was a member of the committee of the Volunteers in Clifden when the split occurred and I'll never forget the Sunday that a British parliamentary representative for Connemara visited Clifden to try to rally support for the British position. This man was very critical of the nationalists and heaped abuse on the Volunteer movement which he repeatedly referred to as the 'Volunteers of Ireland'.

While his overall sentiments and opinions didn't come as a big surprise to me, I was still taken aback by the vitriol which he heaped on the then leader of the Volunteers, Eoin MacNeill. MacNeill was somebody whom I'd known on a personal level for many years and I could feel my blood begin to boil, the more this representative ranted and raved. Eventually, I had heard enough and I stood up and let the individual know what I thought of him. I was only just getting into my stride when a group of the speaker's lackeys threw me head-first out the door of the main hall and onto the road. My old friend Liam Mac Fhlanncha, who had joined in my protest, came flying out the door a moment later.

That same night the British representative decided to address a gathering of armed Volunteers where Liam and I heckled him once more. We asked him straight out what right did he have, an individual who had no connection whatsoever with the nationalist movement, to address a company of Volunteers and advise them on what political strategy they should adopt. There was no drilling or athletic training held that particular night as the debate on which side the local 'drilling sergeant' would take, raged on amongst the company's leaders. As it happens, the drill sergeant who was absent that night would take the side being proposed by that British government representative, a move which would put a damper on the activities of the Clifden company of Volunteers for some time afterwards.

In fact, a large number of men from that Clifden company ended up enlisting in the British army during the Great War. One member of the Clifden company fought in the First World War and then returned to live in Clifden when the war was finished. This man was killed by the Black and Tans on the evening of St Patrick's Day 1921 and his death was most likely in revenge for an earlier attack which we Volunteers had committed on the Tans. The tragic irony of that man's life was that he was killed by the very same government and empire that he had at one time fought to preserve – and all because he found himself in the wrong place at the wrong time. One wouldn't have been surprised if he had been executed because he was on 'our side', but the man had left the republican movement years earlier when he joined the British army and no longer had any sympathy for the republican cause when he was killed. This was the thanks the empire bestowed on that man in the end.

Unlike the divisions and uncertainty that characterised certain elements of the Clifden Volunteers at this time, there was far more unity of purpose amongst the republicans back home in Rosmuc. The Volunteers in Rosmuc had originally been founded by Dr Cusack, Seoirse Mac Niocaill, Páraic Ó Máille and I. The only major drawback that our Rosmuc company had at the beginning was that we were without anybody with a good knowledge of weaponry and military drills to instruct us in the basics. Luckily for us, Pearse visited Rosmuc just a month or two after we had set up the Rosmuc Company. From 1903 (i.e. the occasion of those Irish-language exams which I mentioned earlier) to 1915, not a year went by that Pearse didn't spend a couple of months a year in Rosmuc if he could. Coming to Rosmuc was a nice break for him from the hustle-and-bustle of Dublin and, fortuitously for us, he decided to take over the running of our Volunteer company on this particular visit. Pearse was a member of the Volunteer's Ard Chomhairle at this time and this meant that we Rosmuc Volunteers actually had a 'direct line' to the top of the organisation.[3] Strange as it may seem, we actually had more contact at this time with the main arteries of the Volunteers in Dublin than we did with the Volunteers in Galway.

The Gaelic League's West Galway Feis was held in Clifden on 28–29 June that year (1914). It was the biggest feis in Connacht at that juncture and large crowds of Volunteers travelled great distances to attend. This two-day event was the biggest gathering of people in Clifden since the era of the monster meetings at which Daniel O'Connell had spoken so many years before.[4] The only significant difference between the two eras was the fact that when O'Connell had spoken all those years before he had addressed an enormous crowd of illiterate and downtrodden people in English, a language which the majority of them could not understand. In contrast with this, those attending this feis were an organised body of independent-minded and patriotic people, the majority of whom were English-speakers, but who were being addressed in Irish, a language which they also understood.

People came from far and wide to ensure that the Clifden feis was a major success. Cluad de Ceabhasa gave up two weeks of his time to help with its organisation and the Gaelic League sent us Páraic Óg Ó Conaire to help also.[5] Cluad de Ceabhasa, Óg and I all lodged in the same house for the duration of the feis and Cluad's bedroom was next to mine. One cold June night I was going to sleep in the bedroom when I noticed that the quilt was missing from my bed. I hunted around and found it on Cluad's bed. Just as I was leaving his room, quilt in hand, who should appear at the door but Cluad.

'What's this?' he said.

'Nothing,' I replied. 'It's just that this quilt has to go back onto my bed.'

'But, that's my quilt,' said Cluad, and he tried to grab it off me.

'Sure, isn't that the same quilt I've been using for the past month?'

Cluad had a hold of one end of the quilt while I had the other. A tug-o' war ensued, one of us pulling against the other. That quilt must have been made of strong stuff! Neither of us would give in and now there was a stalemate between us. Next thing Páraic Óg Ó Conaire came down the stairs.

'What's going on here lads?' he asked. 'Is it a tug-o' war that you're having?'

'There's no way that I'm going to sleep tonight without my quilt,' I said.

'But, it's mine!' replied Cluad.

'By God, I don't see any solution to this problem other than to split the difference between you.'

Páraic went into the bedroom and came back out, razor in hand. 'There's a nice edge on this', he said, running his finger along its edge.

I saw a split-second of opportunity just as Páraic re-appeared and I pulled hard on the quilt forcing it out of Cluad's hands. Every time Páraic met either Cluad or I the next morning, he couldn't stop sniggering. It turned out that he was the one who had switched the quilt from my bed to Cluad's. And all for a bit of fun! Cluad thought it was the woman of the house who had made a mistake while I had assumed Cluad had swiped it.

There was a big meeting of Volunteers organised for 29 June, a gathering which many of the same Volunteers who were attending the feis would also attend. Many of these Volunteers made camp in tents just outside Clifden town and the night before the Athenry event they decided to practise their drills. The poor people of Clifden were woken in the middle of the night to the sound of their drills and practices. The townspeople got such a fright that they didn't get a wink of sleep from then onwards. What was really killing me was the fact that I was going to miss the Athenry gathering because of my involvement in the organisation of the feis. 'Duty calls', however, and I had no choice in this regard.

While Cluad was in Clifden we came up with the idea of translating the Volunteers' drills and routines into Irish. This would help improve the Irish of those Volunteers who weren't fluent at the same time as they were practising their movements and athletics. We spent a while translating the various technical terms and orders into Irish but one phrase that stumped us immediately was 'Reverse Arms'. Not only did we have difficulty translating the term, we also weren't entirely clear how to perform the manoeuvre. 'I don't see any solution to our quandary other than that one of us goes down to ask one of the local police,' said Cluad.

The local barracks was only a few hundred yards down the road from us and Cluad made his way down there to get a demonstration of 'Reverse Arms'. I couldn't go down there given that I wasn't on good terms with the police; my name was listed in their 'black book' because I had been seen by them wearing the uniform of the Irish Volunteers. So the bold Cluad walked into the barracks and asked them to explain the term 'Reverse Arms' and demonstrate it. He got short shrift from them, I can tell you. He was told to clear off and thank his stars that he wasn't thrown into prison immediately. Not unnaturally, the police detested the Volunteer movement at this juncture. In fact, they were required to send weekly updates on the progress or otherwise of the Volunteer movement to their local district area leader.

While working in Clifden, I met a grand-daughter of the poet Mícheál MacSuibhne.[6] She lived locally and was in her late fifties at the time. She was a woman who was known for her knowledge of diseases and healing, and was particularly noted for her skill in curing bones and cartilage problems. A fluent Irish speaker herself, she knew only a small amount of her grandfather's poetry. A thin, short and swarthy-faced woman, she worked very hard at her healing trade and to ensure that her children did not go without.

It was at that year's Oireachtas that I first got to know O'Rahilly, who was both in charge of *An Claidheamh Soluis* and a member of the Volunteer's Ard Chomhairle.[7] Not everyone appreciates how much work O'Rahilly did at this time to further the printing and publishing of the Irish language. It was O'Rahilly who first ensured that the two Roman letters 'S' and 'R' were integrated into the orthography of the Irish language. A quiet yet alert man, he was straight-backed and tall, with thick black hair and a pencil-thin waxed moustache of the same colour. He had responsibility for the purchase of the Volunteers' uniforms and I know for a fact that he spent a good deal of his own money on this. I had first approached O'Rahilly in the hope of sourcing a few rifles from him. These guns were required for those parts of Connemara where the Volunteers were badly in need of them. I made this request in Mrs Power's house on Henry Street in Dublin and although he didn't have any guns available at that time, he did provide me with a gun for my own personal protection; a gun which I held on to until it was confiscated from me after my arrest during Easter Week 1916. The government in Ireland at this time viewed O'Rahilly as a major player in any likely insurgency; so much so, that they sent large numbers of extra troops into his native county, Kerry. It was the then head of the British army, General Friend, who gave the order in relation to County Kerry.

'His name might be "Friend" but he's no "Friend" of mine,' I heard O'Rahilly say once in reference to that colonel at a Gaelic League ard-fheis.

9

Divisions within the various Nationalist Organisations

The longest journey I ever made by bicycle was one I made to Croagh Patrick.[1] Along with a couple of others, I left Rosmuc one morning on *Domhnach Chrom Dubh*, the last Sunday in July, and cycled to Clifden.[2] After that we travelled by horse and car to the foot of Croagh Patrick. We climbed up to the peak of the mountain after which we came back by horse and car again to Westport. Having got a bite to eat we headed for home once more. One of the things I remember most about that trip was the heat. It was a very hot day, even for Ireland, a day where the toughest thing to deal with was the hunger and thirst while travelling.

Back in Rosmuc by dawn I hadn't time for any sleep. After a quick wash and something to eat I made for the crossroads at Maumwee by train. My legs were sore by the time I hit the sack that night in MacBoone Street, I can tell you. While a journey like the one I have just described might seem a long one to people today, it was nothing for a travelling teacher to cycle 160 miles in one day back then, journeys which were done on roads that were very rough compared with today. The roads then were narrow and rough, and as you cycled along your bicycle would raise a spray of shale and stones behind you. The turns and twists of the Irish roads often proved the most tiring or difficult aspect of your journey in those days and you were lucky as a travelling teacher if the back wheel of your bicycle lasted for more than six weeks at a time. What made it more difficult again was the fact that we were only able to afford the cheapest bicycle wheels and tyres at this time.

The Oireachtas was what brought me to MacBoone Street on that particular day in 1915. I might have been really exhausted by the time I wheeled into town but it was a happy form of tiredness. That journey was really worth the effort because that Oireachtas proved one of the liveliest and most spirited that I ever had the good fortune to be involved in. As it happens, the house I lodged in also housed many of the principal figures in the Gaelic League, Gaels who burned with the desire for Irish freedom, political and cultural. Thomas Ashe – God be good to his soul – you were amongst this group of inspiring people![3] A true Gael to the very core of his being, Ashe was a singer and musician of some repute. I saw him again a short time after this, as he circled alone around an English prison yard, his hands clasped at the small of his back. He had been sentenced to solitary confinement but even then he did not allow the coloniser to break his spirits. As I watched him from the tiny window of my prison cell that day, I noticed the quick movements of his fingers, as if playing out a secret rhythm. It was as if psychologically he had transported himself to a lively music session somewhere at home, as if he was still playing his uilleann pipes in his mind.

One year after I spotted Ashe in that prison yard, he had again taken the fight to the foreign invader on Irish soil, acquitting himself with such bravery and resilience that his name will forever be associated with the struggle for Irish freedom. He was sentenced to death for his role in that insurgency but the 'merciful' English commuted his sentence to one of life imprisonment. Ashe was always the life and soul of the prisoners in Dartmoor prison and in the other English prisons where the Irish lads found themselves. Even when times were toughest, Ashe never let it get him down. He was always in good humour and would help cheer up all of the other prisoners. A handsome man who was always smiling, he kept our spirits up in both good times and bad.

The end of the year saw the first split worth mentioning within the Gaelic League, a split that had been threatening for some time. The revolt which was brewing came to the fore more quickly that year due to the growing influence of the younger generation within the Gaelic League. The motion which brought the disunity to a head was one which was listed on the Gaelic League's conference agenda calling not only for an Irish-speaking nation but also for a free and independent Gaelic nation. The motion was passed but there was nevertheless a wing of the organisation that regarded this development as too 'political' in nature. Douglas Hyde resigned from his position as Gaelic League president.[4] Hyde was not a 'political' man but there were two different groups within the League at this stage, both of whom were politicised to different degrees. One group was very supportive of England's role in the First World War while the other was very opposed to England, and this was the first time both ideological wings of the movement clashed. John Redmond's faction had never come up against so politically overt a motion as the one passed that year, neither at the ard-fheis nor at the smaller public affairs committee meetings. Not unnaturally, those of us who were both Gaelic League and IRB members worked hard to ensure that that particular motion was carried at the ard-fheis that year.

Once the motion was passed, however, many of us felt bad that the man who had set up the Gaelic League, and done so much to attract people to the movement, had now been forced to resign from its leadership. There was such disgust at Hyde being forced to make way for this 'hot-headed' or 'foolish' younger generation that the position of Gaelic League president was left vacant for a year afterwards. Eoin MacNeill, who was with us in prison in England, was appointed to the position the following year. I'll never forget the day that Hyde resigned from the presidency. There were men with tears in their eyes saying that we were now left leaderless and without direction.

Redmond and his supporters were always boasting that they had every national movement and organisation under their control. The motion passed at that ard-fheis, where we called for a 'free and Gaelic Irish nation', put them in a difficult position, however. It called on Redmond's faction to abandon all of their remaining pro-British sympathies. One important thing that emerged from that ard-fheis was the fact that nobody could claim anybody involved in the various Irish-language organisations was in any way ambivalent about the necessity of severing all ties with the empire and gaining complete freedom for Ireland. It was at the Gaelic League branches based in Connemara that this defining motion emerged and I am proud to say that it was I who ensured that the motion was placed on the agenda of that ard-fheis.

No Oireachtas was complete without Éamonn Ceannt. A Galway republican, he was a very sociable man who was also a very able piper. In fact, he had the wonderful privilege of being the first Irishman to play music for the pope since the era of Hugh O'Neill. A tall, thin man with black hair and a moustache, Éamonn was a member of both the Volunteers'

Ard Chomhairle and the public affairs committee of the Gaelic League. His death was a great loss to the Irish nation.

I left Dundalk on the Friday afternoon of Oireachtas week. My early departure was because Jeremiah O'Donovan Rossa's body was being brought home from America. His body was 'lying-in-state' in City Hall, Dublin, and I made it my business to attend and to pay my respects. By the time I reached Dublin, there were already thousands of people queuing in orderly lines to get one final glimpse of this noble Fenian. O'Donovan's Rossa's face was silhouetted behind a glass in the casket so that all of his supporters could say a brief goodbye to him. Like everyone else, I only had a few brief seconds to say a quiet farewell to the great man and all I can remember of his face was its intelligent demeanour and his long, distinguished-looking beard. It was the fashion then amongst the older Fenians to sport a beard.

Almost a year before the funeral, a boat transporting guns and other armaments arrived into Howth. Somebody must have tipped off the British authorities about the arrival of the shipment on Irish shores because they were swarming all over Howth that afternoon. Luckily the weapons had already been unloaded from the boat and secreted away in a number of hiding-places where they couldn't be discovered. This didn't stop the British from taking revenge, however. Returning from Howth that very evening, some disgruntled British soldiers opened fire on some innocent bystanders in the streets of Dublin. They killed three people and injured thirty-two others. No wonder the mercury was then rising amongst Ireland's rebels and freedom-fighters.

Pearse didn't attend that year's Oireachtas – or the one the year before that either – as he was quite busy with the preparations for impending rebellion and actually travelled from Rosmuc to Howth and was there for the smuggling operation involving those guns. He went to Jeremiah O'Donovan Rossa's funeral also from Rosmuc and gave that famous oration in Glasnevin cemetery, an oration which he had actually prepared in Rosmuc. I have attended many funerals and public meetings in my time, gatherings where enormous crowds attended. I saw huge crowds at Wolfe Tone's grave in Bodenstown. I witnessed a giant parade in New York on St Patrick's Day once. It was the same in Ireland, where I had partaken in large rallies and processions, some of them pertaining to the Gaelic League or Sinn Féin. O'Donovan Rossa's funeral was a bigger event than anything I had ever seen before, however. The newspapers published the following day said that it took well over two hours for the funeral cortège to make the short journey from the church to the graveyard, such were the masses of people who were eager to pay their final respects.

Pearse surpassed himself during his graveside oration. I had never seen him speak with such emotional force as he did that day. Dressed in the uniform of a Volunteer officer, he led the Rosmuc company of Volunteers on the day. Standing at the graveside, his ceremonial sword at his side, he delivered that famous oration of his in a powerful voice that was at turns both full of hope and carefully controlled emotion. The fact that our Rosmuc company was under Pearse's command meant that we had the privilege of standing right next to the grave as that historic speech was given.[5]

Life throws up strange coincidences and encounters and Jeremiah O'Donovan Rossa's burial in Glasnevin cemetery was no exception. At the funeral that day I met a staunch nationalist by the name of Eimir Ní Uadaill, a woman whose name should never be forgotten when the annals of republicanism are written. Eimir gave everything for the nationalist cause and there was no major event of this era that she did not make a vital contribution to. She also had a better insight than most people into what the life of a travelling teacher such as myself was like at this juncture. Indeed, on that very evening, Eimir invited myself and another travelling teacher to a gathering in the name of George Russell or 'A.E.' as he was better-known.[6] While she invited the two of us out of kindness, I have to admit that such a 'high-society' occasion wasn't really my cup of tea. It would have been impolite to refuse her, however, and we accompanied her to the get-together. There was a big crowd in the house when we arrived, various well-known painters, writers and politicians amongst them. Russell himself was a big, stocky man, a handsome and effusive individual who sported a big, thick beard. While I had little experience of such 'intellectual' gatherings, I couldn't help noticing how welcoming Russell was and how interested he was in us. He expressed a strong admiration for us and an interest in the work of travelling teachers such as ourselves, a fact which I found very gratifying.

During the course of our conversation with Russell, Eimir Ní Uadaill mentioned to him that I had written a couple of books. I could have killed her for mentioning this, however, as a number of people suddenly directed their attention towards me. Like many young people from rural areas, I was still incredibly shy and felt quite awkward in social situations, and the last thing I wanted was for people to begin asking me questions about my youthful literary endeavours. If the ground had swallowed me up at that very moment, I would have been more than happy. Many of the writers in the company sidled over to engage me in conversation. They were more surprised than anything else when they heard that I wrote in the Irish language. That somebody as young as myself was writing essays and books – and in the Irish language, to boot – seemed very strange to these literati, the majority of whom had been raised and educated in an entirely English-language environment. That there were still people in Ireland who had grown up in an entirely Irish-speaking milieu came as something of a shock to them, I think. Little did I realise that night, however, that there were also a number of people in attendance who soon composed elegies for the dead of 1916 – i.e. some of the same people who had stood alongside me at O'Donovan Rossa's graveside that very afternoon – Russell (himself) and Séamas Ó Súilleabháin amongst them.[7]

Russell showed us some of his paintings that night, a number of which were actually hanging where the evening's gathering was in full swing. Those of us who had grown up in a rural area such as Connemara were at a loss as to what to say while he was explaining the various paintings to us. None of us knew about painting or art criticism and all we could do was nod approvingly and make complimentary comments regarding his work whenever we got the opportunity. How could you insult a man who had invited you into his home where you had drunk his tea and enjoyed the good company? As far as I can remember, the majority of those paintings consisted of dreamlike and mythical scenes, figures which were half-man/half-fish and the like. Many of the images were reminiscent of mermaids or other supernatural beings. There was something unreal and unworldly about them, a sense of the ethereal that I didn't notice in other art forms in my later years. While we discussed art and literature that evening, the thoughts of many of us lay with the great man we had just buried that day, the man who had inspired that passionate and historic speech on the part of Pearse, a speech that will never be forgotten.

A few years subsequent to that evening, when both of us

were incarcerated in an English prison, Ashe told me a story about Jeremiah O'Donovan Rossa. The old Fenian's faculties, his hearing included, were in decline for a good while before his death. Once, when Thomas was in America on a fund-raising trip for the Gaelic League, he went to visit O'Donovan Rossa who was feeling somewhat low. As soon as Thomas began speaking Irish, a huge transformation came over the old Fenian. A man who had been raised speaking Irish, O'Donovan Rossa never denied his language or his heritage, no matter how much suffering or imprisonment he was forced to endure.

While the build-up to that Dundalk *Oireachtas* had seen a certain degree of tension between the different factions within the nationalist movement, the feiseanna around the country were almost inevitably occasions for sport and fun. Seán Seoighe was the travelling teacher in the Achill area at this time. He was charged with organising a feis and Páraic Ó Conaire and I were sent to North Mayo for a fortnight to help him out with the preparations. This assignment was like a mini-holiday for Páraic and me since Achill is such a beautiful part of the country and it was a change from our regular routine.

The feis, which was held in an old convent or school, was a great success. We had a concert that evening in Achill Sound, an event that I was put in charge of. Many people attempted to get in free and so I sent Ó Conaire down to the door as 'back-up' to Seán Seoighe. Things got a bit out of control then and a group of youths who refused to pay the entrance fee forced their way in, pushing Seoighe and Ó Conaire out of the way with a huge plank of wood. These wild hooligans hit both Seoighe and Ó Conaire in the stomach with this plank driving them back onto the floor of the hall. This incident was in some ways reminiscent of the toppling of the Bastille, because neither of them ever wanted to work on the door again. Eimir Ní Uadaill was the initial organiser of this feis and, as often happened, the local clergy did nothing to support the event.

One of the most attractive things about both the Irish language movement and the nationalist movement of this era was the sense of community they generated. There was a wonderful sense of camaraderie amongst the Gaels of this era. It was as if we were all one big family. This sense of unity permitted us to overcome any obstacle, whether big or small. For example, Páraic Ó Nia (my closest ever friend and a man who stood his ground at the heart of every battle), Páraic Ó Conaire and I went from Rosmuc to Spiddal for a céilí once. Thirty-six miles over and back was the journey then, but it didn't knock a feather out of us, because we were young and single and we were all mad for music and dancing. It was a lovely morning as we cycled home. We were somewhere near Knock in the early dawn when Ó Conaire, who was out in front, collided with something on the road. He was thrown from his bike and got quite a serious cut on his hand. The obstacle on the road turned out to be a donkey. It was still pitch-dark at that time of the morning and none of us had spotted the donkey which was asleep lengthways in the middle of the road. To add insult to injury, Ó Conaire's bicycle was punctured in the collision and none of us had a puncture repair kit with us.

'You go on!' Ó Conaire advised us. 'I'll get to Rosmuc later on, one way or the other.'

We would have preferred to stay there with Ó Conaire until he was up-and-running again. Páraic Ó Nia, who was a postman, had to get home to deliver the post while I had to go to Tourmakeady, County Mayo for work the next day.

'How did you get on after we left that night?' I enquired of
Ó Conaire the next time I met him.

'Well, I kept walking until I reached Tully. When I spotted
a big reek of turf on the side of the road, I pulled out some loose
sods that I could use as a pillow. I made a small square pile out
of the sods and covered them with my raincoat. Then I lay back
in the ditch there and had a nice sleep for myself. I was woken
by the feel of something breathing on me. It turned out to be a
goat that was nuzzling my face! I fixed the puncture then in the
house of the schoolmaster O'Leary near Na Doireadha.'

Long journeys by bicycle sometimes necessitated sleeping
outdoors in those days. I remember returning home from the
Galway Oireachtas one Sunday night in 1913 when I was
so exhausted that I just had to stop for a rest. I made myself
as comfortable as possible on the side of the road at Lurgan,
between Oughterard and Cross. I was woken by a group of
tinkers who had noticed a bullock chewing on my jacket. I
threw some choice curses in the direction of that same bullock,
I can tell you.

The following anecdote is another example of how different
life was then as compared with today, particularly as regards
the lack of transport infrastructure, telecommunications and
the manner whereby information could be misconstrued or
misinterpreted depending on the context. I was 'away from
home' in Clifden for a few days attending a feis in Castlebar,
County Mayo. Returning on Saturday, I was only just back in
Clifden town when I felt something peculiar was going on.
Everywhere I went, people were staring at me. I walked down
to the local market and it was the same with everybody I passed
at the stalls there. No sooner did I approach a stand or a stall
but the traders there dropped whatever they were doing and

gave me their full attention. It was as if I was somebody famous or I had returned from the war or something. I began to get a bit paranoid and I decided to walk down one of the side-streets to see whether the reaction was the same there. I checked my clothes to see whether there was something odd about my appearance but I couldn't see anything out of place. My worry and uncertainty about what exactly was going on was making me angry by now, and – under my breath – I began to curse anybody I found staring at me or laughing at me.

I couldn't believe it when I got back to the lodgings; both the other lodgers and the people of the house, came up to me and began to shake hands with me. One after another, they congratulated me, slapping me on the back and cheering me. Everybody was speaking at once and I had no idea why they were behaving like this. I thought I was losing my mind! 'Congratulations', they were all crying out as they clapped their hands together. The landlady first sensed my bemusement and cut 'straight to the chase'.

'Have you seen the newspaper?' she asked.

'How could I have?' I answered. 'Sure, I was on my bicycle for hours and only just got home from Castlebar a few minutes ago!'

The landlady showed me the paper then, where I read a report of my recent marriage! The report was a detailed one, listing all of the guests who had supposedly attended and the wedding presents which each of them had given. It would have been hilarious except that many of the nicest of the local Clifden people were mentioned as attending this supposed wedding. This was really embarrassing. Worse again was the fact that in addition to the local and regional newspapers, the Dublin newspapers took the story and reprinted it verbatim.

There were occasions, too, when misinformation and confusion worked to one's advantage if you were 'quick off the mark'. In Clifden, one day in 1915, I wheeled my bicycle out of my lodgings and laid it against the wall. I was about to hop onto it when two policemen suddenly appeared out of nowhere and made a grab for the bike. Without so much as a 'by-your-leave', they grabbed a hold of the bicycle and tried to wrestle it out of my grasp.

'Where are you going with my bike?' I shouted out, getting a good grip on the bike.

'Let go,' they shouted back.

'You'll have to take me as well,' I hissed at them, 'because there's no way that people are getting my bicycle.'

'Do you realise what exactly you're doing, obstructing the law like this?' the police shouted out.

'I know only too well what I'm doing,' I answered them.

By now, a crowd had gathered around, curious to see what all the fuss was about. On hearing the commotion, Seán Seoighe, who was my teaching assistant in Clifden at the time, arrived on the scene and grabbed a hold of one end of the bike. 'Two against two,' he challenged the policemen, the crowd swarming around. The gathering crowd must have made the two policemen a bit nervous as they suddenly appeared more hesitant than they had moments earlier.

'Hold on tight Seán, whatever you do,' a voice shouted from amongst the watching spectators.

'Don't you give an inch Colm,' another person shouted.

'Never fear,' I shouted back as Seoighe and I 'dug in', redoubling our grip on the disputed bike, as the two policemen tried to force it off.

'The canon,' someone shouted in the crowd.

'Upon my soul, it's the canon,' repeated one person after another as they moved aside to make room for the approaching canon.

'Make way for the canon,' somebody shouted out as the cleric marched into the circle, a big crooked stick in his hand. The same canon never went anywhere without this stick of his and God help anyone who got in his way when he decided to wield it.

'What's going on here?' the canon enquired in a loud and authoritative voice.

I'd always been told that you had two-thirds of the truth if you explained your story to a priest before anyone else did. I seized the opportunity immediately.

'These two decided to confiscate my bicycle, without so much as a word to me.'

The canon was a law-abiding man and I could see what he was thinking. The last thing he wanted was to have the law down on him. He stared at the two policemen who tried to take advantage of this interruption in the proceedings to tear the bicycle out of the firm grip which both Seoighe and I had on it. I tried to appeal to the canon's sense of justice then – 'As you can see canon, there's no way that this issue can be sorted out in a calm and rational fashion under the present circumstances.'

The canon thought for a second before twisting around the raised stick like a big baton in his hand.

'If you don't release the bicycle of this decent man here,' he pronounced, 'I'll lash out. Believe me, you won't be the better for it,' he said, his eyes fixed on the two police.

The policemen let go of the bicycle in a slow and deliberate fashion. Then they made their way back to their barracks as fast as their legs could carry them. No sooner had they disappeared out of sight, than the canon asked me what the reason for the dispute had been. I suspect that they were taking my bike in lieu of a fine which they imposed on me for not having a light on my bicycle. The reason I refused to pay the fine was that the name they wrote on the fine was not my real name, but the English version of my name instead.

'Didn't they catch up with you in the end?' asked the canon.

'They sure did. But it was the priest who baptised me and not the police.'

10

Easter Week 1916:
A Glorious Week for Ireland

In those days, it was a genuine pleasure to come across somebody else who was of a similar mind to oneself as regards the Gaelic Revival and the nationalist 'Question'. The question on every nationalist's lips then was – 'When? When would the blow for freedom be struck?' Each Volunteer had to ensure that he was ready for action, an instruction which meant buying a rifle and bullets. I had already bought a gun and fifty bullets in anticipation of the day. We knew that sooner, rather than later, the time for action would be upon us, and we needed to be ready. The fact that Britain was busy on the battlefields of Europe meant that the time was ripe to strike against the enemy.

I was already in Dublin the week before the Rebellion took place, and tension was high as we put our final preparations in place. Everybody was on high-alert, including the British authorities who had their detectives and spies out and were monitoring everybody's movements in anticipation of the battle that lay ahead. In fact, the British had so many spies and intelligence officers on the ground that we rebels had difficulties finding 'safe houses' where our hosts were sympathetic to our cause and yet unknown to the authorities. The British detectives were a diligent and loyal breed and escaping their clutches was never easy. Thomas Clarke's was under constant surveillance, for example; there were never less than two detectives loitering on the corner of Britain Street close to his home. Organisational matters relating to the Volunteers ensured that I had to liaise with Pearse in the weeks before Easter Week.

It is important at this point to provide the context for the growth of the Volunteers in Rosmuc. The way in which the Volunteers developed in Rosmuc had meant that we were more directly under the control of the Dublin-based Ard Chomhairle of the Volunteers, than we were under the regional battalion in Galway. There were two main reasons for this. Pearse himself was our company's leader and we didn't receive any support from the local, regional or county leaders. Suffice to say that there wasn't the same centralisation in terms of organisational activity within the Volunteers in the west of Ireland at this time as there would be after the 1916 rebellion.

Officially, the Volunteers in Galway consisted of one battalion, the catchment area for which lay between Galway city and east Galway. Most of the organisational and military endeavours in Galway officially related to this battalion whereas we in Connemara were left to our own devices, for the most part. This was somewhat strange as the backbone of the west of Ireland IRB was arguably the Connemara battalion. The resilience of our Connemara-based battalion is proven by the fact that just twenty-five of us managed to successfully engage 2,000 police and Black and Tans – this all over a period of two years. This was the political and organisational context which was the backdrop to our communications with Pearse regarding our tactics and instructions before Easter Week. I explained all of the 'politics' and the local territorial 'issues' that were the background to the Volunteers in Galway to Pearse as best I could. While he would have been aware of many of them already, it was important that everything was as smooth as possible on the organisational and communications levels, given that we were about to go into battle with an enemy as powerful as the British. Having explained the complexity of the situation to him, Pearse had a quiet think for a few minutes. He surprised me somewhat then because his solution to these various 'issues' seemed to relate to our Rosmuc company only indirectly.

'The best thing for you (i.e. the Rosmuc company) to do is for as many of you as possible to attend the mobilisation in Galway city next Sunday.' As I later realised, Pearse was planning how to 'integrate' the Connemara (Rosmuc) company better into the regional Volunteer movement. He had to play politics too. My understanding of what Pearse intended was that subsequent to the Galway mobilisation on the following Sunday, our Rosmuc company would be treated more 'equally' by the committee who ran the Galway battalion of the Volunteers and would be better 'integrated' into the county and regional structures generally.

God Almighty! Little did I realise as Pearse and I said our farewells to one another that day, that this would be the last time I would ever shake hands with the man who changed the direction of Irish history more profoundly than anyone else – from the Battle of Kinsale onwards. Nervous that I might be late for the mobilisation in Galway the following Sunday, I left Rosmuc that morning at the crack of dawn. The wind was against me cycling into Galway, the sky dark and showery-looking. Luckily, the weather cleared up by early morning, the sun rising in the sky. I covered that forty-five mile journey carrying a faulty gun and about fifty bullets, without any major mishap. It was still early morning when I arrived into Galway town.

I had a short rest and attended Mass at Woodquay church.

Then I made my way to the mobilisation point. Imagine my surprise when I was informed that the mobilisation had been cancelled. Apparently, somebody had been sent to Dublin the previous day to get all of the orders relating to the forthcoming rebellion from the IRB senior council, orders which would then be communicated at the mobilisation. I decided to stay there with all of the other Volunteers who were also awaiting the arrival of this messenger from Dublin. It turned out to be a long wait because there was no sign of the messenger either on that day or the next. We later learned that Eoin MacNeill had sent this messenger to Limerick first and that Galway was his next port of call. Unfortunately, the messenger had been delayed in Limerick.

By now, all of us waiting in Galway were on tenterhooks. To make matters worse, having hung around Galway for the weekend, rumours began to filter through on the Monday that the rebellion had already begun in Dublin. Increasingly agitated, and with no sign of the promised messenger, we decided that we had to take action ourselves.

I was sent to Mayo to see what news they had or what instructions they had been issued with. As it happens, I knew the Mayo Volunteers' leaders as well (or even better) than I did the County Galway leaders of that era. I set off for Mayo on my bicycle, travelling by the back-roads to avoid any curious bystanders who might notice a stranger passing through. The Mayo Volunteers were gathered together in the City Hall in Castlebar and were awaiting instructions, much as we were in Galway. They too had yet to receive any orders from Dublin with regard to what our next steps should be as part of a national rebellion. Given that the Mayo battalions had no extra information, I decided not to delay, turned right around, and cycled straight back to Galway. On returning to Galway, I heard some very bad news. A raid had occurred on the Volunteer leaders in Galway and they had been taken into custody. Now, there was nobody to provide leadership in Galway should the enemy initiate an attack on us. A sense of despair fell over many of the Galway Volunteers. This didn't last long, however, as the following morning news filtered through from Mayo that the Volunteers there were already in action and were taking the fight to the British occupiers there.

My spirits were raised and I decided to head for Mayo again to join in the fighting. On arrival in Castlebar once more, I discovered that the supposed rebellion in Mayo had never happened and that the story we'd heard was only a false rumour. I turned my bicycle in the direction of County Galway once more. I knew for a fact that there was now fighting in Athenry and I decided to cycle there straight away. Come hell or high water, I would be in action tomorrow, secure in the knowledge that I would finally be taking the battle to Ireland's oppressor.

As the saying goes: 'Talking the talk and walking the walk are two very separate things.' That's how it worked out for me at any rate. I had had very little sleep or food in the previous four days and I stopped at a house in Cong, where I knew the people well, to have a break. I knew the people there would give me a welcome and a bite to eat. Unfortunately, I had barely set foot in the house when the door was forced in by three policemen who made a beeline for me. I spun around and pulled out my gun. The police made a rush for me and I fired. The shot went astray and I fired again, but this time the gun jammed.[1]

Within a split-second the police had my shooting arm twisted behind my back and had forced me backwards onto the floor. Once they had me down, these three burly policemen had no trouble disarming a young, thin fellow like myself. I was taken into custody by two policemen, both of whom received promotion and a commendation from the king of England's representative in Connacht for their troubles; I heard this later on. Once the police had me in their clutches, they put me behind bars. I was taken to the local barracks and thrown into a cell there. As I was put into the cell, they released a big, dirty-looking dog from the same cell. At least my imprisonment had resulted in freedom for somebody! As they saying goes – 'Every cloud has a silver lining'.

The police must have considered my capture a major coup or they must have thought a rebellion had already begun, because before that night was out, there must have been at least two dozen policemen who arrived at the barracks to view me or to take turns guarding me. A stream of senior officers trooped in and out of the barracks during the next twenty-four hours. I never heard such discussion and official claptrap spouted as I did during that twenty-four-hour period. All the to-ing and fro-ing and the intense preparations for battle on their part were mirrored outside the barracks too, it appears. Every road to and from Cong was black with policemen questioning anybody travelling the roads. There were police in the fields and in the shelter of the ditches. They were posted along every stretch of stone wall also, all in a last-gasp effort to ensure that the chains of occupation were reinforced tighter than ever. At some point during the night they put some shackles on me and led me out of that filthy cell.

Given that motor cars were still rare then, I was placed on a horse and cart with three armed policemen guarding me. I'll never forget their swagger and the evil looks they were giving me as they sat in beside me on the cart. There were twenty policeman out in front of the cart and roughly the same number behind us. We set off at a good trot across the plains of Moytirra, through Ballyhale and on into Ballinrobe. It was late at night by the time we reached that town and I was thrown, shackles and all, into another cell in the police barracks there. The shackles had been attached so tightly back in Cong that my wrists were bleeding at this stage, but it made no difference to them.

A few agonising hours later and I was brought out of the cell again and placed in a motor car, where, once more, three policemen joined me. As before, we had a police escort. Two other motor cars filled with police accompanied us, one in front and one at the rear. I got some abuse during that car journey, I can tell you. Those three policemen called me every name under the sun. They insulted me, my family and anybody whom I ever knew or was related to. I never heard such foul language in my entire life and I hope I'll never hear such evil conversation again as long as I live. It was as if the three policemen guarding me were competing with one another to see who could be the most hate-filled and disgusting. At one stage, the two policemen sitting either side of me placed the muzzles of their rifles in my ears in order to 'blow my brains to bits if the mood came upon them' – as one of them kindly informed me.

Life is strange. Four and half years later one of the two policemen who was in the back seat of that car with me that night was killed in a shoot-out between the IRA and the Free State army during the Civil War. He was loyal to his masters until the very end – for all the good it did him. I spent the rest of that night in the Castlebar police barracks. At nine o'clock the following morning, I was brought under heavy guard to the town jail. That first day in prison was one of the longest ever! My initial welcome to the jail involved being thrown into a freezing cold bath. This was just a taster of what was ahead because I suffered regular beatings and torture, both physical and mental, in that place. For the first few days they starved me. At their own regular meal-times they tormented me by making sure that the smell of food wafted into my cell, while not a bite passed my lips.

Within a day or two, I noticed how heavily guarded this jail was and assumed that there must be some very high-profile prisoners incarcerated there. There was no section of the prison, either inside or out, that didn't seem to be crawling with soldiers so that there was virtually no chance of escape. New batches of soldiers arrived regularly under cover of darkness as you never saw them appear or disappear during the day. That the prison was also a centre for young, 'novice' soldiers was also clear to me on the few occasions that I was released from my cell to be fed. I would see these novice soldiers performing endless marches and drills and practising new moves with their weapons. As I soon found out, the vast majority of these young soldiers were just kids, aged between sixteen and eighteen, teenagers who had been forced to enlist in the British army against their will.

The prison guard on my landing was a middle-aged man who was slightly hunched and sporting a grey moustache. He was one of those people who never seemed to get angry, a man who feared his superiors and who was even more afraid of us – the 'Shin Feeners' – i.e. the term he used to refer to prisoners such as myself. On arrival in the prison this man had led me straight to my cell, while intoning the rules and regulations of my new prison home. 'The only glory you'll find in this place is by keeping your cell clean,' he told me. Then he spent the next quarter of an hour explaining the rules and regulations of the prison to me. It was a very warm day and by the time he was finished, the warder was bathed in sweat. He opened my cell door and showed me the various items that were in there including a number of Catholic religious texts, a small table, a bed, a stool and various items of cutlery. The way he spoke to me you'd swear that this was the first time I had ever seen such items of furniture.

'I'm warning you now. Dress your bed and keep your cutlery clean.' He brought in two pillows then and demonstrated how he wished the bed to be made. 'You do it now,' he said. I gave it a go but I obviously didn't do it according to his standards because he told me to do it again. He made me repeat the procedure three times before giving up on me, claiming that I wasn't capable of doing it properly. We moved onto the cutlery then and he demonstrated how he wished to see them scrubbed. I had to scrub them twice a day, I was informed and they needed to be so shiny that I could see my own face in them. I actually had the temerity to ask the same warder for a mirror at a later date. Needless to say, he told me where to go.

'You're in the wrong place if it's a mirror you're looking for,' he informed me angrily. 'Keep scrubbing the arse of that dish there. That'll do you. That's all the likes of you is used to anyway.'

In addition to the various cleaning regulations, there were particular rules that we had to follow relating to the positioning of our cutlery. For instance, we had to leave our plate on the cell-floor, the edge of it leaning against the wall of the cell at a particular angle. The position in which the plates had to face meant that they were always wobbly against the wall and more likely than not they would fall over. Just when you thought you had them set in the right position, the plates would topple over and you would be tormented trying to get them back into the right position again before they were inspected. I was attempting to do this balancing act one day when the whole lot toppled over with a big crash. Next minute there was the rattle of keys and the door was pulled open.

'Was it here that the racket was?' the warder asked. 'It sounded like the world had ended. Set those plates up again. Do it again until you have it right.' Then he went out again.

While I would consider myself a good judge of character, this particular prison warder was a man I could never figure out. He was a contradictory individual. Just when you thought he was being nice to you, he would suddenly turn on you and treat you really badly. One day he appeared at the door of the cell and, without a word, grabbed me by the collar of my jacket. 'Get this jacket off. You'll get it back when you leave this place.' He even took the Tricolour badge that I was wearing. Another night he came rushing into the cell just as I was going to bed and grabbed one of the blankets off the bed.

'You'll have to make do with one blanket tonight. There's so many of your crowd in here tonight that I haven't enough blankets for everybody. Haven't I spent half the evening over in the home for mentally ill people looking for blankets for you lot? Just when I thought I had enough, even more of your crowd arrived in. There's so many of you taken prisoner now that I haven't got blankets for even a third of them.'

I gritted my teeth and kept my mouth shut, but I felt like telling him that it was a pity he hadn't stayed over in the mental home because there were many people there who weren't half as crazy as he was.

One night I was fast asleep when the warder who controlled the keys woke me with a start. 'Get up,' he ordered. 'If you have any personal possessions, get them together and be ready to leave!'

He hurried out the door then as quickly as he had come in. Bizarrely, he left the cell door wide open. I poked my head out the door only to see two soldiers standing guard at either side of the entrance. It didn't take me more than a few seconds to get packed, since any few possessions I had fitted into the pockets of my coat. The soldiers told me to accompany them and they brought me downstairs to the first floor landing where a group of other prisoners were already standing under heavy guard. The prisoners were divided into two separate groups and I was told which group I had to join. Over the next quarter of an hour, more and more prisoners arrived onto the landing, one after the other.

I recognised almost all of them. Joseph MacBride from Westport, the brother of the major who had been put to death after Easter Week was there, as was Seán Ó Corcoráin who was still just a teenager. This lad, who was full of crack and devilment, was killed a short while after this by the Black and Tans during the War of Independence. Another loyal Irishman who was there was Páraic Dóras, the man who was the editor of the newspaper *Mayo News*. I'd known him from the very first day that I became a travelling teacher. In fact, Páraic gave me my first ever cigarette. I wrote one of my first Irish-language pieces for him when I was house-bound in Westport years earlier – stranded due to the very bad weather. It was when I presented him with that essay for his newspaper that he handed me that first cigarette. It was that cigarette that I was reminded of just then as we were counted and marched into line by the soldiers on that landing. If only I'd realised when I accepted that first cigarette, how many of those same cigarettes I would end up smoking over the coming years. When we'd all been accounted for, we were brought under cover of darkness to the local train station. It was still night when the train pulled away from Castlebar station. The train pulled into Dublin as the early morning light was spreading across the countryside.

We were ordered off the train immediately and marched down O'Connell Street and up to Trinity College, Dublin. Some of the buildings were still burning on O'Connell Street from the rebellion of a few days previously. The houses and official buildings on O'Connell Street were absolutely wrecked, having been bombed by the British naval ships based out in Dublin Bay.

We were brought to a halt outside Trinity College where we were left standing for hours. As we were brought through the streets on the walk to Coolaney, British soldiers hurled a frenzy of abuse at us. They went from one man to the next mocking us and removing any Catholic religious items we were carrying. Any rosary beads, crucifixes or other holy items were confiscated. Our long quarantine outside Trinity College completed, the shouting and roaring of the British officers and soldiers came to an end and we were marched to Richmond Barracks. This barracks was a veritable fortress of British soldiers. It was also a constant hive of activity with army personnel constantly running here and there. Every informer, spy and lackey of the British state in Ireland must have been in and out of that place on a regular basis.

We were all interrogated at length by various policemen and British detectives on arrival at Richmond Barracks and when they had enough of that we were all locked into a large room which was entirely bare except for another twenty men who were there already. Exhausted from the long hours of marching and standing, we all sat or lay down on the freezing ground wherever we could find a space. I was very lucky that I was wearing my tweed overcoat when I'd left Castlebar Jail the previous day. This coat came in very useful now. We were all weak with the hunger as we hadn't had anything to eat since the previous day. Eventually the British soldiers sent in some dog biscuits to us and a big bucket of a stinking watery liquid that was supposed to be tea. We were left in this room from the Friday until the Monday.

We heard an incredible amount of commotion and bustle on the Saturday. We were forbidden from looking out of the one barred window that was high in the wall of this room and so we couldn't see for certain what was going on. All we could tell was that there was an enormous amount of to-ing and fro-ing and a large volume of orders and instructions being given within the barracks. We could sense that all of the British army personnel outside the walls of our room were on red alert. Naturally, we prisoners were all frightened at what might be in store for us. It was anybody's guess what might happen to us or whether torture or execution might be our eventual end.

We eventually found out that all of the commotion was because of the arrival of Asquith – who was due to visit the prison that day. He had arrived in Ireland the day before apparently and was said to be inspecting how well the rebellion had been suppressed. Although we had been warned not to look through the tiny window that was high above our heads, we climbed on each other's shoulders to have a glance outside. About midday, we saw Asquith arrive through the entrance of the prison. It was difficult to see him clearly as he was at some distance from us and he was surrounded by a small squadron of officers and bodyguards. The only thing I made out about Asquith was that he was wearing a silk hat that was too small to cover his grey hair, which was long at the back. A short man, he was sporting a black overcoat and this hat that was propped high on his head. Apart from the officers encircling him, there appeared to be a prisoner, whom none of us recognised, also standing to attention and waiting to meet him.

The newspapers of the day later claimed that the British prime minister had discussions with the prisoners and that these discussions were very constructive. As far as we knew, however, the only prisoner he spoke to was that unidentified prisoner whom he met at the entrance to the jail.

To give Asquith his due, the prison conditions did improve slightly after his visit. The morning following his visit we each received a small piece of bacon, a piece of bread and even a cup from which to drink the tea. From that day until 15 May when I was transferred from that prison, the food and the all-round conditions of that prison improved somewhat.

It was rumoured at the time – and there are people who would claim the same today – that Maxwell, the head of the British army in Ireland, had constructed a trench in Arbour Hill, into which he was going to throw the bodies of 300 of us whom he planned to execute.[2] The rumours were that it was Asquith who vetoed this move and thereby saved our lives. Personally, I don't think that there was any truth in this. My own view is that the executions of the 1916 rebels ended because of our close links with America. That the Americans wanted an end to the executions of the 1916 Volunteers and indicated as much to the British is a much more likely explanation for the fact that the policy of executions ended. This, and the fact that John Dillon lobbied hard in the British parliament to put an end to the bloodshed. It's these people, rather than Asquith, whom the likes of me has to thank for the fact that I wasn't fertilising the soil of Arbour Hill.

It was the same afternoon as Asquith's visit that I found myself served with a summons to appear before a military court on Monday morning, 15 May. We all received the same summons around this time, a summons which said that we were charged with our part in an armed conspiracy against the king. We were also charged with attempting to usurp the laws which that same king oversaw. There were a range of appendices and sub-sections to each of these various summons.[3] It was in these sub-sections where I was charged with a number of very serious offences, including the allegation that I had attempted to assassinate three members of the crowned forces. On the appointed Monday morning, I was brought in front of the court under armed guard. On my way into the court, I met Páraic Ó Fathaigh, a man who was a teacher like me, and who was on his way to face trial. We were both brought into the court where we were flanked by two guards, eight soldiers and two officers.

Ó Fathaigh and I were tried before a British army general who was assisted by two colonels. If there were three people whom one felt less hopeful of expecting any mercy from, it was these three individuals. The minute I saw them, I knew I hadn't a hope. An army lawyer was the prosecutor and I wasn't allowed to speak in my defence or have any legal representation. The cases were over within minutes. Mine took just five minutes and it proceeded as follows. The army lawyer detailed the evidence against me. He was then questioned briefly by the British officers on a number of small points, but I wasn't allowed to say anything. The proceedings completed, I was led out into another room accompanied by a guard.

Who did I meet in that same room but Eoin MacNeill, believe it or not. Eoin's court case was being processed at the same time as Ó Fathaigh's and mine. If we were going to end up in that trench in Arbour Hill, we'd be in illustrious company anyway. Conchúr Mac Fhionnlaoich, the son of Cú Uladh appeared in the same room too.[4] All of us who were tried that day were sent to Kilmainham Jail that very same afternoon. Three days was all we spent there, thank God. As someone who spent time in custody in over thirty barracks and prisons, I can honestly say that Kilmainham was the coldest and filthiest of the lot. The reason it was in such a poor state was because it hadn't been used as a prison for a long time before the 1916 rebellion. Once the rebellion was over and they had nowhere to put many of us, we were just thrown into this damp hole.

At night we had to sleep on a blanket on the filthy freezing ground because there was no furniture in any of the cells. On our third night there we were ordered from the cells as dusk was falling and brought to the first floor. A bastard of an officer began to read out our names one after the other and as he read them we were ordered to line up one after the other. Then he went to the top of the line and read out the court's judgment from a few days previously. He went down the line and read the judgment of the court as it related to each and every one of us. We were all found guilty of treason against his majesty's government.

When he reached me in the line, he informed me that I was sentenced to fifteen years imprisonment. Then he gave a short cough and added, 'But, thanks to mercy of the court, five years of that sentence have been suspended.' Then he moved a step forward and spoke to Páraic Ó Fathaigh, who was behind me in the line. He went through the same rigmarole with him except that Ó Fathaigh was sentenced to twenty years, reduced to ten, 'by the mercy of the court'. The whole rigmarole that this officer went through as he delivered the sentences seemed very strange to us who had never seen the like of it before. He started with what seemed like some kind of a 'rhyme' that he obviously knew by heart. Then, when he came to the end of this, he would pause momentarily before delivering the terms of your actual punishment. It was as if he was trying to frighten you somehow. Then the ritual went like this: 'You (he'd give the name of the prisoner) have been found guilty.' He'd pause again then or give a small cough and read out the terms of your sentence.

Once everybody had received their sentences we were sent back to the cells, the same cells that had housed Pearse, Thomas Clarke and the other leaders of the Easter Rising before their executions. One of the soldiers who was guarding us showed us the exact place where our leaders had been shot. The walls were pockmarked with the bullets that had killed each of these heroic Irishmen. A few days after our sentences were pronounced, we were transferred in prison vans to Mountjoy prison. This prison was in better condition than Kilmainham, which we weren't sorry to see the back of. In Mountjoy we were officially moved from the custody of the British army and transferred to the responsibility of the state. We were now considered common criminals and treated as such.

The cell I was assigned in Mountjoy had previously housed no less a luminary than Éamon de Valera. Proof of this was a piece of slate on the wall that had been constructed as a calendar and under which de Valera's name was signed. In fact, the very morning that I arrived at Mountjoy was the same day that he was transferred to Dartmoor prison in England. We had barely arrived in Mountjoy when we, too, were informed that we were to be transferred to a prison in England. Two days in Mountjoy and our next transfer was announced. They were keeping us constantly on the move.

Once again, the English came like a thief in the night. It was nightfall when we found ourselves transferred to the cattle-boat that was leaving the docks at the North Wall for England. There were twelve of us in all and we were placed in the hold next to the shuffling and bellowing cattle. Whilst it was rough and dangerous to be squashed in beside the cattle who were slipping and sliding everywhere, we were initially glad that they were beside us as the cold was biting. We were under no illusions of course. Given that there was just a wooden frame between us and the churning waves, any accident aboard this cattle-boat and we would all be drowned within seconds. It wasn't long before the warmth of the cattle gave way to a more choking feeling. All of us, men and animals, squashed in together at such close quarters and breathing on top of one another like this, meant that the air soon became clogged with our breathing. It became very difficult to breathe, a suffocating feeling that was so frightening we began hammering on the hatches. Eventually our captors had to open the hatches that led to the deck to let in some air.

There were a dozen or so of us down there, the majority of us Galwaymen. Most of us knew each other quite well already. One man, Mícheál Pléimeann, was already a close friend of mine. A middle-aged man, he had already suffered a good deal for Ireland by then, but his trials and tribulations had only made his dedication to the cause of Irish freedom stronger. Although he was advancing in years, he fought alongside the other rebels that Easter with the energy and verve of a young man, such was his patriotism and love for Ireland. So too did his four sons. As a young man he had been one of the strongest men in the west of Ireland, a man who had no equal when it came to weightlifting. In his prime, he had worked on the construction of the large bridge at Crompáin Choill Sáile in Connemara, a place where his feats of strength had achieved renown both far and wide. Believe it or not, it was a woman from the Coineasa family who had finally beaten him in a competition involving weights. I can honestly say that I never met a man who was as young at heart as this man. A poet and a stonemason, he belied his years even while incarcerated in various horrible prisons with the rest of us. He even composed two songs while in prison – *Convict 95* and *O'Donovan's Kid* – both of which were very popular on the west coast of Ireland for many years afterwards.

Interestingly, the officer who was the superior of the British soldier guarding us on the journey over to England was a very friendly Irishman, a man who had been born in Dublin. He showed his solidarity with us on many occasions during our transfer from Ireland to Dartmoor. He made sure that we never went hungry or thirsty, and on a number of occasions he made sure that we were 'protected' from bystanders who came to look at the 'rebels' or hurl abuse at us. These people came to stare in the windows at us as we were brought into a waiting-room in a train station somewhere in England (I can't actually remember where it was). We must have looked pretty awful by then. Three weeks growth of beard, unkempt wild-looking hair and filthy clothes from weeks spent lying on the ground – we looked a right state. Having said this, the vast majority of the people who came to roar abuse at us were without doubt the dregs of society. They shook their fists at us, mocked us and threatened to kill us. It was the usual behaviour that you got from them. One fellow was so worked up with his shouting and gesticulations that he actually put his hand through a pane of glass in the station's waiting-room. He had to be dragged away by one of the guards, his hand bleeding heavily.

A bizarre incident happened then. A giant of a man suddenly appeared. He must have been at least eighteen stone in weight with massive shoulders and his legs were nearly as wide as they were long. He was so heavy that he was sweating profusely and had to stop every now and then to catch his breath. He walked over to the waiting-room where we were huddled and stared carefully through the window at us, whispering to himself as if he was observing some strange animals at the zoo for the first time. A look of disappointment came over him and we realised then that he had come to look at us expecting to see some strange two-headed creatures with many eyes. He turned away from the window to where a woman was calling to him. 'They look the same as any other people,' he shouted to her in a resigned tone before walking away. We had a few strange incidents like this before we reached the forbidding walls of Dartmoor.

Dartmoor was a mean-looking place that was situated on the side of a mountain in what looked like the middle of nowhere. It was an eerie-looking place that was perpetually shrouded in mist. This damp fog would fall thick and fast, creeping into the cells like an intruder. This mist had an evil smell about it and it never lifted, summer or winter. It was as if this smog reflected the malevolent mood of this foul prison. Once this evening fog fell it changed the atmosphere and appearance of everything. Even the small bits of furniture in the cells seemed to change shape. The exterior of the prison was surrounded by a huge moat, which had guards on either side of it, thereby making the chances of escape very slim. To get anywhere near this moat you would have to negotiate some very imposing walls, all of which were incredibly high and thick, with bricks on which were hundreds of iron spikes. Even a bird would have found it difficult to escape from there! If by some miracle you had managed to escape you would then have had to make your way across miles and miles of dark moorland. There was nowhere for an escaping prisoner to hide on the bare marshes that were regularly whipped by the wind and the rain. Aside from the omnipresent mist, these never-ending moors were all so alike that it was difficult for someone not to get lost out there. It was said that escaping prisoners could run for miles and yet find themselves so disorientated that they unintentionally stumbled back into the prison once again.

We republican prisoners were billeted in the oldest section of the prison. This section had been built by American prisoners-of-war who were captured by England during the American War of Independence. The buildings here were constructed of huge granite bricks that appeared indestructible. The height and thickness of rock here rendered these walls unassailable.

I would be mortally ashamed to describe the body search that we were subjected to on arrival at Dartmoor. The prisoners had to get used to this pretty quickly given that these searches were carried out three or four times a day subsequent to this. Suffice to say that there was no orifice or part of your body that they didn't check for anything you might have concealed there. Your mouth was searched very thoroughly as were your ears, your nostrils, between your toes and your fingers and in every part of your hair.

Most of the republican prisoners in Dartmoor knew each other very well already. We had fought, drilled and suffered alongside one another in the years before this and would do so again in the future struggles that lay ahead. Each month there were usually new republican prisoners arriving to this fortress on the moors. A week after our arrival, Eoin MacNeill arrived in Dartmoor and that first morning that we were let outdoors for recreation Éamon de Valera instructed us all to stand to attention before MacNeill's arrival in the exercise yard. Providing a military guard of honour for this renowned one-time republican Volunteer leader was the least we could have done to demonstrate our huge respect for MacNeill.

De Valera had us organised and standing to attention a few minutes before MacNeill appeared in the yard and it was just as well. I knew MacNeill for years before this and I didn't recognise him when he arrived in the yard. His appearance had changed completely. His beard was gone, his hair was shaved and his prison uniform had rendered him unrecognisable. I'd never seen anyone whose appearance had changed so drastically. This military display caused consternation amongst the hierarchy of the prison, from the governor down to the warders who patrolled the landing. They must have felt intimidated by it, as they were only used to dealing with so-called 'common criminals'. These same criminals would have been in fear of their lives if they had dared to order other prisoners or 'gang leaders' to do anything. We republicans had completely flummoxed them with our strict regulations and rituals. That this was obvious was indicated by the fact that we were subjected to increased monitoring on a round-the-clock basis after our display in the prison yard that day.

The seven months I was in Dartmoor were spent making cloth sacks. The endless sewing while hunched over the bags in the gloom of that prison took its toll on my eyes after a while. By August, I had a serious problem with my eyes and I went to the governor of the prison to request permission to see the prison doctor. I got short shrift from him, however. He was abusive and told me to go away. This proved a stupid move on his part, however, as a few weeks later I was in real trouble and had to be transferred to the prison hospital. I spent two weeks lying in complete darkness, a blindfold over my eyes. What this treatment was supposed to achieve, I'm not sure. I removed the blindfold myself after nearly two weeks and was shocked when the prison walls appeared bright green!

De Valera must have heard about this strange 'experiment' that was being conducted on me as he complained to the prison authorities that I was being mistreated. Unfortunately for him, he was punished for his 'insubordination' and found himself in solitary confinement and on bread and water for three days. De Valera was also ordered to spool flax for these three days as part of his punishment. He refused to this, however, arguing that he was a political prisoner and not a common criminal. The authorities in Dartmoor obviously considered de Valera a formidable adversary, as both he and Dr Richard Hayes, were transferred to Maidstone prison just three days later.

As Dartmoor was situated deep in the English countryside, various sights and smells came to us that reminded us of home. The smell of the fresh hay that was cut during the summer in the fields surrounding the prison walls seemed the sweetest-smelling grass ever known to man. Early morning and late afternoon was when the smell of the hay would drift in with that ever-present haze that drifted across the moors there. Maybe it was the fact that we were locked up for long periods of time or the fact that we could never eliminate the foul-smelling damp that clung to the walls of our cells. Whatever the reason, the smell of that cut grass was one of the few beautiful aspects of Dartmoor during the summer. It was like a drug that you inhaled for as long as possible. Many of the prisoners were so fond of the smell of that cut grass that it's surprising the prison authorities didn't try to 'ban' the smell somehow.

Prison life was lived on rumour and counter-rumour with

every tiny snippet of news digested and re-digested and analysed for what it might possibly mean. Sometimes you received news by accident or by a 'slip of the tongue' which somebody had made. I experienced this on many occasions including during those summer weeks when I was confined to the 'dark room' because of my eyes; a cell that doubled as the prison hospital. I was like somebody who was lost in a strange limbo-like world with that blindfold over my face and the sheets that functioned as blinds on the cell window and that were there to block out any form of light that might sneak through. When the warders left food inside the cell-door I was completely disorientated and would fall on my way over to find that plate of food. On this particular day, there was a rattling at the door and some warders appeared and pulled me from the bed. I was led into another room where a doctor removed the blindfold and examined my eyes. I was alone with this doctor who initially informed me that he was also a British army officer. After his words of introduction neither of us spoke to one another, as was often the case in these situations. When he was finished his examination he didn't refer to my eyes at all. The only thing he said was: 'You all won't be here for much longer.'

Sure enough, two weeks later we were transferred to Lewes prison which was situated thirty miles south of London. I was kept in that 'dark room' until a few minutes before we left Dartmoor when I was brought out to join the other prisoners. A day spent in prison feels a good deal longer than any other 'normal' day. It's worse again if you're separated from all other forms of human contact and you're kept 'in the dark' (literally). More difficult again was the fact that there was no mental or physical stimulation there at all. I couldn't read or write or do any form of work either.

One day while musing on my predicament I remembered the traditional methods of poetry composition as employed by the Celtic druids and poets of Ireland in a previous era. Rather than writing down anything as part of the composition process, the poet usually went to a lonely place in the hills or an isolated hut somewhere, shutting themselves off from the world for a certain period of time. They would then compose these incredibly complex metric poems in the dark, emerging only when the entire poem was completed. If they could do this in previous centuries, then why couldn't I also give it a try here in the 'dark room'? Who knows? Maybe I could compose a poem that would outdo some of the greatest poets who had produced poetry in prison – poets such as Villon or Oscar Wilde, for example!

I began composing some lines in my mind. Then I began to repeat these lines aloud so that I didn't forget them. I was soon lost 'in my own world'. The external world of the prison, the dark room and the countryside beyond the walls no longer existed for me and my poetic juices were flowing. I became so caught up in the poetry that was coming to me thick and fast that I failed to hear the door of the prison hospital cell opening. The assistant governor of the prison appeared accompanied by a group of guards. Although I couldn't see them, I could tell by their voices that they were disturbed by what they were hearing. They let it slip that they had been listening outside the door of the cell for some time. They informed me then that I was obviously 'losing my marbles' and that if I didn't shut up and get a proper control of my mental faculties, they would send me to somewhere that was more suited to the likes of me – i.e. a prison for the mentally insane. Having issued me with this warning, they left me on my own in the room again. After they were gone, I cursed this awful place where a man couldn't even enjoy the one simple solitary pleasure that was left to him, i.e. composing a poem by himself.

I took heed of their warning, however, as I had no wish to find myself transferred to a hospital for the insane. For the record, here are a few verses of that poem that nearly got me into trouble in a British prison:

THE GREAT PENINSULA

Many's the fun-filled night
I was joyous and happy with drinking
In the villages where young and old are so welcoming
That was before my life changed and I was locked in a dark prison
I was locked away
For the love of my country
And for challenging the tyrant
They can't cage my memories, however
Or destroy my dreams of Inver Mór
What a beautiful place
That home to fish and periwinkles
It is here that the sailing boats fill the waters
They glide across the waves in full sail
It is here that the birds are never silent
They never let up on their haunting music
At dawn or at sundown
In the morning or the afternoon
It is here that there is real fun and joy
This is the place where young and old enjoy one another's company
Come feastday or holy day
It is here one finds women of exceptional beauty
Their hair silky and golden
Any of them whom I ever left lonely
I remember them now with sorrow

I think of them all still where they live on the edge of the tide
I recall them all now in my thoughts
I think of them all there still in Inver Mór
Wandering the country as a travelling teacher
I did my work with great joy
I spread the message of freedom wherever I travelled
I tried my best to undo that slavish and colonial mentality no matter where I went
We may have been oppressed for centuries but we will never lose our spark of freedom
Our spirit – let it never be quenched
Now … everybody – let us raise a glass
On behalf of the true and loyal men of Inver Mór!

We endured a great deal in prison but one of the toughest punishments of all was being separated from other prisoners or being placed in solitary confinement for weeks on end. Even if you weren't sent to solitary confinement as a punishment, the fact that you were kept in a cell on your own nearly twenty-four hours a day meant that you rarely got to speak to anybody else. I'd say that I barely spoke more than 100 words in the full seven months I was in Dartmoor. Other than the priest who came to listen to my Confession, I barely had a conversation at all. You can't really blame people who have spent long periods in prison if they become very 'enclosed' and speak very little later in life. Even the priest was sullen enough at times. One day shortly before Roger Casement was hanged (grace to his soul), I decided to enquire of the priest who did his rounds what the latest news on Roger's case was. He was on his way out the door, having listened to my Confession, when I asked him what had happened to Roger. The priest shot me a brusque reply but didn't tell me anything. Shortly afterwards I heard through a different source that poor Roger had been sentenced to death. There wasn't a dry eye in the place the day that Roger was executed. Each of us offered up the sacrifice of the Sunday Mass and Holy Communion for the soul of Roger, one of Ireland's heroes.

How you managed in prison depended to a large degree on the prison warders, the governor and the other prisoners (i.e. those prisoners who weren't Irish republicans like us). There was one prison warder in Dartmoor who really had it in for me. Whether he was the same with all of the other republican prisoners, I'm not sure, but he never lost any opportunity to torment me in any way he could. The same man, who was getting on in years at this stage, had also been a prison warder when some of the old Fenians including Thomas Clarke had been imprisoned there years earlier.

On arrival in Lewes prison we were informed that we would now be treated as prisoners-of-war. This wasn't actually ever true, although conditions did definitely improve there as compared with Dartmoor. The biggest improvement in our situation was the fact that we were allowed to associate freely with one another when we were in a communal area or on recreation. This was a huge thing for us. The rules regarding contact with the outside world were also more liberal than they had been in Dartmoor. In Dartmoor we had been allowed to send one letter home every four months, whereas in Lewes we could write a letter once a month. Other than this, the food, the clothes and the general conditions were more or less the same as they had been in the prison on the moors.

Lewes prison is in southern England and is surrounded by some rich farmland. In the distance you could see big chalk quarries and beautiful trees and gardens in the suburbs of the town. The prison itself was an enormous red-brick building, the red giving it a warmer appearance than many of the other prisons I passed through at different points of my young life. While we had been in Dartmoor, Count Plunkett had been elected in a by-election in County Roscommon.[5] He was the first republican candidate to defeat the representatives of Redmond's party in any Irish political contest of that era. As it happens there was a prisoner in Lewes with us – Joseph Hennessy, may his soul be in Heaven – who was elected in a similar manner at this juncture. The fact that the republicans did not put forward any particular policies, the fact that Easter Week had ensured a change of mood in the country, and the fact that Hennessy was a candidate who was also imprisoned in England at the time that he stood for election, all ensured that he was elected in a similar fashion to Plunkett.

The thing that worried some of us who were then in Lewes was the fact that nationalism might be putting too much emphasis on the constitutional route and tending towards the more conservative approach adopted by Parnell and some of the Fenians in the past. In the immediate aftermath of the 1916 Rising, it was our view that we needed to adopt a more radical approach and 'seize the day' in accordance with the new nationalist mood that had swept Ireland. There would never be a better opportunity to drive the British out of Ireland once and for all. This was how we read the political situation at this point. Because many of us were now in Lewes prison, we were able to debate at our leisure the best future political approach our movement should adopt. The debate became so hot-tempered and polarised at one point that we eventually decided to have a vote on the issue. Should we continue with our effort to seek a free and independent republic or should we adopt a more constitutional approach which would ultimately involve years of diplomacy and no guarantees of success in the longer term?

I couldn't for the life of me understand how there were men amongst us who had put their lives on the line for a free and independent republic only a year earlier and were now happy to settle for adopting a more constitutional approach. I felt embarrassed and ashamed that this was the case. Another aspect of the debate within republicanism at this time which irritated me related to the Irish language. Despite the fact that we organised Irish-language classes for anybody who wished to attend, there were many of the prisoners who hadn't the slightest interest in the language. In fact, there were some amongst them who went to German language classes instead, a decision which I found very peculiar! Our efforts to promote the learning of Irish in the prison meant we set up our own newspaper. This newspaper was, of necessity, produced secretly, and was a handwritten publication as a consequence. We called this bilingual publication *An Buabhall* and Páraic Ó Fathaigh was its Irish-language editor while Thomas Ashe was the editor of the English-language material. When we organised a strike within the prison a few months later, the prison authorities discovered the existence of our newspaper and confiscated all copies of it.

Initially we taught Irish-language classes while 'on the move'. Whoever was teaching the language walked the yard with three students at a time and the language was taught both orally and aurally in this fashion. Those who were interested improved their knowledge of Irish very quickly in this manner. Éamon de Valera was able to recite the entire text of 'The Midnight Court' without any hesitation. The same was true for Conchúr Mac Fhionnlaoich, who had Céitinn's poetry on the tip of his tongue.[6] We began a branch of An Fáinne within the prison.[7] Since we had no rings that we could attach to our lapels, we had to use green needles instead, the same needles that we used to sew floor-mats as part of our prison-work. We appointed Joseph Hennessy the leader of our Fáinne branch and we made it one of our primary aims to be assigned a proper status as political prisoners. We decided to put a plan in place to intimidate the authorities into assigning us political status in the correct sense of the word. We wanted to frighten the prison authorities into the realisation that we were a very organised and disciplined outfit who wouldn't give up until we had achieved what we wanted.

Pentecost Monday was a beautiful day, the hills bright-green and the sound of children's voices coming from where they were playing in the streets outside the prison. It was just after Pentecost when we were let out into the prison yard under armed guard to exercise for an hour, as was normal. Twenty minutes later Éamon de Valera, Eoin MacNeill and Thomas Ashe stepped forward out of our group and presented the representative of the prison governor with a letter. The three men turned on their heels and all sixty of us roared out with our battle-cry – *'An Phoblacht Abú!'* – ('Up the Republic!'). Our shout rang out, frightening the racehorses on the hills of southern England and alarming the prison officers there. The recreation period was immediately brought to an end and we were all escorted back into the cells. The weather was humid and thunder was in the air. The air was dead and it became very difficult to breathe, so difficult that we all broke the windows in our cells. We had arranged to do this in unison at a particular time of the night. As many of the prisoners, we republicans included, were fond of singing, we had decided that the end of a particular song was the signal for all of us to smash the windows in our cells. The song in question was 'May God save Ireland'.

In fact, the people of Lewes must have considered us reasonably good singers because they used to come up every evening and listen to us from outside the walls of the prison. Whether it was because they were unhappy with the interest the locals were taking in our singing or not, the prison authorities decided to separate us and we republican prisoners were transferred to different prisons throughout Britain.

The prison authorities did their best to try to crush our spirit before transferring us to different prisons around Britain. Every ploy, whether physical or psychological, was employed in an attempt to break our resolve. The few sticks of furniture that were in the cells were removed so that we had to sleep on the floor. Any plates or dishes were confiscated so that we had to eat our food off the floor. I'll never forget the second night I spent sleeping on the floor of that cell. The thunderstorms were so violent that night, I had never seen anything like it. Eoin MacNeill, who was in the cell next to mine, shouted in to me to spread myself out as wide as possible on the floor but well away from the broken window.

The following Saturday myself and five other republicans were tied together on a long chain and transferred. George and John Plunkett, both sons of the aforementioned Count Plunkett, were attached to the same chain as me. We had no idea where we were being transferred to. All we knew was that we were brought to the local train station. On arrival at the station, I recognised Mícheál MacStáin, a journalist who had been sent over from home and who was keeping the Irish people aware of our protests for political status in the British prison system. Mícheál didn't have a chance to get any real information from us in relation to our protest. It was actually we who received some information from him as he shouted to us as we were led past under heavy escort. He told us that we were about to be transferred to Parkhurst prison. It was an awful pity that all of us didn't speak Irish as we could have spoken to each other privately at that moment, even within the presence of our captors. Mícheál took the same train as we did. He wanted to follow us to verify our final destination.

As mentioned previously, I was having many problems with my eyes during this period of my life. I suffered constant pain with them and there were times when I nearly went mad with the pain. While in Lewes prison, Thomas Ashe had half-jokingly advised me to ask the prison doctor for a guide dog as used by blind people. The prison doctor in Lewes was a very serious type, however. He wasn't a very approachable individual at the best of times. When I finally plucked up the courage to ask him whether there was any possibility that I could get a guide dog, it actually took him a few seconds to understand what I meant. He told me straight out then that there was no way that he could supply me with such a dog. He did inform me that I could apply to the British secretary for home affairs for such a guide dog, however, and that he would support me in my application. 'If your request for the blind dog is granted you will have to submit a further application to the minister requesting a kennel and food for the dog.' In addition to this advice, the prison doctor provided me with a pair of dark glasses which I was actually wearing on the day that I was transferred to Parkhurst prison. The journalist Mícheál MacStáin saw me wearing these special glasses as the six of us stood chained to one another waiting at the train station that day. Apparently, people in Ireland had already heard about the request I'd submitted to the British government for a guide dog. The sight of me wearing these dark glasses obviously bothered Mícheál a good deal, because he contacted the parliamentary representative Laurence Ginnell, who asked the following question in the British House of Lords on 15 June 1917:

> Mr Ginnell asked whether Mr Colm O'Geary, one of the Irish political prisoners in England under sentence of secret Courts martial, has become blind under the prison treatment; on what grounds his request for a little dog to lead him about has been refused; and, what justification is offered for chaining this blind man in addition to handcuffing him?

> **Sir G. Clare**: Two ophthalmic surgeons have been consulted owing to complaints made by O'Geary about his vision. They both report that his vision is practically normal in both eyes. Nothing is known as to the alleged request for a dog.

Ginnell's enquiry in the House of Lords and Clare's reply resulted in two eye experts examining me in Parkhurst prison where we republicans were still refusing to take part in the daily 'work' of the prison, a 'strike' which was the central plank in our ongoing campaign to achieve full status as political prisoners. These experts gave me a very cursory examination and left the prison again, copies of Clare's official reply (as outlined in the House of Lords) in their pockets. Rumours were circulating in Ireland that I was now completely blind, rumours which really affected my family given that they couldn't be sure what the truth was.

It was late on the Saturday evening when we arrived at Parkhurst prison, where I had the misfortune to be assigned to one of the cells where the condemned men were housed before execution. Just as I was falling asleep that night, I heard the sound of rattling chains near to where I was lying! The rattling of the chains stopped as soon as it had started and I tried to get back to sleep again. Just when my heart had stopped pounding and I was on the point of dropping off again, another rattling sound came from the cell next to mine. I couldn't believe my own ears. All sorts of terrifying thoughts flashed through my mind and I felt a cold sweat breaking out on my forehead. Was I hearing the death-rattle of some poor unfortunate who had once passed through this cell on his way to the gallows?

I got very little sleep that night. The morning light provided the answer to the mysterious rattling noises. As we were released from our cells for the exercise period, I was led past the cell next to mine, where I noticed a prisoner asleep on the stone floor. The same man was tied with a huge chain which encircled his hands and his feet. The slightest shift of position on this man's part during the night and his chains made that eerie racket.

That morning we were forced to join a group of the 'lowest' rabble in the exercise yard. Not unnaturally, we refused to mix with these prisoners and immediately separated ourselves from them. This scenario had obviously been planned beforehand by the prison authorities as they immediately descended on us and dragged us back to the cells where we were locked in again and put on bread and water for three days. We escalated our campaign for political status from this time onwards and did our best to break every prison rule that we possibly could. By the time I came before the prison governor to be assigned my punishment, I had contravened virtually every rule in the book, and was told that I wouldn't be permitted to send a letter home for the next three years. Nor would I be allowed to receive any visitors for the following three years either. Any small privileges I might have been privy to before this were also 'gone by the board' now, of course.

The greatest irony of all was that this draconian punishment was handed down to me only hours before I was set free. We had no idea, of course, that we were about to be set free and we were continuing with our protest for political status, despite the continual punishments, both mental and physical that we were subjected to. The very day that I was handed down my own punishment, I was forcibly shaved by a number of warders. They had a hell of a job trying to hold me down as I fought these three warders like a tiger. Eventually, they tied my hands behind my back and strapped me to a chair. In the end, they did a very poor job of that shave, despite the various roughhouse tactics they had to employ.

We were transported by both boat and train from Parkhurst to London and it was on this journey that I witnessed an example of Irish goodwill and nationalist fervour that I will never forget. Hundreds of people were at that train station when the transfer was taking place. Many of them were just there to stare at us out of curiosity while there were a certain number there who had turned up to shout abuse at us. One loyal Gael wasn't going to be inhibited, however. As we were rushed in groups onto the train, this man shouted out proudly at the top of his voice: 'Three cheers for the Irish rebels!' before being swallowed up by the crowd. On our way into London, some local women threw bricks at the windows of the carriages that we were in. None of us suffered any injury luckily, although some of the windows of the train were smashed to pieces. We spent just one night in Pentonville prison, but, I can honestly say that I got the best night's sleep in fourteen months in that prison. To top things off, the priest who said Mass the following morning (Sunday) spoke very highly of us and even used some Irish during the Mass.

Officially, we had been transferred to Pentonville so as to be 'cleaned up' and provided with 'proper' clothing before being transferred to a prison in Ireland. What we suspected was afoot, however, was that we were finally about to be released from custody. While we waited for our new prison clothing to arrive in Pentonville, some of us took the opportunity to visit the grave of Roger Casement who had been executed there in August 1916. Our visit to his grave was a very sad one. In the end, we were each fitted out in tattered clothes that looked like they had been stolen from a bunch of tramps. We were also forced to wear pairs of 'civilian-type' shoes, all of which were battered and broken. When they were finished with us, the prison authorities placed us on a train that left two hours before the 'regular' train. This was so that nobody would know that we had been officially released. We were a tired bunch by the time we reached Holyhead where we waited for the boat to Ireland.

11

Free Once More

Never believe anyone who has spent time in prison and who tells you that they were not happy to be released. You never saw as happy a group as we were the day that we were informed our freedom was imminent. We arrived back in Dublin to a hero's welcome. We got a great reception, hundreds of people cheering and waiting and wishing us the best. There were bonfires all over Ireland to celebrate the fact that we had stood up to the British imperialist system. Rich and poor came up to us and invited us into their homes. Everybody we met shouted their praises and wished us the very best for the future. Those people who were against us just stayed away. It was clear that there had been a huge sea-change in the attitudes of the Irish populace since we had last been in Ireland. The Easter Rising had changed Ireland completely. The negativity and hostility we had experienced just one year previously was gone now. In its place was a new-found hope and pride and a growing nationalist fervour.

The writer Sean-Pháraic Ó Conaire was amongst the people who welcomed us. Appropriately, his book of short stories, *Seacht mBua an Éirí Amach* (1918), was just about to be published and he was seeking donations from people to ensure that he could pay the printing costs. He used the occasion of our welcome home to canvass as many people as possible amongst the nationalist sympathisers there, in an effort to raise the necessary money. I had my doubts as to whether he would manage to get any money at that welcome-home gathering, given that most of the people there were as poor as himself. How wrong I was, however. I later heard that he managed to collect a good deal of money towards the publication of his book on that particular day. Although I was completely broke myself at the time, I still managed to cadge the necessary six-and-seven from various people – money with which I was subsequently able to buy a copy of Páraic's new book.

Páraic was a stocky, short man with twinkling eyes. When you met him his eyes were always smiling. He had the mischievous look of somebody who was about to tell you a good story. When he was young he had a big head of hair, wild-looking and uncombed. The same hair had thinned a good deal by now and he was even going a bit bald at the back. Physically, you'd have sworn he was out of proportion somehow, as if his head was too big for his body. Personality-wise he was a mixture too. The innocence of a child and the wisdom of old age all wrapped in one. I met him was one day when I was back in Galway. He was in great form that day and he told me about a lecture that he had recently given to the city council. He'd been invited to speak about literary issues by the council group concerned with the economic development of the city. A large group of city business-people, many of whom had become very wealthy through their respective businesses, had attended. Páraic had found the irony in the situation hilarious. Here were people, many of whom had been very successful in business, listening to a bohemian like Páraic, a man who hadn't a penny to his name. 'That's not all,' Páraic said. 'Sure, who ever saw business people the likes of them showing the slightest interest in literature?' He gave another roar of laughter and disappeared up the road. Speaking of Páraic, he played a good trick on me, when we were getting the Volunteers to take the pledge against drink, during the ceasefire of 1921. Páraic had been staying in Kilkieran for a while and, because he was an outsider to the area, I thought he would be the ideal person to read out the pledge to the company of Volunteers there. They would take much more notice of him than they would of me, I thought. Páraic said he would be happy to do this, although I could have sworn that I detected a tiny smile at the corners of his mouth. I divided the Volunteers into two groups on the evening in question and ordered them to listen to this visitor whose duty it was to read out the pledge to them. I had written out the words of the pledge on a piece of paper for Páraic beforehand and as far as I remember the words went as follows:

> I swear before God that I, as a Republican Volunteer, will abstain from any alcoholic drink on any occasion that I am in the active service of my country.

'Now men!' said Páraic, having scanned the note that I had handed to him, 'Everybody raise their right hand and repeat these words after me – without fear or hesitation.' The hands went up and Páraic took a step backwards as if to put some distance between the men and himself. He gave a small self-conscious laugh.

'Ready now!' He read out the pledge, in a slow and steady voice. 'I swear – before God – that I – as a Republican Volunteer – will abstain from – any alcoholic drink – on any occasion – that I am in the active service – of my country.' What did Páraic do then but continue speaking and include an addendum of his own to that oath as follows: 'except when I get thirsty – or when the opportunity presents itself – to have a drink – so help me God.'

Believe me, that was the last time I called on Páraic to issue a group of Volunteers with the pledge.

On another occasion someone asked Páraic to settle a dispute between two men regarding the ownership of a dredge they had both used for collecting scallops. Páraic explained his decision to remove the dredge from both of these men and give it to somebody else who would make good use of it as follows: 'If those two men had any respect for themselves, they wouldn't spend their days squabbling and threatening each other with legal action.'

Immediately before our release from prison in England, John Redmond's brother, William, the then leader of the Irish Parliamentary Party, died in France. He was killed fighting for England in the Great War. Before his death, William Redmond had been the elected representative for County Clare. Given that there was now a vacancy there, one of our main subjects of conversation on the train journey to Wales that signalled our release was the forthcoming by-election. Who should we republicans nominate to stand for our party in that election? This burning question now occupied us. It was during this long journey too that we heard that de Valera had been asked whether he wished to stand for the Republican Party in the by-election. De Valera now went from one carriage to the next consulting with all of us regarding what we would do in his position. Given that de Valera had been our leader in prison, not one of us was against him putting his name forward. In fact every one of us, to a man, pledged to support him in every way that we possibly could if he did decide to seek election.

A couple of days later, when everybody had had a chance to return home and readjust to normal life, a group of us met in Fleming's Hotel, Gardiner Place, Dublin. At this meeting we set out a strategy for winning a seat in the Clare by-election. While the vast majority of the people at the meeting were in favour of putting de Valera forward as a candidate in the by-election, this didn't prevent a very heated debate from taking place. There was a good deal of anger amongst some of those in attendance regarding some of the tactical errors that had been made during the Easter rebellion of a year earlier. That the same people who had been complicit in these errors would now be part of de Valera's back-up team for the forthcoming by-election was questioned by a number of delegates. A ferocious row ensued, a row that was resolved only when de Valera stood up and said that there was no way that he would allow his name to go forward unless everybody agreed to resolve their differences and back him. De Valera's intervention put an end to all of the tension and back-biting.

At this same meeting, we also decided to petition both the American president and the head of the American Congress. The petition requested that America help Ireland to carve out a separate national identity for herself on the world stage, when Europe was re-configured subsequent to the First World War. We already had a good precedent for this given that the then American president had just recently announced that the world now belonged to the smaller nations and that they should no longer feel bound by their often-tyrannical imperial pasts. The same president had even gone so far as to say that the Great War, which was then at its height, was really being fought so that the smaller nations could have their freedom. Dr MacCartan placed this petition before both the American president and the American Congress in Washington on 23 July 1917.

The majority of the ex-prisoners who attended that Dublin meeting moved to County Clare for the fortnight before the by-election to help with de Valera's canvass. The campaign was fast and furious and became quite heated and controversial at times. It involved a huge and sustained effort and, given that it was the first election I was ever involved in, I threw all of my energies into it. Our efforts really paid off in the end because de Valera was elected with a surplus of 1,000 votes. It was during that fortnight in County Clare that I met Thomas Ashe for the last time. He was at one of our campaign meetings in Feakle, a meeting where the majority of the people were against us. Before the meeting, Ashe was on the podium with us that night although he didn't speak as far as I can recall. A short time after this, Thomas was arrested in County Longford while addressing a public meeting. He and a few of the other prisoners refused to recognise the prison regime in operation and they went on hunger strike. As Ashe's life ebbed away, the British tried to force-feed him by brutally shoving food down his throat. This rough treatment was enough to finish Ashe off. A greater Gael more committed to both language and country never drew breath. Ashe had a big funeral. Unfortunately, I was unable to attend myself as the western Volunteers had organised a huge gathering at Partry, on the border between Counties Mayo and Galway. Colonel Moore was at that meeting, which was held right next to the place where Lord Claremorris was assassinated during the Land War.

There was an obvious sea-change in public opinion relating to the nationalist project throughout Ireland and in County Clare, in particular, at this juncture. While the majority of the older priests were opposed to us and aligned with Redmond, the younger priests were increasingly helping us behind the scenes. The older generation of clergy were putting their hope in the then forthcoming Dublin conference organised between both the British government and the Irish Party. The aim of this conference was (supposedly) to set up a national government in Ireland on behalf of the Irish people. Our party – Sinn Féin – took no notice of this conference. We knew that the British were only playing games. They were simply 'playing for time' until the Great War was over. This was the primary reason that the majority of the clergy were still against us; they were very supportive of England in that war.

During this period, I found myself working in Scariff, County Clare. Both the parish priest and the younger curate there were very sympathetic to us republicans, but England's lackeys in the area were quite active and opposed to us. Every possible rumour and sliver of propaganda was spread about us to try to turn the people against us. One night we were making our way to a small hilltop village not far from Scariff, a place which was known to be particularly hostile to us. There were more than six of us walking across bog and hill on this particular night and we had been warned to be very careful on our approach to this village. If anyone spotted us, we knew that we might have to make a quick run for it. There was just one house there where we would receive any form of welcome, a house owned by a man who had once been a member of the Fenians.

As we made our way through the countryside, there was an enormous downpour and by the time we reached the village we were all soaked to the skin. This old man met us and accompanied us to the first house in the village where we spent a good deal of time canvassing for Sinn Féin and arguing our party's position in relation to the forthcoming election. After a good deal of debate, the man of the house agreed to vote for Sinn Féin. A few minutes after he'd stated his intention to vote for us, we put it to him that most people in the area considered him to be very hostile to the republican cause. 'Who said that about me?' the man asked, jumping up angrily from his chair. 'Well, the best way for you to put that rumour to bed is to accompany us as we canvass the village, thereby proving to everybody that this lie isn't true.' This man who had supposedly been most hostile to us at the beginning duly accompanied us as we did the rounds of the houses that night. Sure enough, on the day of the election, the entire village voted for us.

12

The Revival of the Volunteers

Once the Clare by-election was over I found myself back working in County Galway again. The day of my return was an auspicious one. There was a huge gathering in Eyre Square for all of the English gentry's supporters because Lord John French was giving a public speech to the masses.[1] Many people were off work for the day and there was a general air of celebration and excitement amongst the throngs of people who were going up to hear him. Many people had been drinking heavily and were shouting out in loud voices, steadfastly proclaiming their loyalty to French and to England. After his speech was over, the crowds scattered throughout the town.

By then I was making my way from Salthill towards the city centre and I couldn't help but notice a number of the scattering crowd staring at me with an ugly look on their faces as if they were angry with me. I had completely forgotten, of course, that I was still wearing the jacket that I had worn during the Clare by-election, a jacket that had a small tricolour badge sewn into the lapel of it. This was what was attracting the stares of a couple of these passers-by but I was oblivious to it. As I walked past Dominick Street, where the police barracks was, I noticed a group of policemen standing at the door chatting to a group of women in shawls who had gathered there to express their admiration for king and country. The women were 'well-on-it' with drink and as I passed by a couple of the police stared over in my direction.

One policeman whispered something quickly into the ear of one of the shawled women and she suddenly turned in my direction. Next thing this bunch of women came running out of the barracks gate and chased me up the street. I had nearly escaped them when one of them made a dive for me and managed to trip me, knocking me to the ground. Next thing they had me pinned on the ground and were pummelling me with their fists and tearing at me. Five or six of them then fought with one another to see who could tear off the badge that was on the lapel of my jacket; the toughest one, who seemed to be their leader and who had initiated the pursuit, won out in the end. She tore it off the lapel with her powerful hands and then punched me a few more times in the face and the stomach for good measure while the others held me down spread-eagled on the ground. Then she threw the badge on the ground and danced on it as if in a rage. The women argued amongst themselves as to whether they should keep me pinned to the ground for another couple of minutes or set me free. Their leader, this enormous and powerful woman who had done the 'war-dance' decided for them, however. She ordered the others to pull me up off the ground into a sitting position whereupon she gave me another few punches.

'Leave him be, now,' she said. 'He has had enough.'

They told me how lucky I was that they hadn't killed me and to get out of there before I found myself in more serious trouble.

I dusted myself off and left that street as quickly as I could. Out of the corner of my eye, I noticed the policemen at the barracks door having a good laugh. I could have been killed that day with that unruly mob beating the living daylights out of me, but they wouldn't have intervened, that's for sure. The gang who had attacked me were Claddagh women. I take my hat off to them. They were as hard as nails and as tough as any man. If their husbands – who were all out fighting for the British army in France at this time – had fought even half as hard as those women did, it is a wonder that England didn't win the war in a canter. The reason that these women were so loyal to England at this juncture was very simple, of course. It was a loyalty based purely on economic considerations. Most of them had family who were employed in the ranks of the British army or the British navy and they themselves were reliant on the weekly remittances these men sent home. Not unnaturally, once the Great War finished and the remittances stopped, the Claddagh people were as nationalistic as any other community in Ireland.

Shortly after my release from prison, the Galway committee of the Gaelic League managed to raise enough money to employ me as a travelling teacher for a couple of months. Most of the League members were also members of the Volunteers and the IRB, so that was to my advantage of course. An unofficial facet of my travelling teacher job, therefore, was to reinvigorate the latter two organisations wherever I went, in addition to my Irish-language teaching duties throughout County Galway. Indeed, I frequently spent more time on my Volunteer work than I did on my Gaelic League duties at this point in time. I could justify this, however, by pointing out that wherever I helped to strengthen or rejuvenate the Volunteers, the Irish-language organisations working in that area went from strength to strength also. All of the nationalist-related organisations were helping one another and working together symbiotically at this point; this was the reality of the situation.

I often recall an incident which took place in the Clifden

area at this time, one which was symptomatic of the ideological trends we were then struggling against. I was teaching Irish in two schools there, schools where the other teachers didn't have any Irish. I always wrote the pupils' names in Irish in the roll book but one day the school inspector visited and reprimanded me.

'You won't get a penny in wages from the Education Board until you change those names to their English equivalents,' he said.

'Over my dead body, will I change them,' I replied.

I had come across a tough nut in this inspector, however. I sent the rolls back to the Education Board in Irish but they were promptly returned to the school headmaster with strict instructions to have them translated. It was only years later that the schoolteachers in that school told me what really happened. I had been pleasantly surprised at the time to have been paid – as per usual. At the time, I was sure that I wouldn't be paid at all given the inspector's contempt for the Irish language.

The Sinn Féin ard-fheis took place in October 1917, in Dublin. Before then, it tended to be a small event, but that year proved very different. A very big crowd attended. The night before, the conference delegates from throughout Ireland were lobbied with a view to selecting Count George Plunkett as the next Sinn Féin president. Although some people would afterwards claim that they had proposed de Valera for president from the beginning, there is no truth to this; I attended all of the meetings beforehand, official and unofficial, and I was there when Plunkett was put forward as the principal likely candidate. Despite intense lobbying from various factions within the party, it wasn't clear in the hours preceding the ard-fheis that Plunkett would have the requisite support to secure election to the position. Support for Plunkett faded away in the final hours before the election when everybody still expected it to be a close-run contest between Arthur Griffith and Éamon de Valera. Sensing the change in political mood, Griffith announced that he wasn't letting his name go forward and recommended de Valera for party president. If it had gone to a vote that day I felt (and still feel) that Griffith would have won in a close-run contest. It never did come to that, however, and the delegates went away happy from that ard-fheis, confident that they had made a good selection in de Valera.

De Valera was a man who had already carved out a reputation for himself as both a leader and a fighter by then. Interestingly, the most important event that week was not the official Sinn Féin ard-fheis – as open to the public; it was what went on behind the scenes. Ultimately, the 'young guns' coming to the fore in Sinn Féin were not happy with the slow pace of political progress and the over-emphasis on sloganism which they perceived at this time. They wanted action and the day after the Sinn Féin ard-fheis concluded, an 'underground' conference was held in Croke Park. At this gathering were many active Volunteers and officers from throughout Ireland including many of the men who had been imprisoned with me in England. Everybody got an opportunity to express their real feelings and put together concrete plans in terms of military strategy. De Valera headed this gathering and Michael Collins acted as conference secretary. A plan was put together to ensure the immediate rejuvenation of all the Volunteer companies throughout Ireland and a new military Ard Chomhairle and a public affairs committee were formed.

While we met for just a few hours that day, we got more work done in that short time than we had completed in the previous two days at the official Sinn Féin conference that year. The proof of this lies in the speed at which subsequent developments took place throughout Ireland. An important seed was sown that day which would come to fruition years later. Through the diligence and hard work of many dedicated nationalists, including a good many of the people in attendance that day, the course of Irish history was changed for the better. Sadly, many of the people who were in the gathering on that occasion are now dead. Some fell fighting the English while others died at the hands of their fellow Irishmen and Irishwomen. Whichever way they died, the country is a much poorer place for their absence.

Subsequent to the Croke Park gathering, I focused all of my energies on the re-organisation of the Volunteers in the west. The Galway Volunteers would be re-organised and would form one big company from then on. Initially, this seemed a good plan but over time it proved unworkable, given the size of County Galway. It proved impracticable to have a well-organised company spread across such a wide-ranging and diverse county. Rather than improving our all-round communications as we had initially hoped, this organisational change actually worsened them. Communications only got better again between the various branches of the County Galway Volunteers once we had reverted to the original system once more.

This same year saw the Connacht feis held in Westport, County Mayo. One of the main organisers of the feis was Thomas Derrig, a man whom I came to know while he was still a student in University College Galway.[2] Thomas was one of the most dedicated people in relation to the promotion of the Irish language then and in later years. It was at this Feis Chonnacht also that the newspaper *An Stoc*, the Connacht-based Irish-language monthly first saw the light of day. Although Thomas had to do most of the organisational work for the Westport feis, he also found time to launch this new newspaper, a project which both of us had been planning for many years. The feis was an ideal occasion for the newspaper launch given the fact that many of Connacht's leading Gaels (and future essay contributors to the newspaper) attended. Father Mícheál Ó Conaire, a dedicated Gael from Claddaghduff in Galway, officially launched the new newspaper. For a while before this, another man dedicated to the Gaelic cause, Pearse McCan from County Tipperary, had offered sponsorship of £50 to any individual or group willing to set up an Irish-language newspaper such as *An Stoc*.[3] With this money serving as our guarantee, it was possible for us to go ahead with this exciting new project. The newspaper's first editor was Tomás Ó Máille while the manager was Father Tomás Ó Ceallaigh. *An Stoc* survived as a newspaper until 1921. After this, the newspaper sided with the pro-Treaty forces and many republicans, myself included, refused to support it any more. Initially, and when I wasn't imprisoned in England, I used to write the column called *Cúinne an tSeanóra*.

13

Nationalist Groupings in County Galway

It is difficult to describe the speed with which the national mood in Ireland changed at this juncture. Everywhere throughout the country new cumanns of Sinn Féin sprang up and every small village and town in Galway had its own one.[1] There was still a hardcore of people in Irish society who hated the growth of Irish nationalism and did their best to denigrate it at every opportunity. Their numbers became fewer, however. Almost all of the younger generation were strongly in favour of Sinn Féin, but many of the older people were 'sitting on the fence' and waiting to see how the political situation in Ireland would pan out. Wherever Sinn Féin and the Volunteers were strong, it was much easier to generate interest in the Irish language, of course. As outlined previously, a conference had been held in Dublin, organised between the English government and those Irish parties who were still pro-British. This conference was known as the Plunkett conference because George Plunkett was its chairman.

The conference concluded, as we in Sinn Féin had expected, with the British the only 'side' who were even half-satisfied with its deliberations. The British government were just engaged in the usual time-wasting and waffle that had characterised their approach to the Irish 'question' of course, and for this reason we in Sinn Féin had had nothing to do with it from the very beginning. Rather than wasting time on what was essentially just a 'talking-shop', we used this period to focus on firmly establishing the Sinn Féin cumanns and Volunteer companies in every parish in Ireland. Ironically, the failure of that British–Irish conference only served to strengthen our hand. We continued to attract more and more recruits, with scores of young men joining us every week.

Another reason for the growth of republicanism at this point was the fact that the then major-general of the British army had sent a letter to Ireland's youth threatening conscription if these young men did not voluntarily sign up to join the British army. Naturally, many Irishmen saw no alternative at this point except to join ranks with the only group in Ireland which was willing to stand up to the British colonial regime – i.e. ourselves in Sinn Féin. The Irish adults who had previously dispensed their 'wisdom' to the younger generations now 'lost face', when, to their horror, many Irishmen were shipped over to England as 'enlisted sergeants'.

There was hardly a Sinn Féin company anywhere in County Galway that we did not appoint one or two members of the IRB to its administrative council. Essentially, the Irish-language organisations and the various political and nationalist organisations worked in a cooperative fashion and, given that the same personnel were in the various organisations, we all helped one another. Arguably, it can be said that the IRB was really the main organisational and ideological bulwark behind the most important of the various nationalist and Irish-language groupings at this time. In hindsight, the fact that administrative and leadership power was concentrated in the hands of such a small few from the same organisation was not healthy and, as history would show, the IRB would eventually let down the cause of nationalist unity. When the Treaty was being negotiated, for example, the IRB's Ard Chomhairle issued a statement calling on all of its members to give whatever support was necessary to the pro-Treaty side.

The beginning of 1918 saw myself and a friend of mine – a man who was on the IRB's Ard Chomhairle – sent around Connemara in order to improve cooperation further between the IRB and the Volunteers. A new battalion of the Volunteers had recently been formed in Connemara, one in which Peadar Mac Dónaill and I were principal officers. Both of us were also members of the IRB, of course, and we decided to 'get one over' on the local officers of the law, if possible. Given that the government didn't direct the same antagonism towards Sinn Féin as it did towards the Volunteers, it was also felt to be a good move to appoint me as secretary of the local district executive of Sinn Féin. The hope was that my involvement in Sinn Féin issues would somewhat deflect any unwanted attention away from my much more serious involvement in recruitment and military matters.

Subsequent to our quick county-wide survey of the various Volunteers groupings, rumours began to spread of a potential link-up with the Germans and a possible 'spectacular' attack against British forces in Ireland. An order came from Michael Collins to this effect and a number of us were issued with secret codes and passwords, the plan being that we would meet with some German army personnel on a submarine in Galway Bay. There must have been some breakdown in communications, however, because, although Peadar Ó Máille (or 'Máilleach Chois Fharraige' as we called him)[2] spent two nights on the sea 'disguised' as a local fisherman, our German contacts never materialised.

Hardly a day or night went by now that I didn't have to attend some meeting or other. I'll never forget one night when I became incredibly weak as I cycled along, crying out for food. It was a very peculiar experience, what we in the Gaeltacht refer to as the 'hungry hill'.[3] I was coming home from a meeting in Cashel when this terrible hunger struck me. I was barely halfway through my journey but I had to get off my bicycle and sit down on the side of the road. I felt weak all over as I broke out into a cold sweat and if somebody had put a piece of iron in front of me at that point, I think I would have tried to eat it. While I had often experienced bouts of hunger while in prison in England, I had never felt anything like this before. It put me in mind of one of my fellow republicans who had been imprisoned with me in Dartmoor, a man by the name of Tim Brosnan. He was never anywhere near full after our prison rations were doled out to us and the poor man suffered so much from hunger pangs that he would chew the leather of his shoe in an effort to alleviate the pain.

I remembered then that the best thing to do, when hit with the 'hungry hill', was to look around for something to chew on and I noticed some sedge growing on a ridge near where I was sitting. I chewed on the end of a piece of sedge and within a few minutes I felt strong enough to get on my bicycle and begin my journey again. Despite the fact that I later went a full nine days without food or drink on a prison hunger strike, I can honestly say that I never felt the same overwhelming sensation of hunger that I did that evening on that lonely Connemara road. Ever after that incident, I resolved to get to the root of what causes the phenomenon known as 'hungry hill'. Some say that this feeling of weakness overcomes somebody who is passing a place where the people do not readily share food. Others attribute it to the fact that a woman has passed that way who has neglected to bless herself by making the sign of the cross.

Another time when I was 'on the run' from the Black and Tans between Derryrush and Shanadonall, a 'hungry hill' struck me. It hit me so hard that my tongue actually swelled in my mouth. I was on the northern side of Loughawee when it happened to me and by the time I reached Féichí Mac Con Iomaire's house in Shanadonall, I was unable to speak. In fact, it took me such a long time again to talk that the people of the house feared that I would never speak again. They were worried that the fairies had put some sort of a spell on me as I passed through Cnoc Mordáin, a place that's reputed to be home to a large band of them.

It was round this time also that the first whispers began in relation to conscription. The rumour mill was alive with the story that all young Irishmen would be forced to join the British army, whether they liked it or not. As it happens, this threat of conscription couldn't have come at a better time for those of us who were promoting Sinn Féin. The villages whose inhabitants had previously been reluctant to join us were now begging to become active Sinn Féin members, something which had not been the case a short time before this announcement concerning conscription, as illustrated by the following anecdote. One day I received an invitation from a Sinn Féin branch secretary to go to Errismore to address their group. Coincidentally, Errismore was also the home patch of the Connemara representatives for the English parliament. Unsurprisingly, there were still many of the country people in this area who were supportive of the British parliamentary representative – the old phrase 'blood is thicker than water' comes to mind in this instance. When I reached the meeting place, the only person in attendance was the man who had invited me!

We chatted for a while as we awaited the rest of the meeting's attendees – or so I thought! A considerable time passed before I asked the secretary what time he intended to begin the meeting.

'Any time you prefer, really,' he replied.

'Where's the meeting taking place, then?' I asked him.

'Right here, is fine,' was his reply. 'I am the branch and the members all in one!'

It was one of those rare and beautiful autumn afternoons, the type of day that only comes along a couple of times during the course of a lifetime. The sun was a golden ball on the horizon. It kissed the ocean waves as the sound of children playing on the shore was carried on the sea breeze. It was completely calm, the heather and the furze resplendent with colour. I passed two peelers as I cycled through Aille Hill on my way towards Galway town. Both of them were big lumps of men. They were both red-faced from the sun, their moustaches thick and waxed. Their eyes narrowed as I passed them by and I could tell by the look of them that I was in for some trouble. They both gave me contemptuous looks but they did not call me aside for questioning as they were often prone to do in those conflict-ridden days.

A few minutes later, however, I glanced over my shoulder and noticed that they were following me. Young and fit as I was then, I quickened my speed on the bicycle and tried to out-pace them. They soon realised what I was trying to do and they too increased speed. It soon became a battle of will and strength and I really began to 'knock steam' out of that road in an attempt to shake them off. By the time I reached Spiddal village I had put some distance between myself and the peelers; I was a quarter of a mile ahead of them, but given that I had had nothing to eat since early morning, I began to feel weak with the hunger.

In Spiddal, I hopped off the bicycle and slipped into a small café run by a local family there. I was barely comfortable, however, when in came my two pursuers, now accompanied by a third peeler. They ordered me to my feet and dragged myself and my bicycle down to the local barracks. I had a bag on the back of my bicycle and it was this that had really piqued their curiosity. The pretext on which I was arrested, however, was the fact that I refused to give them my name in English when asked. They were so keen to go through the contents of the bag that, in their excitement, they even forgot to lock me up. And when they found nothing incriminating in the bag – no secret notes or communications exposing my treachery to the crown – their disappointment was palpable. They threw the bag aside and body-searched me. Once again, to their great disgust, they found nothing of interest.

Night was falling and I could hear the young men of Spiddal gathering outside in the street; they were talking to one another in low voices. Some of the policemen who were in the barracks left and the sergeant went up to his office upstairs, leaving me under the watchful eyes of a peeler who sat next to the fire. No sooner had the sergeant gone upstairs, however, but he was back down again. He left the barracks but returned a few minutes later, a disgruntled look on his face. In and out he went for the next hour or so, his face darker and more angry-looking on each occasion. He was like a hen on a hot griddle. At first I put this strange behaviour down to drink. I thought he was heading out to the pub each time and that he might be drinking for courage. This wasn't the case, however. It turns out that since the only telephone in the vicinity was in the local post office, the sergeant was phoning the head of the police in the Galway headquarters each time to ask what he was supposed to do with me. The fact that his boss was unavailable each time he called was the reason that he was in such a foul mood every time he returned to the barracks. The last time he went out, he returned with a big smile on his face, however. He whispered something to the other peeler and the two of them began to laugh.

In English, then he said to me, 'You are at liberty to go now', before disappearing back to his office upstairs. I completely ignored the sergeant's instruction and pretended that I hadn't heard it. Given that I had been raised speaking Irish only, I could let on that I didn't understand what was being said. When the peeler who was guarding me saw that I hadn't moved after a few minutes, he shouted upstairs to the sergeant and told him to come down. The sergeant re-appeared, a bemused expression on his face. 'If you don't get away fairly soon now, we'll be obliged to show you the road!' he said to me, pulling a huge turnip of a watch from his waistband and checking the time. 'We'll give you three minutes to get out.'

The sergeant hopped impatiently from foot to foot, a nervous look in his eyes. The young men outside on the street had become more raucous now; they were shouting out at this stage and who knew what they were thinking of doing?

'Do you hear that shouting outside?' the sergeant enquired of me.

'*Dheamhan fhios agam céard atá tú a rá, a dhuine choir,*' ('I haven't a clue what it is you are saying, my good man') I replied.

'You are dead r***w,' responded the sergeant and he was dancing with rage by this stage. 'Let's have no more of this nonsense,' he said, glancing nervously at his watch again.

There wasn't a stir out of me, however, and the next minute the sergeant gave two sharp blasts on his whistle. Within two seconds two burly-looking peelers came running in out of nowhere; they must have been out on the street somewhere all of this time. The two of them stood to attention in front of the sergeant while he laid into me verbally – in Irish this time. 'You'll be going out with a bloody nose now, seeing as you didn't do what you were told.' He gave a signal to the two peelers and they grabbed a hold of me under the arms and lifted me clean off the ground. They then deposited me outside the door of the station, and with a look that would strike a stone dead, they slammed the door behind me to ensure that I wouldn't be able to sneak back in again!

This was a period in our history when the civil authorities held absolute control over the lives of the Irish people. You could be arrested at any time without warning and thrown into a prison cell for as long as the authorities considered you a suspect. Having the appearance of a patriot, or even looking as if you were thinking patriotic thoughts – either of these possibilities was enough to get you brought into custody in those days.

14

A Prisoner Once More

1918 was barely under way when a major crackdown by the colonial regime came into force. Tension was high throughout Ireland as people were arrested and imprisoned in big numbers, often solely on the pretext or suspicion of being involved in anti-government or seditious activity. In reality most of the country was under martial law at this time and in addition to being imprisoned without trial, many Irish citizens were murdered or assassinated on the whim of the crown forces. Others who were on hunger strike in the prisons died also. The situation was on a knife-edge, with everybody waiting and watching to see when it would finally erupt into an all-out war. The fact that the British were hinting at imminent conscription only added fuel to the fire and there was hardly a parish in the country whose young men hadn't taken the oath of allegiance to the IRB and were ready to fight tooth-and-nail against any prospect of conscription into the British army. At a special meeting of the Irish Catholic bishops and the Irish republican leaders held in Maynooth, it was agreed that all clergy who had taken the oath would instruct their flock to resist conscription. The support of the Catholic bishops on this issue served to further strengthen the solidarity of the Irish people with one another and their resolve to take the fight to England when the time came.

I was arrested at the beginning of the year on the charge

that I had been training the local Volunteers in athletics. I was sentenced to two months in prison at a special court sitting held in Galway town. At this juncture, all IRB members were under orders to pay the bail bonds immediately; we needed as many men as possible to be free and ready to help in the fight. The head of the Galway Volunteers ensured that I succeeded in getting parole and Cluad de Ceabhasa and John O'Donnell, the latter a one-time parliamentary representative for County Mayo, posted bail for me.

I was travelling all over County Galway now on a daily basis in my role as a travelling teacher. In reality, this was increasingly a front for my Volunteer organisational activities. The truth is that everybody was getting ready for the final showdown between ourselves and the British and, consequently, people didn't have the same amount of time as they did previously to devote to the learning of Irish.

Men, women and children were now 'on alert' and preparing themselves for the battle that was inevitable. Cumann na mBan members were stocking up on bandages and medicines and anybody who had any form of medical training was sharing their knowledge with others within their local community. Young men were reading up on military matters and educating themselves in guerrilla tactics and the use of arms. The elderly were making prophecies or had resorted to prayer in advance of the battle to come. And yet, despite months of intense preparation, we were caught cold when the initial moment of truth arrived.

The enemy swooped at the very last minute and pulled the rug out from under our feet before we could get going properly. It happened on Friday 17 May 1918. That fateful evening, British forces raided the houses and hide-outs of all leading republicans throughout Ireland and arrested anybody they deemed to be plotting rebellion. The following morning saw the newspapers replete with exaggerated accounts of the massive rebellion which the British had cut off at the source. There was talk of a conspiracy between Irish nationalists and the Germans, a conspiracy which the swift actions of the crown forces had managed to avert. It must be remembered of course that Irish newspapers were subject to strict censorship at this point in time with the British even employing a particular individual whose duty it was to censor all Irish newspapers and ensure that everything published in them was completely biased in favour of the British and those countries who were their allies in the Great War.

On each occasion that an attempt was made to initiate a pro-Irish or pro-independence newspaper, the authorities immediately forced it to shut down, thereby excluding the nationalist view from the public arena entirely. In an era when newspapers were the primary source for the public dissemination of knowledge, this made it very difficult for us to put forward our point of view.

Amongst the various plots which had allegedly been exposed was the 'German Plot', where both Germany and Ireland were allegedly involved in a conspiracy that sought to put an end to English rule in Ireland, once and for all.[1] The newspapers were all very pro-British as relating to the First World War also. Propaganda was as important in those days as it is today. The complete stranglehold which the British held on the press in Ireland at this juncture, meant that it was extremely difficult for us to get any news regarding the republican movement or any of our successes released into the public domain.

The day of my arrest I had been overseeing Irish-language exams in the Spiddal area. My work for the day completed, I set off to visit a number of the surrounding villages to liaise with a couple of the different companies of Volunteers. It was very late at night by the time I got to my lodgings and I went to bed straight away. I woke up in the early morning to find seven policemen standing around the bed. At first, I thought I was having some sort of nightmare and I imagined that if I closed my eyes again the sight of them would disappear. It took me a few seconds to realise that this was no dream and that the men in black uniform were really there. Their captain was a big, ugly fellow with a pock-marked face and a grey moustache that was so long and winding that he could have tied it around the back of his head.

'Get up,' he roared at me, shoving his gun into my ribs.

I climbed slowly out of the bed as he ordered me to get dressed.

'Is that your stuff over there?' he said, pointing to some boxes that were in the corner of the room.

Before I had a chance to answer he began to push me around, the gun jutting into my back. 'Forget it. We'll come back for that stuff later!'

They marched me downstairs, some policemen in front and some behind. They led me out onto the street and whether through stupidity or stress, they left the door of the house open behind them. It was then that I noticed they were wearing bullet-proof vests underneath their uniforms. They had obviously been prepared for a shoot-out, and a shoot-out they would have had if I had been awake or had a few seconds warning of their approach. If I had been prepared and had the opportunity to barricade myself inside, there is no doubt that it would have been a bloody affair. This became clear to me as soon as we were outside in the sunlight. I had thought there were only seven of them but the house had in fact been surrounded. As I was led away about twenty other policemen appeared from behind the walls and the bushes that surrounded the house. I discovered later that one of the policemen had sneaked up a drainpipe, climbed in a window and made his way downstairs to open the front door for the others.

Unfortunately for those of us who were using the place as a 'safe house', the woman who owned the house wasn't at home that night. We were all fast asleep when the policemen had initially knocked on the front door, completely on the off-chance. Their suspicions had obviously been aroused when they didn't receive any response and they had decided to surround the house.

None of us in the house that night had heard the slightest sound, we were all so exhausted and 'out for the count' from our constant travelling and moving between one 'safe house' and the next. The others in the house with me that night, all of whom were brought out one after the other, included Thomas Derrig, Francis Muldowney, University College Galway student Martin Murphy and Séamus Quirke, who was killed by the Black and Tans shortly after this.[2]

I was brought to the barracks which was located less than 100 yards from where I was apprehended. I wasn't there long before some other republican colleagues were brought in too. Seoirse Mac Niocaill, the solicitor, and Dr Cusack were the first pair brought in. We were kept there overnight and in the morning they placed us under armed guard on the back of one of their army lorries, after which they transported us to Renmore Barracks in Galway city. As the morning wore on the number of republicans who had been rounded up began to increase and more prisoners were arriving in lorries, most of whom were from the western half of the county.

We were all marched under heavy guard towards Galway station where we were to be placed on the next train to Dublin. To ensure that there were no escapes, the train stopped about halfway between the train station and Renmore army barracks where we were loaded on. It was on the train that we got our first chance to see the national newspapers and were able to get a better sense of what was going on throughout Ireland. According to the newspapers, both the king's representative in Ireland and the chief secretary for Ireland, both of whom denied any knowledge of the 'German Plot', had resigned. Lord John French had been appointed as governor and now took the place of the king's representative in Ireland. A man named Edward Shortt was appointed to the role of chief secretary for Ireland. The newspapers also suggested that conscription to the British army for all able-bodied Irishmen was now very likely. Preparations to that effect were made, with a senior British army military appointee being put in place to ensure the coordination of this conscription project throughout Ireland, a move which hadn't been instigated since the era of Cornwallis in 1798.[3]

That Saturday we all spent a restless night crowded into the tiny cells of Arbour Hill Prison. The guards who had transported us from Galway headed for home so that our new jailers had no idea who was who. Confusion reigned and no sooner had night fallen than we began to protest in a coordinated fashion, making a tremendous amount of noise. Every prisoner was shouting for the warders and requesting this, that and the other. We needed food and drink and we were shouting out about this. We needed tobacco and cigarettes, we needed books and bedding. There was nothing that a request wasn't being put in for and the menacing nature of our threats created a general all-round racket. The guards became frightened then and they went in search of advice on how to deal with us. Various phone calls were made to Dublin Castle, highlighting the urgency of the situation; the guards were afraid that we were about to start a riot in the prison.

A while later, a number of senior members of the prison staff appeared, accompanied by four heavily armed soldiers. They shouted into the cells to us and asked us what our demands were. We called out such a long list of demands that they didn't know where to start. The prison officials and soldiers left then without giving us anything to eat. We spent a restless night together in the cells, the extent of the damage done to the movement by the seizing of so many of our leaders being the focus of our discussions. By morning, we had concluded that there were enough men still free to take control of the armed struggle and we were renewed in our determination to resist the imperialist forces with all our might. This blow to us (Sinn Féin) made us more determined than ever to get revenge on the English and to strike with twice the force on the next occasion that we had the opportunity.

After a few hours, we gave up our noise protest and the shouting died down. We were too hungry and thirsty to keep it up by then and once darkness enveloped us fully, we went quiet. We whispered amongst ourselves and decided to make one last onslaught on the prison doors in a show of force. Altogether, we attacked the doors and the walls of the cells, hammering and kicking them with all our might. The prison doors took an almighty battering but they held firm. Then we lay down on the ground on the black sacks that had been placed there as our bedding.

It was the racket of the doors being hammered again that woke me in the morning. Everybody was up and the protest was in full swing again. We only eased off with the noise protest when some food was brought in to us. Apparently, a decision had been made in Dublin Castle to accede to some of our requests. The prison authorities had decided to adopt a 'softly-softly' approach and, once breakfast was eaten, they undid the bolts on the cell doors. We were released from the cells and allowed to walk around on the landings for a while. Then we were ordered to organise ourselves into one group as we were to be addressed by the senior commanding officer within the prison. Once we were lined up he gave a fairly long-winded speech, the main points of which were as follows: 'For the limited period that you are going to be in this prison, it is not worth your while to initiate an obstructive campaign against us – the prison authorities. I have a written announcement for each and every one of you and the sooner we hand them out the better.' He pulled a small table in front of him and placed a pile of papers on the table. Then he called out our names and we each stepped forward to receive our notice. I received this one:

Order Under Regulation 14.B of the Defence of the Realm Regulations

Whereas Colman [*sic*] O'Geary, Rosmuck, Galway W.R., is a person within the area in respect of which the operation of Section One of the Defence of the Realm (Amendment) Act 1915, is for the time being suspended. And whereas on the recommendation of a Competent Military Authority appointed under the Defence of the Realm Regulations, it appears to me that for securing the public safety and the defence of the Realm it is expedient that the said Colman O'Geary, Rosmuck, should in view of the fact that he is a person suspected of acting, having acted, and being about to act in a manner prejudicial to the public safety and the defence of the Realm, be subjected to such obligations and restrictions as are hereinafter mentioned:

I Hereby Order that the said Colman O'Geary, Rosmuck, shall be interned in Frongoch Camp, and shall be subject to all the rules and conditions applicable to persons there interned and remain there until further orders.

If within seven days from the day on which this Order is served on the said Colman O'Geary, Rosmuck, he shall submit to me any representations against the provisions of this Order, such representations will be referred to the Advisory Committee appointed for the purpose of advising me with respect to the internment and deportation of aliens and presided over by a Judge of the High Court and will be duly considered by the Committee. If I am satisfied by the report of the said Committee that this Order may be revoked or varied without injury to the public safety or the defence of the Realm, I will revoke or vary this Order by a further Order in writing under my hand. Failing such revocation or variation this Order shall remain in force.

(Sgd) E. SHORTT,
Chief Secretary.
Dublin Castle,
17th May 1918.

The commanding officer then instructed us all to gather our personal effects together and to be ready for our departure. He then turned away, surrounded by his four subordinates who encircled him as if they were his own personal bodyguards. The thought crossed my mind at this moment: is it better to be a subordinate or a higher-up in this life? If you are one of the lower-downs in this life, nobody takes any notice of you at all. On the other hand, if you are one of society's higher-ups you don't get a moment's peace as everybody is constantly at your side and at your beck-and-call.

We didn't have to wait too long before our transfer took place. We were brought on an armed lorry to the North Wall where we were placed on a cattle boat under a heavily armed military guard. We were placed in the hold of the ship beside the cattle and the horses as before. The funniest moment came when each of us was given a purple-coloured life-belt which we had to place over our heads. The irony wasn't lost on us. Our captors would have been more than delighted to get rid of a large group of republican rebels such as ourselves, and here they were instructing us on how to save ourselves in the event of an accident or a potential incident with a German submarine. Fortunately, the life-belts weren't needed on that trip and we arrived into the port of Holyhead safe and sound.

We waited there for a number of hours after the boat had docked and just when we thought we might be confined to that stinking hold for a long time yet, we found ourselves transferred from the ferry and brought to an army barracks somewhere in the hills outside Holyhead. The army officers guarding us there told us that we would shortly be moved by train to Birmingham. At this stage we weren't too sure where we were going to end up, as conflicting rumours and reports were continually being passed on to us by the army personnel who were guarding us. Based on the notices that we had received in Arbour Hill prison we assumed that we were being sent to Frongoch in Wales, but we now wondered whether there had been such a level of confusion amongst the prison authorities in Dublin that the administrators in Arbour Hill hadn't been sure themselves of where they were sending us.[4] Whether we were bound for England or Wales, the soldiers guarding us were loud in their threats and outlined in detail the brutal tortures and deaths that likely lay ahead of us. We were so used to these psychological tactics at this stage, however, that we barely noticed them any more. The most vocal of these soldiers was an old British army sergeant who was conspicuous by the fact that he had a glass eye, having lost one of his eyes in the Great War.

'You bunch of spineless thugs. You've had it easy so far but that won't last for long. You have no idea what lies ahead of you as we are going to fight tooth and nail to keep our empire. We'll run you back to where you came from and burn your hides while we're at it.'

'You've done your best to drive the Irish back into the marshes and the bogs for centuries – but not for much longer,' we answered him.

We gave him as good as we got, I can tell you.

There are few journeys on this earth that can be more beautiful than that train journey between Holyhead and Birmingham – if a prison camp isn't your final destination, that is. The train chugged along through the plains, the woods and the mountain passes. The sea rolled against the edges of the cliffs, and all of this under the warm glow of the beautiful May sun. Elderly people and women were the mainstays of the farming lands in these areas and the absence of young men such as ourselves because of the Great War was remarked upon by a number of people on that journey.

It was pitch-dark by the time we reached the train station in Birmingham. The prison vans were already there awaiting our arrival and there were some scuffles between us and the prison guards as they tried to force too many of us into the first two vans. One thing led to another and before we knew it there was a full-scale fist fight taking place on the road. Ourselves and the prison officers were evenly matched and man-for-man we soon wore them down.

Frightened by what they saw happening, the English on-lookers must have contacted the local authorities because a squadron of policemen suddenly appeared and we laid into them as well. Because there was a black-out – a consequence of the British fear of German air attack – it became quite confusing who was who and with the fists flying you didn't hang around to find out. You just kept throwing punches. Eventually the mêlée died down and the British agreed to send out a few more vans to transport us to the prison.

Fists flew again when we got to the prison and this time it was one of the prison officers who started the fight. Once things calmed down again, the prison officer in charge began to read out our names one after the other. Not one of us replied, however, and they were left in a right quandary since whoever had accompanied us from Holyhead had now left. It must have been some administrative hiccup or other, but there was nobody there now who actually knew one of us from the other. The man in charge of us had simply been handed a sheet of paper with our names listed on it.

The governor of the prison was called to deal with this crisis and as had happened in Arbour Hill previously, he decided to make a speech of 'appeasement'. As in Dublin, he too adopted the softer and more diplomatic approach deciding to negotiate with us from the off. 'I know that none of you are in the mood for answering anything now given your long day travelling. I think it's best if you all hit the sack now and we'll all be in a better mood for discussion in the morning.' We agreed to his request, with the proviso that they didn't lock our cell doors that night.

The next morning we appointed three of our own to negotiate with the prison governor and to see what sort of privileges they could garner for us. Dr Cusack, Count Plunkett and Seoirse Mac Niocaill were our three representatives and three better men we could never have chosen. We considered it more advantageous to have a small delegation put forward our point of view rather than all of us speaking together. If we all spoke at once, we probably wouldn't get half of the demands we hoped to get. Ironically, having spoken with our representatives, the governor decided to hold a broader consultation and, that afternoon, he walked around from cell to cell to confirm the requests which we had already delivered via our spokespeople. I don't know how the man kept a straight face when he heard some of the requests that we put to him. Some of them were just ridiculous and we were only mocking the system. Having listened to us, he bluntly informed us that he had been issued with no instructions from the British prison service as of yet as to how he was to deal with us or what type of prison regulations – i.e. whether 'criminal' or political – would apply to us.

Whether for an easy life or not, the governor agreed to our demands with the proviso that he would have to check with his superiors in Downing Street as to whether he could grant them or not. 'In the meantime, you might be kind enough to get us some tobacco and the few bottles of alcohol – to help us pass the time in here?' – our representatives said, without a hint of shame. Instead of rejecting this request out-of-hand as we had assumed, the governor surprised us with his reply – 'Well, I'm heading into the city centre right now and I'll see what I can do.'

The governor was only playing games and stalling until he had spoken to his superiors in the government. He returned that evening with a whole series of excuses as to why he had been unable to deliver on any of the promises that he had made previously. The distribution of every type of foodstuff and alcohol was now organised by a new legal act known as the Administrative Act, he told us. This act stated that each and every individual prisoner in the country had to submit an application for any food or alcohol that was 'outside the norm' – an application that would then be adjudicated upon by a committee of civil servants in the London government.

When the prison governor had previously stated that he had been given no explicit instructions from his superiors as to what regulations or measures were to be applied to a category of 'political' inmates such as ourselves, he wasn't lying. Once he saw that we had our internal system of organisation and discipline, the prison governor had left us to our own devices. Provided we behaved, we were given the run of that section of the prison where we were incarcerated. After a few weeks, we realised that this was likely to be the way that things would remain for the foreseeable future unless we decided to actively agitate for somewhat better conditions. We drew up a new list of demands that we argued would improve our conditions in the prison and ensure that we remained exemplary prisoners in terms of behaviour. Our demands were all minor ones, simple things as relating to food and cleanliness and the manner whereby the prison regime instructed us to organise ourselves. One of the reasons that we focused on small demands at this point, and as agreed communally by all of the republican prisoners, was in case we found ourselves separated from one another within this prison or in any other prisons at any time in the near future.

To say that the governor was surprised the day that we presented him with this list of written demands would be an understatement. He clearly wasn't very used to dealing with prisoners of our 'type'. Presumably, the 'regular' prisoners he had experience of dealing with didn't expect much change in their status or their conditions. They just did what they were told and that was the end of it. Now the governor had a new 'breed' of prisoner on his hands – and we let him know all about it. I think the poor man was initially in a state of shock when we handed over our list of written demands because he told us that he needed a few hours to consider matters. He disappeared then and we didn't see him again until a couple of days later.

Of course, the truth of the matter was that we (i.e. the prisoners) had very little power and were really only 'chancing our arm'. Other than create a lot of noise, break the cell windows or destroy the small pieces of furniture that were in the cells – there was very little that we could do as a meaningful protest. Even if we had created nightly disturbances, the fact that we had a prison landing to ourselves meant that any protests would have affected the other sections of the prison very little.

One thing we republicans were always very keen on in prison was sports. We had barely arrived in that prison when we were out organising teams to play throwing games or handball. If the weather was bad we stayed indoors and organised Irish-language classes or played cards. Actually, one of the 'demands' which we had included on our list as submitted to the governor was a request for a proper wall where we could play handball. The wall that we used had small panes of glass in it which we broke more often than I can remember. In fact, when there was no sign of any visible progress on our list of 'demands', those same panes of glass were broken much more often than they had been before then.

We were in prison during the Irish general election of 1918 and a number of prisoners who were imprisoned with us – Count Plunkett, Brian O'Higgins and Dr Brian Cusack amongst them – were elected. Indeed, Plunkett, who had been the first TD ever elected on the republican side one year previously, was re-elected as a TD for County Roscommon.[5]

Over time, we gradually came to know our prison guards. Two of them were friendlier than the others. One was an Irishman from Belfast while the other was an Englishman. These two men agreed to deliver messages from us to our supporters outside and, particularly, to our fellow republicans who were imprisoned in other parts of Britain. We began slowly with short, coded messages and when the channels continued to work well, we became more daring and sent out longer messages and even letters. Every road has its turning, however, and that is what happened with us also.

One day, one of these two men arrived into us in a very agitated state. In an anxious voice, he delivered the bad news to us. A man had been apprehended on a train in Birmingham station with a large batch of letters, the majority of which had originated in our prison. The prison warder was in an absolute panic. We'd never seen this man, normally very composed before this, look so terrified and we had to sit him down and calm him.

'Don't worry!' we told him. 'If anybody takes the rap for this, it will be us. There is no way that we will hang you out to dry for what has happened. That will never happen.'

The man left our cells a much more relieved man than he had been when he first arrived. After we had debated the ins and outs of this discovery, we agreed that our two prison warder messengers were in no way guilty of selling us out. We were certain of this because we knew by his body language and the questions that we had put to the man. Irrespective of our deliberations, there was no doubt now that the prison authorities would be pointing the finger of suspicion at the prison warders on our landing and the two men who had delivered messages on our behalf would 'come into the frame'.

That day we had a meeting at recreation where we came

up with a plan that would help divert suspicion away from the two guards who had befriended us and which ensured that any potential guilt or blame would be assigned to ourselves alone.

Dusk was falling as the head prison officer made his way back in the direction of the prison gates. He had been back into the city of Birmingham to get a bite to eat and now he was returning to the prison to begin his next work-shift. Suddenly, a big brown parcel flew over the prison wall and hit him on the head. The prison officer fell to the ground as if struck by a lightning bolt. While the parcel wasn't in any way heavy, he just lay there prone on the ground. He must have thought that there was a bomb in that parcel and that he was going to be blown to kingdom come at any second. When no explosion came after a minute or two, however, his courage returned and he rose from the ground. He looked above him and all around, but the night was so quiet you could have heard a pin fall. We watched him from our cells as he hesitated momentarily, unsure of whether he should pick up the parcel or not. Finally, he moved a little closer to it and bent down as if to read the address on it. We saw him bend down and pick the parcel up from the ground before examining it more carefully.

Then, one of life's strange and lucky coincidences happened. Just as the prison officer marched off to the governor's office to show him the parcel, two Irishwomen arrived at the front gate of the prison. These same women were republican sympathisers who would regularly call to the prison gates and hand in cigarettes and tobacco for us. We, who were watching, could hardly believe how lucky a coincidence this was. The fact that two Irishwomen arrived at just the same moment as some of our republican prisoners flung this 'decoy' parcel over the wall was a more fortuitous coincidence than we could have imagined. Our attempt to deflect attention away from the two guards who had helped us had been boosted no end.

From then on, the number of prison officers stationed outside the cells of the republican prisoners was increased. This didn't bother us too much. Now that attention had been deflected away from our two 'sources' within the prison, we were happy. Of course, we had planned the throwing of that parcel over the wall for the same time that the prison officer in question would be returning from the city. We'd spent that afternoon scribbling down pages of complete rubbish on the stash of papers that we'd folded into that parcel. I had actually used that afternoon to compose a poem entitled 'The School', the text of which I enclosed for publication in the monthly Irish-language newspaper *An Stoc*, which we used to publish back in Galway then. The fact that I provide the text of the poem here is not because the poem itself has any great merit in terms of metre or poetic artistry. It is because the original 'manuscript' of this poem spent its initial months – (and indeed the rest of its life) – in the office of the British ministry of home affairs:

THE SCHOOL

Hardly a day passes
That I don't remember my childhood
An innocent time when I was without worry or strife
Rowing along the seafront or swimming in the lake
In the place that fronted our school
Many is the day we spent dazed
In front of our school-desks
When we could have been out in the beach
Laughing, playing and making fun
Many is the frosty morning, our hearts were in a tizzy
The hours we spent slip-sliding happily on the ice

Time passed as it does, we had no need of any clock
Until it was time to return to the classroom once more
Many is the day we shook with fright
The stick swishing through the air
The master mercilessly prodding us to greater effort
Beating the texts into us until we had it off-by-heart
His stick made us dance every morning in that schoolroom
All our friends have left now, they are long-scattered and gone
Some across the sea, others resting in the graveyard
Others are still in jail, we miss them here tonight
Dreaming of the days when we were still at school.

A strange thing happened to me in 1919 while I was still incarcerated. Believe it or not, I was actually handed a prison sentence while I was still in prison. A very sad message was delivered to me one morning in Birmingham Jail. My father was on his deathbed. The prison regime in Birmingham was a very liberal one as compared with many other prisons of the day. In the case of a family member who was dying, we were allowed parole for one week, to visit home. My request for parole was granted and I was brought to the train the next day.

Although nothing was said to me, I soon spotted the detective that they put on the train to Holyhead with me. Believe it or not, he was actually dressed as a clergyman! While he had the 'get-up' of a religious man – to me, at least – it was as clear as day who he was. As soon as I sat into the carriage I reddened my pipe. I happily puffed away and watched amused as the thick clouds of tobacco drifted back in the direction of the 'clergyman' who was sitting behind me at the rear of the carriage. It wasn't for nothing that the other inmates had nicknamed me the 'human furnace' in prison. I loved smoking. There was hardly a moment in the day that I didn't have that pipe in my mouth. It wasn't too long before the 'man of the cloth' was complaining about the stuffiness of the carriage and was asking that I put the pipe out.

'If you can't stand the heat, get out of the kitchen. Isn't that what they say?' I answered the detective-in-disguise.

I started blowing out that smoke like no tomorrow then – just to annoy him. I could sense the man getting more and more agitated but he kept his complaints to himself for the rest of the train journey. He didn't say another word for the rest of the trip and I never saw him again once I took the boat to Ireland.

On the boat I ran into Joseph MacBride, Major MacBride's brother. He too was returning home to visit a seriously ill relative. Like me, a detective had followed him on his journey across England where he was being held at that time in another prison. Anybody who's spent time in prison will tell you that you become a bit institutionalised after a period of incarceration. When you are in prison it is easy to go without a shave and within a month of our incarceration there was hardly one of us republicans who did not sport a big unruly beard. It was only on those few days that I was released to see my father that I realised how much my appearance must have changed. As the train came into the west, I spotted a few people whom I recognised only to realise that they no longer recognised me!

When I eventually got back to Rosmuc, there were people there too who gave me funny looks. I think maybe they felt sorry for me because they suspected that we republicans weren't allowed to shave as part of our prison sentence – i.e. that it was a special part of our punishment. Believe it or not, a few people even ran away at the sight of me – I think they thought that I was one of those madmen that you see roaming the countryside every once in a while!

Everything was all right until we reached the crossroads at

Maumwee. When I hopped off the train there, two policemen were standing against the wall and I noticed the way that they glanced at one another, having spotted me disembarking from the train. Not only must I have looked like a bit of a tramp, with my tattered clothes and my wild-looking beard, but I was also a stranger whom nobody had met at the train station. I hurried out of that station as quickly as I could only to be followed by the two policemen and a police sergeant who suddenly appeared out of nowhere. I acted completely oblivious to them and had reached the end of the town before they caught up with me.

I was stopped then and asked the usual questions. What was my name? What was my business in the area? How long would I be in the vicinity for?

To say that I got a frosty reception from them when I gave them my name is an understatement. At first they swore that I couldn't be who I said I was. The 'suspect' whom they knew of as 'Colm Geary' was a much younger man than me, they claimed. They ordered me to turn around and walk back with them to the police station. Given that the three of them were armed, I didn't really have much choice in the matter. I did what I was told but we had barely marched a few yards up the road when a motor car came flying along the street, its exhaust pipe spluttering. The driver of the car – (a man who shall remain nameless) – jumped out and shook my hand. 'Well, if it isn't himself!' he said laughing.

'Don't tell me you know this individual?' the sergeant asked incredulously. 'Keep away from him.'

'Stay away from who?' My friend stepped forward and placed himself between me and the policeman. 'I'll never abandon any true friend of mine,' he said, fire in his voice, 'what do you intend doing with this decent man?'

'Hang him if necessary,' the big mullet of a sergeant answered spitefully.

Something of a stand-off took place then between the police on one side and my friend and I on the other. The police now reverted to their previous 'charge' that I couldn't possibly be who I claimed to be, while my friend contradicted them and assured them that I was telling the truth. In the heel of the hunt, I was frog-marched up to the police barracks under suspicion of being an escapee from an English prison. Only when the proof came through from England that I was on temporary parole, was I allowed to go on my way again.

The day that I was due to return to Birmingham prison was the day my father died. I sent a telegram to the prison governor in Birmingham and he gave me permission to stay on for the funeral. The day after my father's funeral found me on the long journey back to England. Nobody was more surprised than the prison governor the day I arrived back at Birmingham prison.

'You're obviously not tired of our company yet,' he mocked as I reported to his office. 'Did you not get our message? We sent a message stating that you were entitled to a further week's parole.'

'That's the first I heard of this,' I said.

I was more disgusted than surprised by the fact that this message hadn't been relayed to me. Not unnaturally, given that my father had only recently died, that I'd missed this extra week's parole really upset me. I mulled over it so much that when we were finally released from Birmingham prison, I made it my business to enquire from the governor whether he had been only joking about that extra week's grace or not.

He assured me that what he had told me the last time I'd been in his office was indeed true. The governor had sent a message granting me the extra week's leave but the message had been delivered to the police station that served the Rosmuc area. Such was the esteem in which the local RIC held me that passing on the message had slipped their mind.[6]

On the surface of it, one would imagine that a prison was the last place where you would find poitín – especially a prison in the very heartland of England. Believe it or not, however, I actually managed to smuggle a full bottle of this raw whiskey back into Birmingham Jail. So much for security! The poitín was badly needed at the time because there was a terrible flu in Britain and the prisons were full of it. This flu was one of the most debilitating sicknesses I had ever seen. There was one day when three of the prison guards collapsed while on duty, they were so affected by this flu virus.

Whether it was the fact that everybody had a swig of this Connemara poitín or not, (incredibly) not one of the eighteen republican prisoners in Birmingham prison got that flu. God was on our side with regard to the food situation also. There was a huge food shortage in England at this time, and in the prisons the situation was very difficult. You wouldn't believe the tiny amounts of food the other prisoners in Birmingham Jail had to survive on at the time. I honestly don't know how there wasn't a revolution in Britain then given the dire conditions that people were living in.

Ironically, though we were just immigrants to England at the time, we actually had more to eat than the other prisoners, thanks to the food parcels that our relatives regularly posted to us from Ireland.

I was only back in jail a few days when a guard searched my cell. They regularly did spot checks in the prison so there wasn't anything unusual in this. Sometimes they searched only the cells and the yards. On other occasions they frisked us or performed body searches. This particular guard was thorough and he soon located the bottle of poitín, half of which was already gone. He gave the bottle a shake, a questioning look on his face.

'It's a pure wine from Connemara that's in that bottle,' I said to him.

To be honest, I wasn't too worried that the guard had discovered the poitín. What could they do to me after all? Put me into prison, where I already was? And that's the way it turned out. The guard let me keep the poitín and nothing more was said about it.

That bottle of poitín became one of the most prized and joked-about possessions amongst us republicans. Amazingly, the fact that none of us came down with that terrible flu meant that the poitín was only used very sparingly over the following months. I actually managed to spare some of it for the night of our release from Birmingham prison when we had a good party. When we were finally released we all had a small glass of that same poitín on the train that left Birmingham the day of our release. Two people whom we gave especially generous helpings to were the two guards who had been so nice to us while we were still locked up. Given that they were unfamiliar with the strength of poitín, they were soon in flying form and were roaring and shouting and singing all of the way back to the ferry in Wales, along with the rest of us. I have my doubts as to whether those two men ever got a promotion in the prison service after the carry-on that night – especially given that we prisoners gave them a big cheer and a round of applause as we said our goodbyes at the ferry port.

Normally, when you are in prison for an indefinite period, rumours begin to circulate a few weeks or months before your release. That was the way it turned out for us also. In Birmingham prison the rumours were that we would be released for Christmas. This rumour was so commonly believed for a month or two before our release that, eventually, it nearly assumed the status of fact. The rumour also went back to Ireland via our smuggled letters and our relatives at home were so happy for us that they sent us lots of small cakes and biscuits so that we could celebrate the day of our release in style – i.e. with a big feast. They were so generous that we received a whole load of small food packets, some of which were brought in legally and some of which were smuggled in. Eventually we had so much food for our celebration that we had to find somewhere to store it. We hid it in one of the empty cells that was on our wing, one to which we had easy access.

Inevitably, a few of the prison guards discovered this secret stash of ours and began to dip in and out of it when they were hungry. One morning, a few weeks after the occasional item had begun to disappear from our stash, one of our two 'friendly' guards arrived into cell. The man had a look of fear in his eyes. He was nearly more stressed-looking than the day he had arrived into the cells to tell us about the interception of the letters and parcels earlier in the year. He was very on edge, his eyes glancing nervously about him like a man who had a story to tell. The man was even making us nervous because he wouldn't make eye contact with any of us.

'What's going on? Has a war begun again or are you here to deliver some terrible news from home?'

'Not at all,' the man answered, 'but you' pant'y tempted me an' I pinched you' big tu'key; the bloomin' guvne' caught me goin' out the gate with it. The governor must be suspicious now that you fellows have a secret store of food in here somewhere.'

The poor man was almost shaking with fear. You'd swear the

man had committed a major crime against us! To be honest, we nearly burst out laughing. Now we knew who the main culprit was in relation to the pilfering of the hidden store of food. Believe it or not, this man felt so guilty about stealing our food that he actually said to the governor that we had given him this turkey as a present.

When the governor came to investigate the issue in the company of the aforementioned nervous prison guard, we all went along with the prison officer's lie. That same man had been generous to us in countless other ways and we weren't going to land him in any trouble.

One condition which we republicans had argued for upon our initial arrival in Birmingham prison was that we should be allowed to read whatever newspapers arrived at the prison without anybody censoring them first. The governor had accepted this request on our part and subsequent to this the newspapers had been passed around the prison each morning from one cell to the next. One particular morning, however, there was no sign of the newspapers arriving. Having made a number of enquiries in the prison, we decided to send a message to the prison governor asking whether he knew what had happened to the daily newspapers.

The response from the governor's office was a strange one. The messenger came back with the newspapers but with certain columns carefully cut out and removed. There was hardly a page that hadn't been doctored.

Our response was as defiant as usual. We wouldn't read the newspapers that had been subjected to the scissors of the censor.

The response from the governor's office was equally defiant, however. They began playing us at our own game now because they just continued to send us the newspapers each morning, but with various articles removed. When we returned the newspapers and complained of the harsh censorship that was being imposed upon us, we were treated to a litany of excuses as to why this was happening – each explanation more ridiculous than the last. 'The picture that was removed was a photograph of some race-horse which had been seriously injured at a race meeting somewhere.' 'The photo was unsuitable because it depicted a train crash.' 'The photo was of an injury the king of England had received recently.' 'The story that was on that page wasn't worth reading.' You wouldn't believe some of the ridiculous excuses we were given for the fact that the newspapers were being censored. Eventually we found out the real reason that this censorship was going on. De Valera and some other prisoners had escaped from Lincoln prison shortly before this and the prison authorities didn't want us to hear anything about it.

15

A Representative of Dáil Éireann

The Great War had ended a few months before and England was in recovery mode. There was more food available and the ordinary people's lives began to improve slightly. Word came through that we were to be released, having served ten months of a prison sentence. During that time, two good men had passed away while they were still incarcerated in an English prison – Pearse McCan and Richard Coleman.

When we got home to Ireland we found that cooperatives had been set up throughout the country. The vast majority of the Irish people were involved in the setting-up of these cooperative ventures, the only exception being the big shopkeepers. Anybody who had a pound to spare was investing it in the cooperatives because they remembered the era when the shopkeepers and the gombeen men had torn the soul out of the Irish people and they were loath to let it happen again. The sense of idealism that lay behind the creation of the cooperatives was wonderful but the people didn't have the expertise to maintain them. Unfortunately, these cooperatives fell apart only a few short years later. The reasons for their demise were twofold really. On the one hand, the Irish people had little experience of putting in place the foundations or structures to develop such innovative ventures. The infrastructure in Ireland was very poor and had declined even further during the period of the First World War.

It was further destroyed with the violence and pillage that the Black and Tans committed in Ireland. In my own opinion, the main reason that the cooperative stores failed was because the people who were in charge of them had no training in how to manage them and no knowledge of trade or business.

After our release from prison, it became more difficult to promote and organise the Volunteers than it had been previously. People were afraid that they might be drafted into the army if they had any military experience. With the struggle of day-to-day life, people had nearly forgotten what the First World War had really entailed. When the draft had been as good as compulsory, we had been forced to lobby scores of older men to enlist in the Volunteers. Now the opposite was true except that we had great difficulty generating any interest amongst the younger men.

I spent a short while in County Roscommon at this juncture where I was working at my normal job of travelling teacher. People have short memories. It seemed that everybody had forgotten about the First World War already. Many of the men had joined the Volunteers in an effort to avoid British army conscription. The day I arrived in the area I went to see the parish priest of Athleague, Canon Conroy, to plan how best to re-energise the various branches of the Gaelic League and the schedule of Irish classes in the area. Although he didn't have any Irish, Canon Conroy, who was an elderly man at this stage, was a noted scholar and intellectual in his own right. A loyal Gael, the canon had a great respect for nationalists and freedom-fighters and the fact that I had been imprisoned in various English jails led him to insist that I share dinner with him in the parochial house. He spent the meal questioning me about various aspects of the nationalist movement, past and present. He suddenly launched into a big 'spiel' in honour of Daniel O'Connell. If he said that O'Connell was the greatest Irish leader once, he must have said it ten times: 'If only we had a leader of his calibre today,' he argued, 'we would be much closer to achieving our aim of independence from England.' I kept my counsel for a while but the canon 'got on my goat' with this theory and I eventually felt compelled to respond. 'O'Connell had his chance to strike for freedom. He had his chance and he failed!'

The priest's face dropped and I heard him mutter as if I wasn't in the room at all, 'Such zeal! He hasn't learned sense yet!'

Luckily, I kept my mouth shut after this because, as I discovered later, I might have found myself in trouble if I had continued with that discussion! When I left the canon's house later that afternoon he handed me a package wrapped in newspaper. Inside it was a copy of a book called *Beatha Dhónaill Uí Chonaill*. Who was its author but the canon himself? If I could have cut my tongue out there and then, I would have. There was me arguing O'Connell's merits and faults with a man who had written one of the few biographies of O'Connell ever published, a biography where he'd outlined the Irish leader's entire philosophy. I was mortally embarrassed every time I met that elderly priest afterwards.

Dáil Éireann was up-and-running by now.[1] Ministers had been elected with responsibility for the various different government departments. For these departments to function effectively it was necessary to raise money throughout Ireland. Michael Collins, the finance minister, had the primary responsibility for the fund-raising side of things.[2] He divided each county and electoral area into various smaller sub-divisions and selected individuals for each area whose responsibility it would be to raise money 'on-the-ground'. I was one of the people chosen for this work, north County Galway and Connemara being my designated areas for fund-raising. At this point in time, County Galway was officially divided into four separate electoral areas.

As you would have expected, the British hindered our attempts at self-determination in every way that they could. None of the Irish newspapers were permitted to carry announcements in relation to the fund-raising efforts we were initiating to develop our own governmental structures. We weren't allowed to organise any public meetings in relation to the new structures and you risked immediate imprisonment if you were caught in possession of any literature pertaining to such activities. Although everything was done in secret, I managed to raise over £4,000 within the space of six months in the two electoral areas I was assigned to. It was £1 here and £2 there and it was the ordinary man in the street giving what he could afford.

From the beginning of the fund-raising initiative, I had to decide on a good 'cover story' in case the authorities found me in possession of some of this money. I therefore took on the disguise of a travelling salesman who was selling clothes and shoes. I bought a small suitcase, some clothes samples and various samples of boot polish. I also carried a notebook in which to write down my 'orders' for the products from the shopkeepers and I tied the case to the back of my bike as I went about my business. My 'rig-out' was a good one but it didn't prevent me from being searched regularly by the authorities. Anybody who travelled for a living back then was a source of suspicion and if I had to untie my suitcase of 'samples' and open it once, I had to do it a hundred times. My 'official' customers were the members of the local Volunteer branches that we were either setting up from scratch or reviving and strengthening once more.

One day I was in a shop in Kilkerrin near Glenamaddy, County Galway, where I was collecting some money for Collins' fund-raising project. I had barely put my foot inside the door when three policemen appeared. They grabbed me and without a word to anyone I was dragged out onto the street and brought around to the back of the shop, where I was stripped naked. They even pulled off my shoes and socks, making a great charade of searching me thoroughly. They clearly felt that they were 'onto something' because the look of disappointment on their faces when they found nothing incriminating on my person or in the travel case was something to behold. I was told to clear out of the area as quickly as possible or face the consequences. The sergeant, a man by the name of MacMurchú was furious that I had 'got the better of them' and was practically dancing with rage. He brought his face close to mine and introduced himself in a voice that spoke of a deep-rooted sense of self-importance. He was foaming at the mouth he was so furious and he detailed the various injuries he would inflict on me if I ever dared show my face in the area again!

'Diarmaid MacMurchú. Yeah, I've heard of your crowd,' I said to him, giving him as good as I got.

I was on the point of cursing his family and all the generations before him, a prelude to a certain bout of fisticuffs. The other two policemen pulled him away and I was promptly escorted out of the town.

One night of heavy rain I was cycling home from a meeting in Glinsk near Glenamaddy. The wind and the rain became more and more violent until it was soon a full-scale gale. I was forced to dismount from the bike and, bent double against the wind and the driving rain, I made my way slowly to the gate of a nearby house. The piercing glare of a torch almost blinded me and two policemen suddenly appeared out of the gloom.

They had a good stare at me and then carted me and my bicycle off to the police station. The two of them were on a total high and they taunted me all the way to the police barracks. 'I might have given them the run-around for a while but they had finally caught me.' Whether they'd confused me with somebody else or not, I wasn't too sure. They certainly seemed to think that they had apprehended a master criminal! This was obvious from the crowing and the whooping of the two of them. The fact that my face was 'blackened' and the fact that they had arrested me in such atrocious weather conditions led them to think that nabbing me was a major 'coup'.

When they asked me why I was trying to disguise my face by covering it in black 'ink', I came up with some feeble excuse or other. I didn't know what they were talking about to be honest. It was only when they handed me some water and told me to wash off the ink that I realised they weren't 'having me on' – my face was indeed painted black. The realisation hit me like a bolt of lightning! Shortly before this I had bought a soft black hat. I had worn it a good deal but this particular night was the first time the hat had experienced the full force of an Irish rain-shower. It had been subjected to a veritable deluge of water that night and unknown to me the dye in the hat had begun to run. By the time I was arrested, my face was plastered with this black dye. When the commanding officer of the barracks came to question me and saw for himself the way the hat had 'faded', he, too, realised what had happened. By mid-afternoon of the following day, news had filtered through that there had been no major crime committed in the vicinity the previous evening. Suddenly the 'coup' that was my arrest seemed like little more than a damp squib and I was immediately released without charge. The only sobering thought I was left with after that whole experience was this. How many times in decades past have innocent people been unjustly accused and then convicted of crimes in which they had no hand, act or part? If some crime had indeed been committed in the vicinity that night, I would surely have been the one 'fingered' for it.

People wouldn't believe it today if you told them that Carna was then the most difficult place in which to raise money for the National Loan project, but that is actually true. Every time I visited the village, the police were on me like a bad rash. I had to box clever there just to make contact with our supporters, never mind raise any money for the loan project. I had to use a dance, 'The Siege of Ennis', in the end to get to speak to any of the locals. While uniformed police and undercover detectives looked on, I swung from dancer to dancer in the local hall and explained the ins and outs of the Loan Fund to them above the sound of the music and the stomping feet. I had to be careful because in addition to the undercover police who were trying to mingle with the crowd, I suspected that there were one or two locals there too who were ready to tip them off. In an attempt to sift out our real supporters from the spies, I pretended to be a 'visiting dancer' who was organising a separate class in order to teach the dancers a new dance. This gave me the opportunity to speak to people individually and for a longer period. It all worked out in the end, thank God and two or three locals were appointed who would look after the collection in Carna. Little did the police realise that night that behind the whoops and shouts of the circling dancers, important 'matters-of-state' relating to the newly independent Irish republic were being planned and set in motion.

It was during this period, too, that the first independent courts of the Irish republic were instituted. To have our own court system, completely independent of the British system, had been an aim of ours for decades and we now tried to get such systems set up, initially on an 'underground' basis. Those of us amongst the Irish Volunteers who were charged with instituting the new legal systems had a difficult job on our hands, particularly regarding the enforcement of sentences handed down by the new courts. The most difficult aspect of the whole process was the fact that we had nowhere to imprison criminals who had been found guilty of crimes against the local people. At first, we tried to operate a form of 'community justice' based on mutual consent. The alleged perpetrator and the aggrieved party were brought together to see could an agreeable solution or form of compensation be decided upon. If both parties agreed to an 'appropriate' resolution, then the case was brought to an end in a way that was acceptable to everybody.

In cases such as robbery, the accused was brought to a parish or country where nobody knew him to assure the 'independence' of the arbiters. This necessitated blindfolding the prisoner and transporting them to a different area. It was always amazing how frightened people became when you produced the blindfold. The blocking out of the eyes and the subsequent disorientation of the prisoner had a psychological effect on people that was powerful. On many occasions the sight of the blindfold was enough to make a 'small-time' criminal admit to his wrongdoings there and then.

I remember one criminal who was imprisoned for a short time when the blindfold was in common use. In his case, it wasn't the blindfold that was his biggest problem. The man was dangerous and prone to outbursts of extreme violence so we had to put two Volunteers guarding the room where he was being held. One of these Volunteers had an unbelievable appetite. He was always hungry, so much so that they said he would chew his way through the iron bars of a prison cell if there was some food on the other side! Unfortunately for this prisoner he was guarding, this particular Volunteer was eating all of the prisoner's meals in addition to his own. Eventually we had to assign this Volunteer to another job because the poor prisoner was fading away.

Mention of the 'era of the blindfold' puts me in mind of a conference that was held in Galway at which the minister of education in the First Dáil was the keynote speaker. There were a large number of priests in attendance and everybody was full of enthusiasm and new ideas in relation to the implementation of a more 'Gaelic' education system and the revival of the Irish language. It took a while for the issue to raise its head but eventually the discussion came around to this, one of the thorniest questions of the time. What could be done about those clergy who were involved in education but who were actively opposed to the use of Irish? Fr Michael Griffin, who was murdered by the Black and Tans shortly after this, turned to me in the middle of the discussion and said: 'Maybe … you could give us your opinion as to what to do in relation to this Colm?[3] You know the lay of the land better than anyone through your work throughout the country as a language teacher/organiser.'

All my frustrations at the years of dealing with clergy and administrators hostile to the Irish language must have come to the surface all at once then because I said: 'I see only one solution to this problem at this stage, Father. Now that we have our own legal system in operation, we should punish those who obstruct us in our work, whether lay people or clergy. Punish them all equally and give them a dose of the blindfold while we're at it.'

While many of the conference attendees laughed uproariously at my comments, others didn't think it was so funny. Some of these people were aware, of course, that I was involved in the new 'underground' judicial system and they understood the irony in my comments better than most. But that I would suggest using the blindfold on a 'man of the cloth' didn't go down too well with some of them, I can tell you.

I got to know Terence MacSwiney when I was on the finance committee of the Gaelic League. The committee used to have its regular meetings in Fleming's Hotel, Dublin, and MacSwiney would be there, sitting quietly in the corner. He was a man of few words but a real thinker all the same. He was also very dedicated to the revival of the Irish language and foresaw the dangers for the Gaeltacht areas a long time before many others did. It was Terence MacSwiney who helped me secure an area Irish-language organiser specifically for the Connemara area. This was after I explained to him the pressures the language was facing from English even then in the Connemara area. Terence MacSwiney's name became known and revered even in the furthest corners of the empire after his act of resistance against British rule in Ireland. MacSwiney was an incredibly brave man, a man whose strength of character was indomitable. The fact that he survived seventy-four days on hunger strike before succumbing speaks volumes for the man.

Early one Sunday morning I awoke to the sound of truck engines and other vehicles outside on the street. It took me a moment to get my bearings. I was in a house in the village of Tuam. The man who was in the next bed to mine was a cattle-dealer who had arrived the previous evening for the Tuam Fair which was starting on the Monday. The man had shaken me awake because the street outside was crawling with soldiers and police. This cattle-dealer, a large, red-faced man, was in a panic. He was trying to pull his trousers on over his ample girth, hopping around the room in a strange ungainly dance. He leaned against the wall to steady himself and peered through the curtains.

'They've fanned out in a circle around the house,' he whispered. 'They have the place surrounded, I'd say.'

Two seconds later and the crashing boots were on the stairs. Soldiers and policemen smashed the doors of the bedroom open. They had come for me but the poor cattle-dealer found himself under suspicion now too. They questioned him and searched him as I got dressed and they discovered a green-covered notebook amongst his possessions.

'What's with the green notebook?' they asked him.

'That notebook is for my job,' he answered apprehensively.

'Are you a ballad-singer so?' the officer demanded, examining the notebook in greater detail.

'No sir. I am a cattle-jobber.'

'What the hell have these songs to do with buying cattle?' and he began reading out some skit of poem/ballad in what he thought was a humorous voice.

'It's Old Moore's,' the dealer responded and went back to packing his stuff.

A policeman intervened then and began to whisper to the army officer who was asking the questions.

The cattle-dealer was left in peace and I was brought to Galway Jail by lorry. There were six Sinn Féiners in the cells already when I got there. They had been there for a long time already, all held without trial. None of them had had any charge proffered against them and it was the same for me. No charge had been put to me in the house in Tuam either and when I heard nothing after a few days, I asked to speak to the prison governor. When I eventually got to meet him, he told me that he had absolutely no idea why I had been imprisoned. If I had been accused of any crime, he certainly hadn't heard anything about it. That very day the seven of us went on a hunger and thirst strike. After the third day, I felt my appetite for food recede. I felt myself becoming weaker and by the seventh day I was beginning to feel a numbness in my limbs. The lack of water was making me dizzy and my heart was racing by day nine. Three of us were brought to the hospital in Galway on the same day, we were that weak.

It was stretched out in that hospital bed that I first met Tomás Bairéad.[4] He was working as a reporter with the *Galway Express* and was doing a piece for that newspaper (a paper which was strongly pro-nationalist) about the hunger strike. Shortly after his interview with me, the Black and Tans made smithereens of that newspaper's printing press.

Little did any of us realise the day of that hospital interview just what an excellent writer of the Irish language Tomás Bairéad would later prove himself to be. That day in the hospital he was more interested in guns and in rebellion than he was in literary matters. While he was certainly aware that I was a member of the IRB, I wasn't actually aware myself the day of his hospital visit that he, too, was deeply involved in the IRB. This was how secretly the IRB's cell-like organisational structures were organised at the time. I later discovered that he was a leading IRB member in East Connemara and that he regularly swore new members into the organisation. I also later found out that he was amongst a group of men who attacked the police station in Gortmore, Rosmuc, and wrested it from the control of the local police. Bairéad had only been in Galway city a few years (at most) by then and before this he had been involved in operations with the Moycullen company of the IRB.

When I met him that day in the hospital, he was responsible

for the Irish-language material published in the *Galway Express*. Sean-Pháraic Ó Conaire regularly contributed long essays to the newspaper and his writing particularly fascinated Bairéad. I remember him asking me a good many questions about Páraic's writing and his high levels of productivity. It always amazed him how 'clean' or error-free Ó Conaire's manuscripts in Irish were and Bairéad was always burning with curiosity as to whether Páraic wrote the manuscript straight out like that or whether there were any previous drafts from which he might have expunged mistakes.

That day in the hospital Bairéad demonstrated a great knowledge of prison life and I remember being struck by this, little realising that he was already very involved in the IRB at that stage. I remember him asking me such specifics as: What major prisons in England had I served sentences in? Who had been the prison guards on that wing of the prison? When he began to enquire as to whether such-and-such a prison alcove or landing was still there the last time I'd been 'inside', I confess that I became slightly suspicious of him. Little did I realise that he was actually doing 'informal' research for some of the short stories he would later write – stories such as *Costas an Ghiorria*, a story about the prison experiences of a republican prisoner, which later appeared in his collection *Cumhacht na Cinniúna*.

While in Galway Jail I found myself elected to the local (Galway) County Council. I was elected to the position of chairman on the County Council Board for Oughterard. This board was the first rural-based board in Ireland that decided to accept the jurisdiction of the First Dáil. From its inaugural meeting onwards, the Oughterard board jettisoned any and every association we had with the British administrative regime that had previously operated in the area. We also made sure to destroy those disgraceful motions that the Council Board had passed in previous years condemning the Easter Rising of 1916. Our Oughterard board was responsible for another first when we voted overwhelmingly to conduct every aspect of our business through Irish. The executive board of Galway County Council initially accepted this and agreed to conduct their business with us through Irish from then on. Those individuals whose predilection was for long and boring speeches in 'fancy' English soon abandoned that promise, however, although I – amongst others – never spoke a word of English at any council meeting.

16

The War of Independence

It was midday on 20 April 1920 when we drove the RIC out of their new barracks in Maam Cross. A hundred of us came together the night before the attack for some last-minute preparations. The attack was going to be a risky one given that we had just three old-fashioned shotguns for weapons. Even those three guns were far from reliable and there was always the fear that they would jam or give up on us in the middle of the battle. We got our three gunners into position and under the cover of darkness, a group of us sneaked closer to throw fuel and other flammable liquids at the walls so that the place was like a tinderbox ready to go. We retreated again and within seconds the bullets were flying. The element of surprise was on our side and we soon forced them out of the barracks and into a small wooded area that was near the edge of the road. There was no let-up on our side and the barrage of shooting continued for quite a while on both sides. Unfortunately, we Volunteers were the first to run out of ammunition. We had feared as much and as the shooting came to a stop, our boys were forced to retreat to a vantage point at a slightly safer distance. The air went still again and once the police thought we were gone – after half an hour or so – we saw them emerge from their hiding place in the trees. We were lucky in that none of our men had been injured or killed. The only major blow we had suffered was the capture of our quartermaster Páraic Ó Nia. The burning of this police barracks in Maam Cross was one of the first major acts of resistance in Connemara since Páraic Ó Máille had taken on the police that night in 1918 when they came to arrest him in Munterowen East for his alleged role in the 'German Plot'. We left the scene of the ambush as daylight was breaking and had the satisfaction of watching the eight policemen scramble here and there in an effort to retrieve any files or items of furniture from the blaze. Their salvage operation turned out to be a complete waste of time. The once-imposing barracks was burned to the ground. As you'd expect, the local authorities were very annoyed at what had happened and anybody who was suspected of being sympathetic to the Volunteers now expected a knock on their door.

Anybody who was known to have links with Sinn Féin was equally suspect now and a number of our members left their homes for fear of reprisal or in case they would be imprisoned without charge. While the 'regular' police force were no 'soft-touches', such was the irritation with our successful attack and the silence of the local people that the British decided to adopt a more ruthless approach. They sent the Black and Tans into the area, 'officially' as a form of back-up to the local police.

As far as we could make out, the raggle-taggle militia that was the Tans was composed of two types. On the one hand, they comprised the 'lowlife' of British society, murderers and rapists who would have spent their lives behind bars if the British government hadn't 'set them loose' on the Irish people. The other group who made up the ranks of this ad-hoc force were former British soldiers who were unemployed now that the First World War was over and who were well trained in both guerrilla tactics and the use of weapons. It was hard to know which of these two elements was worse. While the second group had the bravery of mercenary soldiers and feared no battle, big or small, the first group – i.e. the majority of them – were very dangerous simply because they had no respect for anybody, themselves included. They were reckless and acted without any apparent restraint or regulation. They were also extremely violent and murdering somebody in cold blood was second nature to many of them.

To give just one example, they didn't recognise any of the widely held protocols with respect to captured prisoners and anybody captured by the Black and Tans could expect torture and a death as brutal as anything they might ever imagine. Unfettered cruelty was the norm for the Black and Tans, they generally 'half-killed' a prisoner rather than executing them properly 'from the off'. Republican sympathisers and nationalists of every hue and description were regularly taken from their homes and subjected to a fierce beating. The semi-conscious victim was then tied to the back of a lorry and dragged along the road until he or she was torn apart in what can only be described as the most horrific form of death imaginable. Sometimes the person was still alive, albeit critically injured, after such brutality, and the Tans would pull out their fingernails and toenails and either burn or shoot their victims. People were buried alive sometimes, suffocated even while they were critically injured.

The British had 100,000 soldiers in Ireland at this point in addition to these armed thugs and militias. This was the formidable foe our tiny republican organisation faced and yet we took them on nonetheless. We re-started the fight for Irish independence again, a fight that we Irish had been fighting for 750 years by then. My life had been a crazy one for a while by this juncture. I travelled a twilight world, moving constantly between a succession of safe houses and hide-outs, often under cover of darkness. I never stayed more than one night in any house for fear of capture and could never even stay long enough anywhere to eat. I might be only just gone when the door would be banged in and the searches would begin.

Séamus Quirke was murdered in Galway at this time. I'd known Séamus for a good many years and his death was another terrible blow for morale. I'd got to know him first when we shared lodgings in Galway city, both of us arriving in the 'big town' for the first time from our respective rural villages. Even as a teenager, Séamus was deeply patriotic, as committed a Gael as you were ever likely to meet. Of average height, he had the look of somebody who had seen a good deal of life as a young man. The worn look on his face was not so surprising in one way. Not only did he hold down a day-job, but he was also active in the Volunteers and in the Irish-language movement. He worked very hard even at a young age. I often heard him getting up out of bed in the middle of the night to deliver a message to one of the Volunteers or to help in an emergency somewhere. He could cycle twenty miles in the night and still be sitting at his desk at nine o'clock the following morning.

Tragically, on the night of his murder, it was the Black and Tans who dragged him from his bed and shot him to pieces. They did the same to Mícheál Breathnach in Galway and Seán Mac Eachagáin in Moycullen. Breathnach was linked with Sinn Féin and a number of other nationalist groups at this time. He was also a well-known and well-loved figure in Galway city since he was a member of the city council and one of the city's leading businessmen. A wealthy and successful businessman, he wasn't averse to spending much of his own hard-earned money on the Irish 'question' nor on other causes which were to the benefit of the poor and the downtrodden Irish.

Mac Eachagáin was an equally idealistic and committed individual, a man who was never found wanting and a man who was willing to make the ultimate sacrifice for Ireland. At a meeting of two of our battalions of officers in Connemara was the last time that I ever spoke to Mac Eachagáin. This meeting, under cover of night, took place in Barna Woods where we also undertook some practice with explosives.

Our ambitious plan, which we were putting the final touches to that night, was the launch of simultaneous onslaughts on four different police barracks in County Galway. By coordinating such an attack at four completely different locations throughout the county, all on the one day, we hoped to inflict maximum chaos and mayhem on the forces of occupation. Amongst the four barracks we were targeting was the police station at Gortmore, Rosmuc, which was where both my battalion and my home place were located and I was given particular responsibility for the explosives operation there. Needless to say, I was paying particular attention to the instructions that were being issued that night during the final practice drills. So too was Mac Eachagáin, as he was assigned to provide us with special support during the attack. One issue which was a constant headache for us at this point was the question of munitions. We were always short of weapons, and efforts to find, transport and hide new guns and ammunition sapped much of our time and energy.

The brigade had a meeting in a house owned by Breathnach in Clarinbridge where Peadar Mac Dónaill the commander of our battalion and I proposed a possible solution to the arms shortage, one which wasn't accepted by the brigade in the end. The plan we proposed involved four of us going in a car dressed in the guise of British army officers. We would drive into a number of police barracks where we would supposedly be about to deliver the police with a list of names of the people whom we suspected were local Volunteers and needed to be brought in for questioning. Once inside the barracks we could imprison whoever happened to be on duty at the time and then make off with any guns or munitions that we could find there.

The death of Fr Michael Griffin shocked the entire country and a good deal of the world beyond the shores of Ireland too. His murder was a shocking event and what made it worse was the way his body was missing for a week before his corpse was eventually discovered. Fr Michael, a noted nationalist and a great supporter of the Irish language, was a chaplain in the parish of Rahoon, in Galway. He was abducted by the Black and Tans who arrived at his home during the night and took him away. He was taken away and murdered and his body was found, thrown in a bog hole, in Barna a week later.

When I think back on those days now – with the benefit of the hindsight of a full two decades later – it seems amazing that we organised any kind of coordinated resistance against the British at all. When you consider how many centuries the British had been here and how many thousands of army personnel, lackeys and spies they still had in Ireland, it was a wonder that we were able to organise anything at all without them knowing about it. Smashing their intelligence networks would, in fact, become one of our main aims from then on. It wouldn't prove easy of course. In fact, the destruction of the British network of spies and informers in Ireland would prove the most difficult aspect of the War of Independence.

As regards the organisation and administration of the Volunteers on a regional basis, there were still major problems that frequently drove us in Connemara to distraction. The

Volunteers in Galway were still organised in one large brigade for administrative reasons but this arrangement simply didn't work. Connemara itself was too large to be part of just one brigade, never mind the rest of County Galway, and now that the battle was hotting up again, the need for better cooperation and more efficient administrative procedures was vital. Luckily, it was decided soon after this to split the County Galway brigade into a number of smaller battalions which were then further sub-divided according to area to make our communications and all-round operations more efficient. The battalion I worked with became known as the West Connemara Brigade. The Volunteers were also re-named at this point and were now known as the Irish Republican Army (IRA).

Since the majority of the officers in our brigade were 'on the run' at this point, we decided to re-group and set up a training camp in Glenlusk. We needed to run over all of the military basics, especially with our most recent recruits, and I was selected as commander of this new training camp. While our group in Glenlusk training camp might have been lacking in military finesse, we were the most enthusiastic and wholehearted bunch of men who ever came together. They were so eager to take the battle to the British that they couldn't wait to get into the fray. It made no difference to them that they were taking on one of the biggest empires in the world, a task which would have been extremely difficult even for a force that was properly armed, unlike us!

Shortly before going to the training camp, I had managed to raise £60 amongst the people of Rosmuc to buy weapons. Peadar Mac Dónaill, another of our group leaders, had raised some money too and between the two of us we knew that we could buy a few guns, albeit not that many. Peadar Mac Dónaill and Seán Ó Fiacháin went to Dublin and they were arrested without charge and held for a week there, a fact which delayed the beginning of our training camp slightly. The men stuck to their task, however, and as soon as they were released they managed to secure a small number of guns. One regular visitor to our camp was the Celtic scholar Tomás Ó Máille, then a lecturer in Old Irish at University College Galway. Ó Máille was addicted to tea and when he came to visit he just drank one cup of tea after another. In fact, the only person I ever saw drink more tea than him was Patrick Pearse. Pearse could drink six strong cups of tea, one after the other and they wouldn't knock a stir out of him. Ó Máille wasn't quite as obsessed with tea as Pearse was but he wasn't far off it either![1]

Tomás Ó Máille – may his soul be in Heaven – was a very easy-going man. He had a sort of a childhood innocence about him and to look at him you would never have thought that this man was a highly regarded scholar. He could talk to anybody on their own level. He wasn't 'aloof' from the ordinary people in the way that many scholars could be. He was a reflective man and although he wasn't a native speaker of Irish, his conversation was always reasoned and interesting. When all was said and done, I don't think Ó Máille was a great man for conversation. He was more of a thinker than a talker in my view. When he found himself 'on the run' later on, he joined us in the hills where he had a huge fascination with nature in all its aspects. He would examine pieces of rock and shale that had fallen from the escarpments higher up on the mountains, for example. He took a great interest, too, in all of the different mountain streams and rock pools that were in the area.

It was while I was in charge of the Glenlusk training camp that Galway County Council passed a motion advocating that the 'peace' of the then status quo in Ireland remain as it was. In fact this controversy caused quite a stir in Galway and in the rest of Ireland. The controversy generated by this motion caused a fuss that it didn't actually warrant – given that the motion was unrepresentative and was illegally passed by just a few council members – i.e. British lackeys – in the first instance. The motion was especially unrepresentative given that any council members who were publicly associated with Sinn Féin or the IRA were 'on the run' or unable to attend the council meetings. In addition, the motion itself should never have been passed in the first place given that it wasn't even listed on the council meeting's agenda for that evening and there were hardly more than six council members (out of a total of thirty) in attendance that night. The reason the motion garnered such publicity in the first place was the fact that a local journalist tipped off the national newspapers, who then competed with one another to see who could 'break' this ridiculous story about the new 'peace' in Ireland and take credit for this peace in the process.

17

Taking the Fight to Connemara

There were twenty-three of us altogether in the training camp. I will run through a list of some of the men who were in the camp so that you get an idea of what each person's responsibilities were. Peadar Mac Dónaill and Seán Ó Fiacháin were the leaders of the men in the camp while I had responsibility for the training; Máirtín Ó Conaola was the spokesperson for the men; Riocard Seoighe, second-in-command, first battalion; Colm Ó Gaora, commander, second battalion; Séamas Mac Conrí, commander, third battalion; Gearóid Mac Parthaláin, commander, fourth battalion; Mícheál Ó Conaire, an Caladh; Seán MacCoineasa, Donncha Ó Catháin, Stofán Ó Mainnín, Seán Mac Conrí, Roundstone; Páraic a Bhailíse, Peadar a Bhailíse, Páraic Ó Máille, Pól Mac Pharthaláin, Tomás Ó Cadhain, Tomás Ó Madaín, Criostóir Ó Braoin, Liam Mac Conaola and Seán Mac Conrí, Cuilleach. Tomás Ó Máille and his brother Éamann joined the group the day of the battle in Munterowen East and there were many others who weren't in that training camp but who joined us when the going got tough. My own brother Micil was amongst this 'floating population'. Like myself, he was 'on the run' non-stop and living the dangerous twilight life of the fugitive.

That group of Volunteers was as multi-talented a collection of individuals as you would find anywhere. There was the doctor of philosophy and the teacher amongst us, the travelling salesman and the blacksmith, the butcher and the baker, the TD and the shepherd, the engineer and the tour guide, the shopkeeper, the tailor and a range of other trades people and sales people. Given the wide range of skills and attributes amongst us, it didn't take us long to put a decent makeshift camp together even if it was in a very wild and isolated spot. In fact, if any night was to be a test of our resolve as a unit, it was the very first night that we came together as a group.

The night appointed for our mobilisation was bitterly cold. It was as wild a night as was ever seen in that part of Connemara. Our meeting place was at the foot of the Twelve Pins in the small village of Doirín na mBláthanna. The hailstones that fell that day were so sharp that they would have whipped the nose off a stoat. By the time everybody reached the meeting point they were in a right sorry state. Drenched to the skin and numb with the cold, the majority of us had walked upwards of twenty miles across bog and mountain to get there without attracting the attention of the authorities or their lackeys. Given that most of us had very few possessions anyway, we were completely reliant on the local people for any replacement clothes and for our food and drink for the duration of the camp. Having to rely on the locals really bothered us because we knew that they often had even less than we did. Worse than this again was the fact that we knew the locals would give us the last bit out of their mouths. We often went hungry, but given that many of us had been 'on the run' for a few years at this stage, we were used to going without. It was different for the locals and we felt guilty about that. The fact that every man and child in the area, whether Volunteer or not, was suffering and going without only made us more determined than ever to succeed in our struggle for freedom.

Once we had our camp set up, the camp leaders had a meeting almost immediately to decide what British targets we should focus on from the outset. We were a small and poorly armed group taking on the might of the British military regime so we had to be strategic about our targets and realistic about what we could achieve.

We drew up a list of villages and towns which were suffering heavily under the yoke of this military regime. The truth was there was no village in the county where there weren't housefuls of people being harassed on a constant basis. Continual searches and interrogations without any charge and torture, both psychological and physical, was routine at this stage in an effort to 'force' false confessions from ordinary Irish people, the majority of whom had no political involvement whatsoever. Given that every village was subject to continual repression, we felt it best to focus our attention on those villages and towns which were experiencing the brunt of the oppression. We all agreed that the town of Clifden was the worst in this regard and that the hinterland around the town was completely under the control of the British. Striking here, right at the enemy's heart was the most effective thing that we could possibly do. The previous November saw Tomás Ó Faoláin, a native of Clifden, executed by the British. He was put to death a few days before Bloody Sunday, a day when our organisation struck at the very heart of the British intelligence system in Ireland.[1] Twenty British spies were gunned down at various locations across Dublin city, all within the space of one evening.

The fact that our friend Tómas Ó Faoláin was only just cold in his grave was a huge motivating factor for us. We were itching for revenge. The night before St Patrick's Day 1921, was the date we pencilled in for an ambush on the British in

Clifden. That night we launched a furious onslaught on the police headquarters in Clifden. After a two-and-a-half-hour gun battle, two policemen lay dead and we managed to capture some munitions to boot. We disappeared back into the hills, our ambush a huge success.[2] None of our men were killed, nor did they suffer any injury. We melted back into the rain-sodden hills that night with a new flame of hope in our bellies. We were on a new high and we needed to be because the long march from Clifden back across that harsh and bitterly cold landscape would have destroyed lesser men.

Negotiating our way through those marshes and hills wasn't easy in daylight but trying to retreat swiftly across this same terrain at night was a veritable nightmare, especially since the snow was lashing down in sheets and the temperature was below freezing point. One of our men almost drowned in a particularly flooded area of bog and everybody's fingers and feet went numb. In the end only sheer human will kept us going. A lack of food meant that we all collapsed under our tents and makeshift shelters when we eventually got back.

Our unofficial reconnaissance point on the way home was a remote cliff-face which was at a safe distance from Clifden, a place known as Aillenaveagh. A bare rump of ground at one of the remotest sections of the Twelve Pins, it was miles from civilisation. The only landmark of any note in the area was an old herdsman's hut, a place that hadn't seen any sign of life for many years. Three of us had tidied this place up somewhat and hidden a tiny amount of food for when we were on the retreat. We dragged ourselves into the hut and divided out whatever food was there amongst us. Having rested for a short while, we continued with our trek back in the direction of Doirín na mBláthanna.

Our Clifden ambush occurred on the evening before St Patrick's Day and the British response was almost immediate. The following day – St Patrick's Day – saw a show of force by the British in retaliation for what we had done. The British attacked and burned a number of buildings in the town and dragged people from their homes in an effort to terrify the entire local population and frighten them against doing anything to help us in our rebellion. The homes of Connemara people considered in any way sympathetic to republicanism were the primary targets of the Black and Tans, i.e. the thugs the British employed to smash the houses to pieces and then burn them to the ground. The Mac Parthalán's family home was burned down as were the houses owned by Liam Mac Fhlanncha and Meaití Seoighe. When all was said and done, the Tans were really just a bunch of bullies and cowards, a group who relied on terror as their primary weapon. Proof of this was the fact that the Tans needed two trainloads of soldiers as 'back-up' for their dirty work on St Patrick's Day. Seán Mac Dónaill, a man who had fought in the British army during the First World War was killed that day and Liam Mac Fhlanncha's brother, Peadar, was shot and seriously injured. Initially, the reports were that the Tans had murdered both Peadar Mac Fhlanncha and Seán Mac Dónaill but although seriously injured, Peadar managed to pull through in the end.

Clifden, a town which had been seen as remaining loyal to British law, was given its 'reward' for that loyalty that night.

One of the best outcomes of that night's work in the long-term was the fact that the British mollified their terror campaign against the local people in Connemara somewhat. Realising that we couldn't have undertaken an attack of such ferocity without the help and support of the locals, they put an end to the policy of summary hangings and beheadings which had struck such fear into the hearts of the Connemara people before this. They realised that this policy had proved counter-productive.

The road between Screeb and Maumwee is a lonely one. All one sees are rugged hills and desolate mountains for as far as the eye can see. Autumn and summer sees an explosion of purple-flowered heather on these hillsides, while in the winter, the mountains are all brown sedge and wild grass. Intermittent rock formations aside, the terrain here is open and empty, a landscape that is entirely without shelter or habitation. There are no woods or thickets for miles, the scrub on the fringe of Derravonniff the only hint of significant vegetation. The only break in this desolate landscape is the huge bog on the eastern side of Derravonniff, the lake known as Loch Chora Uiscín to the west and Camus Bay which juts forward and criss-crosses the junction between Screeb Bridge, Clais Dubh and the bridge at Fornaois. Two or three times a week we watched as an armed patrol of policemen and Tans passed through this area travelling from Maum to either Camus or Lettermore.

This regular patrol was the only significant British presence in the area west of Clifden. There were normally six in the group and they were armed to the teeth, each man carrying a rifle, a handgun and grenades which were visible in special pockets sewn into the side of their jackets. We were very keen to get our hands on that ammunition, the grenades in particular. We knew that we could do some damage with those grenades if we only had a few of them. An ambush on this small convoy somewhere along the lonely Screeb Road seemed like our best chance. A surprise attack in this deserted landscape and we could melt into the hills again before they had time to call up any reinforcements. It seemed like our best opportunity and no matter what way you looked at it, it was definitely a lot easier than trying to attack one of the fortress-like barracks that the police, soldiers and Tans moved between on a constant basis.

Our camp was based in Gleann Cais at this time, but we wasted no time setting out for Screeb once we had the details of the ambush planned carefully.[3] Our group walked to Maumgawnagh and then travelled on to Maumean, then down to Knocknahillion and on to Oorid, where we made camp for the night. The next day we moved through Seana Bhéarra and veered eastwards to Knockadaff and Cora Uiscín ending our journey in Glentrasna.

Fate seemed to intervene on the side of the British then. They suddenly appeared on the road very early the following morning, a change to their routine which caught us by surprise. They weren't due until the next day and so we decided to bring forward our ambush, the only difference being that we would now attack them when they were on their return from Screeb instead of when they were on their way there, as previously envisaged.

We divided our troop in two, one group positioning themselves at the head of the old road into Glentrasna while the others hid themselves in the undergrowth near the Protestant chapel of Derravonniff. The group at the head of the road were instructed not to open fire until the police patrol had passed the point where the last of our men was hiding in the scrub and when they were literally right opposite where our main shooters were waiting. The group hidden in the scrub were to open fire first, the idea being that we would have the enemy caught in a circle of fire and unable to move either forwards or backwards without being shot at.

We settled into our positions off the edge of the road and waited for the sounds of their motorbikes and the roar of their truck coming back along the road. It turned out to be a hell of a long wait as, breaking with their previous patterns of movement, the police didn't return until late that evening. The April weather was pleasant but there was still a cold bite in the air, especially if you were sitting still for hours on end. Now that we were in position, however, we had to wait patiently, even if that waiting went on for ten or eleven hours as on that particular day. The warm sun was disappearing behind the evening clouds when the signal came from our scout that they were on their way. We shook the stiffness from our bones and got the adrenalin pumping. Sure, enough, it wasn't too long before the police patrol came into view.

Travelling at a nice steady pace, they were perfectly set up for us to take them out. Two of the group passed opposite us. Another two followed fifteen yards behind, accompanied by one Tan bodyguard. We waited for these fellows to pass beyond a certain point, when one of our leading marksmen was assigned to open fire. Once we heard his gun go off, we were all to open up with our rifles, and hit them with a ferocity that would knock the life out of them. Whether it was the long day's wait or the fact that one of our men was overly nervous, I'm not sure, but one of our men pre-empted the marksman's first shot and opened fire before the small convoy were in the circle we wished to ensnare them in. Strangely, our man aimed his shot at the Tan who was at the very rear of the convoy, a man who was actually the furthest away from us.

For the two policemen at the head of the convoy, this shot was a warning which gave them a few seconds grace. They leaped from their truck and ran for the shelter of some bushes at the side of the road. The second two men leaped from their motorcycles, turned around and ran for their lives. So, too, did the Tan, when the first shot missed him. He didn't get very far, however, as a second shot got him and he fell onto the road mortally injured. Now that they had some cover in the bushes, the policemen put up a tough fight. The battle raged for a good half an hour, bullets flying back and forth at a furious rate. Eventually the fight came to an end and the policemen called out to say that they were giving themselves up. One man, a police sergeant, was so wound up that he fired twice from close range as one of our men made his way towards him to confiscate his weapons. Amazingly, both of his shots missed their target. As the sergeant was dragged from his hiding place in the scrub, he began whimpering, snivelling, and pleading for his life in a loud voice. The man went on and on outlining all the good deeds he had done during the course of his life and why he didn't deserve to die. It was the strangest performance ever.

In the end we let that police sergeant go free having stripped him of any guns or ammunition he was carrying. We found two bottles of poitín in the sergeant's greatcoat; two bottles that would serve us well as a 'pick-me-up' and a medicine for chest complaints in the months afterwards. The sergeant's comrade, who was lying injured in a dip in the ground, died from his injuries within a matter of minutes and we left the Tan there on the road, looking more dead than alive. The other man was either dead or had run away early in the fight because we found no trace of him in the scrubland round about.

The enemy's revenge was swift. That very evening, just as the news of our ambush was still being relayed across the countryside, the authorities made their move. The first target was my parents' house in Rosmuc. Five lorryloads of soldiers, police and Tans arrived in Rosmuc and went on the rampage. They tore our family's place apart and then burned it to the ground in a fire that could be seen for many miles around. An iron tongs was the only thing that was left after the fire had run its course.

'On the run' at the time, my brother Micil visited the place where we had all played as children a few days after the house was burned down so that he could see the devastation for himself. His joke about that tongs would remain in the family repertoire for many years afterwards. Noting that the tongs was the only remnant of the life that had once thrived in that place, he teased me for years afterwards. 'You always wanted that tongs but, sure enough, you got it in the end!'

While nobody had been killed or injured (thank God), in the burning of our family home, it still had a profound effect on me. Rather than dishearten me, it only strengthened my resolve to take the fight to the English and their collaborators. To my mind, that house had a significance which went far beyond the personal. It was a house within whose walls the struggle for Irish freedom had been discussed and debated for many generations. It was a house that had harboured rebels and patriots, fugitives and people of the road. Within the whitewashed walls of that small cottage, seven generations of people had related their hopes and their dreams and its destruction was therefore the end of something unique. The burning of that cottage set me thinking once again of all of the histories I'd heard from the members of my own family but also on the communal history of the Irish people as a whole. When your home and the home of the seven generations that came before you is razed to the ground, there is no greater motivation for striking at the heart of the oppressor. No wonder the Irish cottiers of the Land War had taken the fight to the unjust landlords of the nineteenth century with such unanimity of purpose.

Four other buildings in that part of Connemara were burned to the ground in revenge for the Screeb ambush, in addition to my home place. Pearse's cottage, which had lain empty since the Easter Rising of 1916, was burned to a cinder, as was the schoolmaster Páraic Ó Conghaile's house in Gortmore. The Achagáin family's house in Derravonniff was destroyed, as was a cooperative storehouse that had only been set up a few years before this in Camus. Ironically, these reprisals on the part of the British police, which were intended to frighten the local people, only succeeded in having the opposite effect. The people who had supported us loyally before the ambush simply re-doubled their efforts, while some of the people who had been indifferent before this came over to our side now that the oppressor had shown his true colours.

Let nobody be under the illusion that we ever had a huge rush of recruits to the cause, however. There was always a large number of people who were happy to live from day to day and cared little whether Ireland was free or not. Indeed, we even had to 'conscript' a few extra young men locally to increase the numbers in our training camp. Some of these men would probably have remained indifferent and 'on the sidelines' if we hadn't persuaded them that it was in their interest in the longer term to join us in ridding the countryside of the scourge that were the British and the Black and Tans.

As part of the 'community justice' we imposed fines on people who actively opposed us or collaborated with the authorities and provided them with information on us. Although many of us felt that such individuals deserved death for their treachery – after all, the Tans would have killed us without the slightest hesitation if they had captured us – we decided that monetary fines were more politic in the long-run. We had plenty of proof that there were always people who were willing to collaborate with the most blood-thirsty Tans in the vicinity.[4] While these people never comprised a large group, they were there nonetheless.

The morning of 23 April found us still holed up in our training camp, a camp which we had transferred to a place near Munterowen East shortly before this. The morning was quiet, the silence broken only by the tread of our look-out who marched slowly up and down a gravel track that led to our hide-out. The sentry stared across the hill-sides fronting the horizon, and he thought he saw some movement in the dawn light. He stopped and stared more closely. In the distance some black dots were moving quickly down the side of a mountain boreen, more quickly than was normal for cattle or sheep. Horrified, he realised that the figures making their way through a gap in the hill at Kilmeelickin were actually police, some of whom were riding motorbikes. The look-out ran back up the hill and, within seconds, we were awake and on the move, grabbing whatever ammunition and supplies we could carry. Some men had their wives and children with them and our first priority was ensuring that we got them out of danger as quickly as possible.

The black dots on the horizon had become bigger now and we could see twenty armed police coming towards us, moving from the direction of the crossroads at Na Gruigeallacha. As a couple of our men led the women and children out of harm's way, the rest of us got our guns primed and watched as the oncoming police came as far as the turn in the road at Munterowen East. The police still had to cross a river before they would be within shooting range of us. Strangely, it was as they were making their way across the makeshift ford of rocks that served as a bridge that they began shooting randomly in the direction of where our camp had been only moments before. This tactic of theirs played straight into our hands. Not only were their shots wildly off-target but the fact that they were still negotiating the large rocks that served as stepping stones in the river meant that they were on the back foot from the very off. They had left themselves open to our snipers and their rapid progress in our direction came to an abrupt stop. As our retaliatory shots came thick and fast, they were forced to dive for cover. After that, it was a game of cat-and-mouse on both sides. A volley of shots would come from their side and we would respond in kind, the location of the shooter changing all the while. This gun battle continued for a good many hours and it wasn't until midday that the firing tailed off on the police side.

Afterwards, the newspapers gave a false account of events that day, a description of events which bore no relation to what we had witnessed. We expected this, however, as the newspapers of the day were under the firm control of the British regime then and were simply propaganda mouthpieces for the empire. Subsequent newspaper reports, which called the day 'A long day of fighting in Connemara', claimed that one policeman had been killed and two others injured in the shoot-out. They also claimed that a large number of us had been killed during the gun-battle, this despite the fact that not one of our men suffered any injury, thank God. The true account of what happened that day was somewhat different.

Some of our men had managed to manoeuvre their way across the hill so that they were behind the policemen's position. When the police found themselves being fired on from both the front and the rear, they panicked and assumed that they were now surrounded. They imagined that we had them encircled and when our men's shots began to raze the ground adjacent to their position, the police decided to reduce their fire and beat a retreat. We were sure that we had them where we wanted them now and we were looking forward to confiscating their twenty or so rifles and all of their other equipment once they had given themselves up or retreated. Capturing such a huge amount of weaponry would ensure that we could function very effectively as a military outfit for some time to come.

Just as we thought the battle was ours, however, the day's events took a strange twist. Unknown to us, a police truck had sneaked quietly into a dip in the ground, to one side of the police. The driver must have got the truck into a downhill roll and then cut the engine so that the momentum of the hill had carried it forward unknown to us while the gun battle was at its fiercest. A string of curses came from our lads as they saw this truck putter slowly into view. The low hum of the truck's engine was the signal for our snipers to open fire once more but the truck continued on its way, as if oblivious to our bullets. Was the driver of this truck crazy? Could he not hear the crack of our bullets as they struck the bodywork on his truck? The truck seemed to cut out then and we were sure that one of our bullets must have hit home. We were wrong, however. As the police sprinted from the brush, they leaped into the truck and it began to move forward again. We re-doubled our efforts and really opened up now with our guns. We watched the windscreen shatter into 1,000 pieces as our bullets riddled their vehicle.

Amazingly, however, the truck kept moving forward as various policemen threw themselves onto the moving truck from a sandbank they were hiding in at the side of the river. We shot one man as he leaped into the truck but the truck got away in spite of our best efforts. We took the opportunity then to back up the hill towards somewhere less open where we couldn't be spotted so easily. We must have crawled a good 700 yards in total, all the way across two stretches of bog as the police who remained hidden in the sandbank tried to pick us off. Our retreat into the hills was slow and tortuous but we knew that with the truck getting away, it wouldn't be too long before the police would return with plenty of reinforcements. We had a system of sorts operating during our retreat and as two or three of us broke for cover, another small group of us opened fire on the enemy position in order to protect them. At one stage it was my turn to burst for cover and I looked behind me only to spot someone following hotly on my heels. It was Tomás Ó Máille and he was running somewhat awkwardly as he had something gripped tightly in one of his hands. It was a pocket handkerchief and he seemed to be more preoccupied with protecting whatever he had wrapped in this, than he was with the danger of his being shot in the back.

'What's that you have?' I shouted at him as we ran for it.

'A handful of hen's eggs. We'll need these badly before too long, given the food situation.'

There couldn't have been many of those eggs that survived that mad sprint across the bog that day. They were already dripping and broken in the handkerchief as it was. The police snipers must have spotted us then because the whine of their bullets was suddenly all around us and we had to make another dash for it. Seconds later one of our men, Séamas Mac Conrí, spotted what was happening. He came to a stop about twenty yards ahead of us and, steadying himself, he opened fire on the sniper's position, thereby giving Ó Máille and I some precious seconds to sprint clear.

As expected, the police arrived in droves that evening, eager for revenge. It seemed that they were intent on eradicating this 'problem' in the hills once and for all because, within the hour, they had returned with lorry loads of Tans. They sent seventeen lorry loads of police and soldiers from Galway with another seven lorries arriving from Clifden. Twenty-four lorry loads of men to hunt down a tiny raggle-taggle rebel army. They weren't taking any chances this time. We retreated further into the wilderness, climbing higher into the hills where the terrain was much more difficult to negotiate and where we had a good vantage point over the whole area. We watched as the police burned down the makeshift shelters that had formed our old camp and fanned out slowly across the bog. They had machine guns with them and they seemed intent on using them. We saw them riddle an empty shepherd's hut and gun down some horses and cattle that were tethered there with these heavy machine guns. They knew that we were probably watching them from our vantage point in the hills and it was as if they were intent on putting on a show of force to frighten us into submission.

We could hear their shouting and roaring and their cursing of us from on high. When they were within a few hundred yards range of us, our snipers began to take pot-shots at them just to annoy them. Their response was to open fire with their machine guns and shoot wildly and indiscriminately in the direction of the hills. What we wanted to do of course was to draw them into the hills so that we could engage with them in the wilder terrain that we knew like the back of our hands. If we could get them to come further into the hills, we could pick them off more easily, especially now that darkness was beginning to fall.

Despite their shouts and whoops of bravado, however, the police and Tans were too smart to fall into our trap and no matter how often one of our sniper's bullets slammed into the tussocks beside them, they weren't tempted to advance any further into the hills. They did come back in an attempt to 'finish the job' three weeks later. Incredible as it may seem, they brought 2,000 men with them to comb that entire terrain and to try to drive us out of the area once and for all. For now, we were safe, however, and as dusk fell that evening our look-outs watched as the Black and Tans trudged back to their lorries, dismantled their heavy machine guns and drove away.

Once the roar of their lorries faded into the distance, our men appeared from their various hiding places in the heather and we gathered to plan our next move. The first thing on our minds was food. It was a full two days since a good many of us had eaten anything and we were weak with the hunger. We would have to make our way down the hills and into the villages where we had friends and family to get something to eat. As we sat there catching our breath Tomás Ó Máille made a prediction which surprised many of us.

'This war is over,' he said.

'Why do you say that?' we asked.

'That's what the old prophecy said,' explained Ó Máille. 'An old prophecy said that the battle would never go beyond the boundaries of An tIomaire Rua or into the mud of Cúl Tuaighe. Today's fight brought us as far as An tIomaire Rua and so the prophecy has come to pass,' said Ó Máille.

Just then, a heavy shower of rain interrupted Ó Máille's hopeful dream for us and we were forced to seek shelter behind some large rocks. While Tomás Ó Máille's prophecy was meant in the best spirit, it would not prove true, unfortunately. The fight for Irish independence continued for a good few years to come. Tragically, Irishmen would shoot and kill each other just two short years later in that exact same spot – An tIomaire Rua.

Come nightfall, we descended the mountains, one after the other, and made our way to Cuilleach, where the locals helped us. They gave us food and drink and we rested there for a number of hours by the warmth of their fires. Around midnight, we set off to climb the hills to the north of us. The moon was out but clouds obscured its light. It was one of those nights when a strange feeling of loneliness fell over the group. Every man was silent and taken up with his own thoughts as we climbed upwards in the blackness, the sound broken only by the occasional snipe which burst out of the scrub at our approach. It was one of those nights when it seemed as if everybody could read the thoughts of the others. Were we really only fooling ourselves taking on the might of the British Empire in this sporadic and piecemeal fashion? Were our efforts really worth it and would the harsh existence of the hunted animal that we were enduring on this hillside make any difference in the end? It was one of those nights when hope and idealism were replaced by doubt and fear.

That night we crossed from Cuilleach and climbed up between the Dá Roighne and onto Baile an Ghabhláin where we passed the night. We spent Sunday and Monday on Benwee where we were constantly on the alert for the police and the Tans. We all took it in turns now to rest or to remain awake because we knew that it was only a matter of time before the authorities came back looking for us. We saw lorry-loads of Tans in the area on the Sunday but they were too far away for us to make an attack on them. The mornings on the mountainsides were bitterly cold now, I remember, and the fact that we had climbed higher and higher for our own safety meant that it was even colder still.

One of our contacts sent an important message to us on the Tuesday night. The police, the British army and the Tans were planning a major operation to oust us from the mountains. They planned to bring in an enormous force of men who would form a circle through the Connemara mountains and sweep them 'clean' of anybody whom they suspected of subversive activity. Our source told us that, as part of this, the British intended to destroy certain bridges and form roadblocks on all of the routes between Connemara and Galway.

We needed to come back with a plan, and quickly. Realistically, we had neither the manpower nor the weaponry to take on the massive force that was coming after us in open country and we had to think of a way of ambushing the British without actually engaging them militarily head-on. There was only one way to do this and this was to play the British at their own game. We decided therefore to destroy a couple of bridges and roads before they did, thereby preventing them from getting access to the mountains at all. If we could prevent their lorries and jeeps from travelling into Connemara in the first place, there was no way that they could cordon off the mountainous terrain that was our base. It would also delay any attempts on their part to transport the large numbers of soldiers and Tans that they planned to send after us.

We immediately set to work and blew up Casla bridge which linked Galway city with south Connemara. We then destroyed small sections of the railway line to prevent rail access to any part of Connemara and destroyed another access bridge – Droichead na Léime near Oughterard. These different attacks prevented any major operations on the part of the army for a while at least – and bought us some extra time in the process. That Tuesday night we moved camp; we walked to Tonamace and from there we crossed Killary. By dawn on the Wednesday morning, we were climbing up the shoulder of An Cnoc Gorm. From there we travelled as far as Corrabeg Valley where we came to a stop. It was here that we decided to set our new camp. An ideal spot, it was situated in a deep glen that was as hidden as it was dark. The mountains were natural barriers here. They were so high that they would serve as an excellent protection for us, surrounding each side of the glen. This area was so remote that neither human beings nor animals ever went anywhere near it. The one downside of it from our point of view was the fact that its isolation made it very difficult for us to get food supplies to the area. Just a day or two after setting up camp there our biggest problem was the lack of food. We were so hungry that we were beginning to get short-tempered and ratty with one another. With the Tans, the police and the army hot on our tails, it was too risky for us to go the long way down the mountains and into any of the local villages in search of food. We had one stale loaf of bread between the twenty of us for that entire week.

God must have been on our side, however, as just then the spring salmon began their return journey back up the Erriff River. 'It is God's will,' we said to one another happily. The fat salmon that the English gentry normally stuff their faces with could be ours now for the taking. Lord Browne was the landlord who controlled access to the salmon pool in Barr Easa and he had various wardens and gamekeepers employed to ensure that nobody took any fish from the local rivers. Three of us headed down to the river the following night, an old scoop net and some home-made harpoons in hand. Ravenous with the hunger, we made for the first ford we could find to see could we catch any of the salmon that would leap through the water there. We were no sooner there when a gamekeeper appeared and told us to leave. Instead of doing as we were instructed, however, we ordered him to fish along with us or face the consequences.

'Once he caught three salmon, he was free to go,' we told him.

Not unnaturally, the gamekeeper was nervous of us because you never saw a man throw himself into the task at hand with such enthusiasm. The first salmon he caught was a whopper of a fish and his relief was very palpable.

'What a beauty!' he said. 'It's a shame to kill him. Mosley would give anything for this fella.'[5]

Before long, we had caught two more salmon, one of which was three pounds heavier than the first one. The longer we were in his company, the more open and friendly the warden became. He was probably getting over the initial shock of seeing anyone other than his own masters lifting salmon from that river. That's what we assumed anyway, because he didn't seem like such a bad sort, once we got talking to him. It probably hadn't occurred to him either that God had put these salmon in the river for everyone's benefit and not just so that the lord he worked for could keep them for himself.

When we were finished fishing, we offered him one of the salmon but he looked at us as if we were only teasing him. 'I couldn't do another day's work as a gamekeeper if I knew that I had stolen one of the fish that I'm supposed to be guarding,' he said, and away he went.

We constructed a tent for ourselves with a large piece of canvas to protect us from the dew and the frost. It's amazing how warm a canvas tent can be even in the coldest weather and we made the tent even more comfortable by layering it with heather and dried mountain grass. At night, we slept on these beds of heather and used our coats as blankets.

There was a good deal of wild heather in this place, the type of heather that had never been pruned in any way, and it made perfect fuel for the fire on which we did much of our cooking. We burned this heather under the outcrop of rock that jutted outwards like a dolmen. The night we caught the salmon at Barr Easa we built up a fire straight away under this cooking rock and having eaten a lovely meal of salmon, washed down with strong cups of tea – we felt like new men again. Rejuvenated once more, we were full of a new strength and vigour and if the entire British army had turned up there and then to fight us, we would have taken them on with relish.

Corrabeg Valley was our base until the evening of 4 May when we decided to make a move and the necessity of fulfilling our Easter duties was the primary motivation for us leaving the mountain that night. The fact that Easter had already passed and none of us had had the opportunity to carry out our Easter duty was making the men uneasy and we organised for a priest to meet us at a prearranged location. The priest met us and we went to Micil de Bhailíse's house on the road between Barr Easa and Bun Dorchaidh. Night was falling by the time our group agreed that there was no point in us going back up to Corrabeg Valley without attending Mass and receiving Holy Communion. Mass was just finished and we were just about to have a quick bite to eat when our look-out ran in to tell us that the British were on their way.

It was still very early in the morning and we ran out onto the road. We could see their lorries in the distance, the headlights lighting up the early morning. We could see at least twenty lorries on the horizon, each of them travelling one after the other in a long line. Although we would have been severely outnumbered, we decided to ambush them if they came within striking distance of us. This was a rare opportunity for us given that the police and the Tans never normally travelled in such large numbers or all together like this. If their intention was to try to encircle us in the hills, as was rumoured, then we would fight our way through any circle of soldiers that they might try to trap us in. As it happens, they never did pass on the road close to us that morning but veered off in a slightly different direction, thereby depriving us of the chance to engage them in combat on that particular occasion. We climbed the mountain opposite us in pairs and we were soon high enough up to see that the convoy of lorries had come to a stop at the crossroads known as Barr Easa where there seemed to be a consultation of sorts going on. It was as if they were undecided as to which road to take from there.

One of the roads went to Leenane and the other towards the mountains of Mayo. Minutes later, the convoy moved forward along the Leenane road. We knew then that it wasn't the Mayo hills that they intended sweeping first and that they would as likely as not be coming back in our direction before too long. We climbed higher and watched them arrive in Leenane where some of the lorries came to a halt. Some other lorries continued further and disappeared out of view. The lorries which stopped in Leenane were now joined by other lorry-loads which arrived from the Clifden direction through Derrynacleigh. They then began to fan out across the hills in what was obviously the beginning of their operation to comb the Connemara hills. We began climbing An Cnoc Gorm with the intention of making camp in Corrabeg Valley. We were still climbing in twos and keeping a safe distance between each pair of us in case the enemy spotted our group moving in formation.

The weather on this particular morning proved to be to our advantage. Showers of spring rain were sweeping in from the sea, thereby ensuring that visibility in the area was poor. Just to be on the safe side, however, we crossed the mountains by following the trail of the mountain streams in case our dark overcoats should stand out against the backdrop of the hills. Halfway through our climb we heard the sound of a light aeroplane. Before long, the sounds of two engines were resonating in the mountain gorges and we came to a halt to watch them soar and dip as they scoured the Twelve Pins and the valleys and glens in between. One of the British spotter planes flew right across Killary while another rose high above the peak of the Mweelrea and travelled across Gleann Umartha before veering southwards towards Gleann na Caillí and our 'hide-out' at Corrabeg Valley. The spotter planes came so close to us a couple of times that it was a miracle they didn't spot us. There was no fear that they could spot our tent in Corrabeg Valley from the air – we hoped – as we had hidden it fairly well in the heather. That the British suspected we had been in the vicinity recently was clear, however; they even sailed two naval vessels up along Killary harbour scanning the bay on both sides.

In the end, they searched every hill, glen, hole, cave, bay and cove between Maam Cross, Clifden, Recess and Leenane. They spent the whole day on that search, a search that was undertaken by the then enormous force of 2,000 men, all of whom were on foot and who had spread out across the hills. This is not to mention the scores of men who were surveying the hill country in both aeroplanes and boats. My own firm belief is that God was looking out for us that day and that is the sole reason that such an enormous posse of soldiers, police and Tans never discovered us. That it was a minor miracle that we weren't captured is without question and I put it down to the fact that we had all just been down the mountain to fulfil our Easter duty the day before this large-scale search took place. Each and every one of our group received Holy Communion at that early-morning Mass in de Bhailíse's house at Bun Dorchaidh.

Now that the British had completed their search, our group had a quick meeting where we decided it probably wasn't safe for us to go back to Corrabeg Valley. Our contacts had warned us that the British had left behind a couple of dozen of their soldiers and a few of their lorries in Leenane which wasn't so far away and this led us to suspect that they would probably undertake some follow-up searches in the hills over the coming weeks. We packed our tent and left Corrabeg Valley behind that same night. We spent most of the night on the march, traipsing across the hills on an 'off-the-beaten' route in case our tracks were later picked up and followed by the British. It was rugged terrain and a few men had mishaps and falls along the way. By the following night we were at the top of a mountain overlooking Gleann Umartha. It might have been the beginning of summer but the peak of that mountain was covered in a black frost. The wind up there had a bitter bite to it and even sleeping in our tent was a struggle. Jumping up and down or going for a long walk were the only ways to try to warm up in an effort to get a few hours sleep. We alternated 'watch' during the night up there, more out of a fear that anybody would suffer hypothermia or frostbite than that the British would discover us.

As soon as the sun came up two of our group headed down the mountain to get some food. They soon returned with two huge cans of hot tea and some loaves of bread and butter. We had all been getting cantankerous with one another because, in addition to the tough weather conditions on the mountain peak, we hadn't eaten for two whole days. The food made a huge difference to us and everybody's mood changed for the better. Refreshed and rejuvenated, we were like 'new men' once more. More than anything it was those two cans of tea which had a huge effect for the better. Not only did the tea warm us up but it also calmed those of us who were used to drinking a lot of tea and were suffering from 'tea withdrawal'.

It was a Sunday and relaxing that afternoon, we looked across in the direction of Cnoc na Cruaiche where it tipped the horizon in the far north. Some of the men began to recount stories concerning St Patrick, patron saint of Ireland, and the Celtic god Crom Dubh. Local folklore had it that Crom Dubh had lived not far from where we were hiding now and during the course of our discussion one man asked what time it was. If it was around the time that Mass was beginning in the villages below, then we should say the rosary together, the man suggested. We all agreed with this man and everybody joined in reciting the rosary in the wan sun of that Sunday morning. It must have been the only time ever that the rosary was said on the peak of the coldest mountain in Ireland!

We spent all of Sunday on the mountain before making for a small village at the bottom. We divided the men into pairs, each pair visiting a different house in the village. The people were somewhat stand-offish when they saw us arriving, however, and we detected a nervousness and hesitancy on their part. We soon found out why. The gun-battle in Ceathrú Cheinnéide had occurred only very recently and this village wasn't so far from there – as the crow flies. For the previous week or so, the locals were constantly on edge, fearing a raid on their village by the Tans at any moment. The fact that we had suddenly arrived in the vicinity had done nothing to ease their concerns.

Although they would probably have felt less worried if we had left again immediately, the locals invited us to stay in their houses. Their concerns with regard to our presence didn't have too long to fester, however, as we had barely settled for the night when a messenger arrived in the area with the bad news that the Tans were on their way through some local villages and were going to raid this village too. Within minutes, our group had congregated on the edge of the village and we were gone off into the dark night once more. We were an exhausted and disgruntled group as we headed out the road that night, and given that we had had little if any sleep for the three nights before this, we were in an angry mood and ready to attack the Tan convoy if they came in our direction.

By dawn, we were halfway up Mweelrea mountain. The weather was cold again and heavy showers of hailstones lashed down on us as we climbed higher up the side of the mountain. It was the lack of sleep that was bothering us most at this stage. Some of our men had gone without sleep for so long that they were becoming dizzy and there was the real fear amongst us that sleep deprivation might become an ongoing problem for us. By now, the constant lack of sleep was nearly as big a problem for us as the Black and Tans.

One of our contacts arrived on the mountain shortly after we had finished our climb and informed us that the story regarding the Tans' raid on the village the previous night had been entirely false. No sooner had we heard this but we hurried back down the mountain again, in the direction of Bun Dorchaidh, where the local people welcomed us with open arms. We spent a few days between Bun Dorchaidh and Mweelrea where we relaxed and got our bodies and minds together again. Then we crossed Killary again and returned to our original camp on Glenlusk.

Our friends and relatives there were able to fill us in on the details of the huge operation the British had mounted the previous week in the mountains. Their stories about the attempted 'round-up' of renegade guerrillas such as ourselves vacillated between the tragic and the amusing. Before proceeding to recount some of the incidents that had taken place with the arrival of the British in the area, they did warn us to remain very vigilant as they believed that there were still a number of Tans (in civilian garb) who had stayed behind in the mountains in the hope that we could still be captured. Those Tan spies hadn't been seen anywhere near Gleann Gais but it was still thought that they were in the hills somewhere around about.

Peaidí Mór who, along with all the rest of the locals there, always welcomed us into his home in Gleann Gais had a funny story about the day the British had formed that enormous circle of men to comb the mountains.[6] They were only just out of bed when the British soldiers raided Peaidí's house early on that morning. One of the British officers questioned Peaidí and when he was finished, he turned to the women of the house to question them also. At one stage during these interrogations, Peaidí spoke 'privately' to a woman who was being questioned in Irish. Hearing this, the officer doing the questioning turned to Peaidí abruptly, saying: 'Sing dumb, you old bloke!' to which Peaidí replied: 'I am very sorry I haven't got that song sir.'

Peaidí related this story to our group as we were making our way southwards to destroy the bridge at Casla again. By blowing up this bridge, we would cut off the only direct road between that part of Connemara and Galway city, thereby preventing, albeit temporarily, the enemy's regular raids into that part of County Galway. In the process, it would also hinder the surprise raids which the soldiers and the Tans still undertook from time to time into the southern parishes of Connemara.

Our battalion took part in more than a few gun battles on both road and hill during the War of Independence but the closest we all came to death was actually not on *terra firma* at all. One night we all took a small boat from Siléar in Rosmuc to Bealadangan. I was carrying a bag that was weighed down with twenty grenades and we had only just left the quayside at Siléar when we struck a rock that was hidden under the water. The jolt the boat took as its keel got caught on the rock threw me forward suddenly and I smashed into the tiller at the rear of the boat, grenades and all. Incredibly, not one of those grenades went off despite the rattle they got when I fell. If one of them had gone off, none of us would ever have known anything about it – we would all have been blown to kingdom come. The boatmen who were with us would never realise how close a shave they too had had with death. They were more concerned with freeing the boat from the rock that had torn the boat's keel. They knew that we had to free the boat, somehow, since the strongest swimmer amongst us wouldn't have made it across the rip-tides that tore through that channel of water.

We got the boat free in the end and it was very late by the time we arrived into Casla. It was too dark to get our explosives primed to set them off the following morning on the bridge and so we decided to stay overnight in a house in Doirín and explode the bridge the following night. It was well past dawn when we reached that house and we didn't bother going to bed but remained by the fire until the people of the house rose in the morning. The people who owned the house were very sympathetic to our cause and their house was known as a 'safe house' that was used by us whenever the need arose.

The family we stayed with were up and about very early the next morning, probably earlier than normal. The woman of the house seemed agitated somehow as she kept going in and out of the kitchen, opening and closing the cupboards. She boiled the kettle at least three times and she produced a dough tray for making bread. Then she washed her hands a good number of times and rooted around in a cupboard in the kitchen.

It wasn't too long before I realised what was bothering her. The poor woman didn't have any food! After a while, a young girl arrived at the house carrying something beneath her shawl and went into the back room off the kitchen. A moment later, the woman of the house took the kneading-trough and disappeared into the back-kitchen after her. We soon got the fresh smell of baking bread and that good woman fed us all with the soda bread and piping hot cups of tea.

We were just finished eating when the three eldest daughters in the family headed out to the bog carrying three creels. They were followed by two boys, one of whom was carrying a loy and the other a turf-spade. Those people were hard people because they spent a full summer's day cutting turf in the bog, and all on an empty stomach. The young people arrived home that evening just as we were about to leave, but the woman of the house and her children insisted that we stay to say the rosary with them. We all knelt on the floor of that cottage and the family offered up the rosary on behalf of our battalion and the cause of Irish freedom. Whether it was this family's humility, their poverty, or a combination of their obvious and innate spirituality and patriotism, I never heard the rosary recited with such dignity and devotion as I did in that cottage that night. The intensity and emotion was palpable in the house and many of us were crying by the end of the prayers. That evening, I was privileged to witness something that was very special, which made a huge impression on me and was something which I will never forget as long as I live.

That night we blew up the bridge at Casla, an action which helped prevent the Black and Tans from terrorising that part of Connemara until the ceasefire which was announced shortly after this. Having destroyed the bridge, we travelled to Lettercallow where we caught a boat to Inver, arriving just as dawn was breaking. The men who rowed us to Inver that night included such renowned boatmen as Cóilín Tom Mhichil, the grandson of Mícheál Ó Clochartaigh, the poet.

The British hadn't given up their hunt for us yet, however. A fortnight later, they formed another huge ring around the hills, this time concentrating on the mountainous areas of southern Mayo and those sections of land in Connemara which they hadn't searched previously. This second search of theirs was the biggest and most coordinated search ever undertaken by the British in the Connacht region but it proved no more successful than their first one. Since we weren't even within the territory that they searched, we escaped capture once more. The irony of it was that they actually came within a few hundred yards of us at one point. In fact, we were watching their every move from our vantage point, hidden in the heather.

We may have lived the harsh life of the hunted animal at this juncture, but that's not to say that we weren't happy and full of the joys of life most of the time. I suppose that we were like one big family really. If one of us hadn't enough to eat, the rest of us tried our best to look out for him and ease his suffering. Everybody cooperated with each other on all of the different tasks we undertook around the camp, whether that task was big or small. We all knew that it was certain death, and a violent death at that, facing us if we had the misfortune to be captured. While this fear undoubtedly lay at the back of our minds, it wasn't something that any of us dwelt upon to any great extent. A worse thought than the possibility of our deaths was the fact that the Tans beheaded and hanged Irish people who had no political involvement whatsoever, simply to terrorise the local population or anybody who was supportive of republicanism or Irish self-determinism, generally.

Looking back on it now, we had many happy times in that tent on the hillside in spite of the difficult living conditions and the fear of death which hung over us. We made our own entertainment, and singing was one of our favourite past-times. Every song you can think of was sung under that canvas. Joyful songs, songs of emigration, nationalist and patriotic songs. When we became tired of singing we performed sketches and mimicked one another for a joke. The only aspect of these entertainments that we were very strict about was alcohol. If we had any alcohol in the camp, not a drop of it was consumed without the say-so of the camp commanders or the doctor who permitted its use for medical purposes. One night, for a bit of crack, we invented a satirical song about our abstemious life in the mountains:

LET US BE DRINKING

Here's to you! Tell us your story brave Irishmen!
Whose fate it is to fight day and night
On behalf of our native land
We who always stand proud
In the heat of war!
We who are never found wanting
when the tumult of battle sounds out!

Chorus
Let us be drinking, drinking, drinking
Let us be drinking until morning
We'll drink to the health of those fighters out on the hills
And those who fell courageously in the tumult of battle
It was back in Clifden
That the sport began
Just when they thought we were dead

We fighters climbed higher still
Into the mountains and the hills

Climbing in the fog
To the highest point in the sky
It was here that we raised our national
flag proudly once more
The battle-cries were sounded again
And we set up our camp in the heart of Gleann Trasna.

From here we struck hard at the 'Big Men' of the occupation
On Screeb Road we attacked them
It was here that we struck at the invader without mercy or pity
It was here the shots flew past our heads
It was here the bullets sprayed us all-around
as if in a spring snowstorm.
The fight began at dawn
The battle rang out as black gave way to white
The Great Tyrant's blood was spilled that day
All day it flowed along the ground
until the sun fell into the sea
They carried the fight to them in Munterowen East
It was a battle that will be commemorated in Connemara forever.

The foreigner was driven back
The foreigner was laid waste upon the plain
Fill the tankards to the brim
Drink to the men who stood firm against the tyrant
Drink to those men until time stands still.

One of our group, a fellow we named 'the poet' carried a bag
full of well-written poems (according to him anyway) with him
everywhere we went in the mountains. And strangely enough,
when times became most difficult for us, 'the poet' would

often have gone AWOL, having disappeared into the desolate countryside somewhere in search of poetic inspiration. Hardly a day went by that he wasn't reciting new verses to us non-stop and tormenting us with questions as to our opinions on his latest publication. In the end he was beginning to drive us completely mad and somebody recommended to him that he visit the poetess Eilís Ní Chaisil who was then living in Connemara. This woman would be able to give him a more impartial and educated judgement of his poetry, it was thought. Eventually our man did visit Eilís but what was said that day, we were never told. The only thing we noticed after this was that the man's enthusiasm for poetry seemed to wane. He no longer disappeared into the wilderness composing new lyrics as he had once done. Eventually our man's poetry phase was no more and one day he informed the entire group that securing the independence of the Irish republic was now a much more worthwhile endeavour than was his composition of poetry.

A month before the official announcement of a ceasefire in Ireland the senior council of the IRA called a meeting of all the brigade officers in Ireland to plan for the setting-up of a new police force in the Irish republic. When the order concerning this upcoming meeting reached me, I was far away in south Connemara and I knew that I would be hard-pressed time-wise to make the meeting which was due to be held the following night in Gleann Chreabh. On my way to the meeting, I had to make sure to call to Baile an Lotaigh to deliver a message, as our training camp had moved there shortly before this and it was actually on the way to Gleann Chreabh. I knew a short-cut that could be taken to Baile an Lotaigh whereby you could cut across the bog at Coirill and come out on the road again at Aitrí. You had to know where you were going, however, as once you got out on the hills and the bogs it was easy to get lost, particularly once the light began to fade. With this in mind, I asked the man who knew that area of Connemara the best to accompany me on the long walk to the impending meeting. A former river warden, this man knew the townlands in that part of Connemara like the back of his hand and we set off as soon as night fell.

It was a beautifully clear and moonlit night. Cloudless and humid, the stars above us were as clear as day. In fact, it was so warm that we had to sit down from time to time to catch our breath and to wipe the perspiration from our faces. Taking the short-cut would only take us two hours at most, we figured. We were walking for three hours, however, before we could admit to one another that we had actually gone astray, somehow. Worse than this, however, was the fact that we were completely disoriented in the darkness and had lost our sense of direction. We had hoped to use the various small streams and lakes on Coirill bog as a general guide but we must have gone severely off course as we didn't come across any water at all that night. In total, we lost a full three hours and we were only able to find our way again once the morning came. I lost my hat; our guide Páraic Mháirtín Uí Nia was frustrated and annoyed at how we had got lost in the first place, and Seoirse Stundún had lost his supply of tobacco, dropping it somewhere in the bog-grass. In our confusion, we had actually walked eastwards and ended up in Boheeshal, six miles from where we were supposed to get out on the road for Aitrí. The 'dizziness' had really played its tricks on us that night but it was a blessing in disguise as we later found out.[7] The Black and Tans had actually raided the village of Aitrí that night and if we hadn't got lost on the marshes, we would have run smack-bang into their patrol. God was with us that night because if the Tans had caught us, we would have found ourselves executed and thrown into the same bog we had gone astray on.

That summer proved to be a very dry one. In fact, the drought that had already begun almost certainly helped to save our lives that night as a majority of the bog-lakes and stretches of water that we had hoped would act as reference points for us were dried up. I got so thirsty on the long walk that night that I was beginning to feel dehydrated. We were near Baile Lios Íochtair, I remember, when we passed what had been a free-flowing stream. All that was left of the stream was a small bog-hole full of stale water but I couldn't walk another ten yards without having a drink of water. I got down on my knees and cupped the water into my mouth with my hands. Imagine my disgust when we began walking again and less then six feet further on, we came across the rotting carcass of a dead sheep. For a few days, I was paranoid that I was going to catch some awful infection.

Seoirse Stundún was so exhausted by the time we reached Baile an Lotaigh that he fell asleep immediately and slept the 'sleep of champions'. The poor man slept for a full two days and nights without waking! Páraic Mháirtín Uí Nia and I were also worn out by the time we got to Baile an Lotaigh and couldn't wait to hit the sack. The informal 'rule' in those days was that whoever arrived earlier than you and had managed to get some sleep, would vacate their bed to give a chance to the latest arrivals. Páraic Ó Máille, who was actually the local elected representative (TD) for the area was already in the bed that I was assigned to and upon entering the bedroom, I found him sitting up on the bed sewing a pair of trousers.

'God bless the work. A spot of tailoring?' I said somewhat gruffly, the irritation of my exhaustion coming through in my voice. 'You started pretty early in the morning, didn't you?'

'I'll be ready in just one minute,' Páraic answered, noticing the edge in my voice.

My shirt was sticking out through the back of my trousers for the last few days. That's how poor people were then. Even a TD had only the one pair of trousers to his name.

Another day, the shortage of clothes was highlighted in a particularly funny way. One of the men in our group was washing some clothes and he hung another fellow's trousers out on the wall of the house that we were staying in. The man who owned the trousers had to stay in bed until his trousers were dry. Unfortunately, a cow that was grazing near the wall took a sudden liking to the trousers and decided to eat them! It took a while for the man who owned the trousers to forgive the rest of us for the fact that his trousers had mysteriously disappeared. For a long time, he was sure that the whole thing was a prank on our part and he just couldn't believe that a cow would actually eat somebody's clothes if it was hungry enough.

For every humorous anecdote that there was relating to those guerrilla days, there were others that could have proved tragic if something had gone even slightly awry. One night when we were 'on the run', for example, a group of us came to a house in Luggatarriff. The weather was atrocious and we were all soaked to the skin by the time we got to this cottage. The woman of the house welcomed us and we were given a bed for the night. Once we were asleep, she hung our clothes near the hearth and took out the guns and ammunition from our holdalls so that they would be dry by morning also. The next morning that kindly woman was chatting to us in the kitchen when she explained that the previous night she had taken out 'those funny-looking eggs that were in your bags and having given them a quick rub with the towel, I just put them over near the fire to dry them out a bit more.'

We never did that tell that poor woman how close she had come to killing the whole houseful of us that night!

I remember the evening that the Irish Republic officially set up its new police force. I was outdoors when the thunder and lightning struck that night and it was terrible. We were between Baile an Lotaigh and Gleann Chreabh, making our way through that difficult and narrow gap that is the way to Gleann Chreabh, when the electrical storm struck with a vengeance. We were just halfway through that mountain pass and we immediately placed our rifles flat to the ground in case the lightning would strike the metal. We had all heard that a mountain top or a hill is something of a magnet for a thunderstorm and we tried our best to flatten ourselves against the earth as the lightning shot down from the sky with a vicious power. The storm lasted for a number of hours and we could only cower in fear as the multicoloured tongues of lightning forked across the sky. Each bout of lightning illuminated the darkness with such a powerful light that, for a matter of seconds, one could see the landscape as far away as Gleann Aighneach, a valley which was many miles away from us. The intensity of the tempest was such that you imagined the unleashed electricity would sever away the top of the hills or slash an enormous fissure in the earth. The storm eased off as we reached our meeting place in Gleann Chreabh. Little did we know then that a ceasefire would be announced only a month after this meeting and that much of the planning and organisational issues we discussed that night would count for nothing.

It was on our way back from that meeting that we blew up Gleann Aighneach bridge, thereby sundering one of our enemy's main access points, a route which they had regularly used for their raids into that part of Connemara before this.

Funnily enough, it was near the end of this period of our armed struggle that I came closest to being captured again. The day before the actual ceasefire was announced a group of us were trekking across the mountains to a brigade meeting that was scheduled for the following day in Glennagevlagh. Our route took us from Baile an Lotaigh to Leenane and from there to Glennagevlagh, a place that is three miles on the Westport side of Leenane. We left Baile an Lotaigh late on the Sunday evening so that we would be hitting Leenane Rock while it was still night. In that way, we would not be spotted arriving into Leenane. I can't explain it at all, but less than three miles from Leenane, a strange mood came over me. All of a sudden, a sense of gloom or despair seemed to have enveloped my whole being. This was strange as only shortly before this, I had felt fine and had been having the crack with the rest of my comrades. Try as I might, I couldn't shake this feeling from me. It was as if a heavy weight of sorts had descended upon me. I couldn't understand this at all, especially given that the meeting presaged a huge change for the better in all our lives.

The following day the ceasefire would officially be announced throughout Ireland. It stood to reason that we should all be letting down our guard somewhat – this evening of all evenings. Instead, a deep sense of foreboding came over me, a feeling I couldn't explain. We were just approaching a 'safe house' of ours when I said to the other men that I had to stop.

'Let's take a rest in here for a few minutes,' I said. 'I don't feel right.'

We called into a house where we were all welcomed and given some whiskey to drink. We had only just sat down when a couple of men arrived into the house with the news that three lorry-loads of Black and Tans had arrived into the village of

Leenane earlier that afternoon where they had taken over Mac Eoin's Hotel. Whether I had some sort of premonition or not, I'll never be sure. One thing is for certain, however. If we had continued on the route that we had planned that day, we would surely have walked to our deaths.

As soon as darkness fell that evening, the owner of the 'safe house' and his son brought us on a new route across Killary – out by boat, thereby bypassing Leenane completely. On more than one occasion that night, we thanked the fates that had interceded on our behalf – I can assure you of that. The following day was a Monday and the previous night saw a messenger visit us from the IRA's senior council with an order instructing us to accept the ceasefire which had been negotiated in Dublin that same day. No sooner was the meeting in Glennagevlagh finished but we set off to hide our weapons and ammunition in a safe place. The war was over.

Endnotes

CHAPTER I: FAMILY AND BIRTH

1   The Galway hooker (Irish: *húicéir*) is a traditional sailing boat with a single mast, a main sail and two foresails (usually coloured dark brown or red-brown) and is distinguished by its unique sail formation.

2   The Year of the French (1798) refers to the Irish rebellion lasting just a few months, which was organised by the United Irishmen, a republican revolutionary group influenced by the ideas of the American and French revolutions.

3   Joyce Country known as *Dúiche Sheoighe* in Irish is a hilly region in the north of Galway which extends into south County Mayo.

4   Theobald Mathew (1790–1856) was an Irish temperance reformer. Born in Thomastown in County Tipperary, the movement he founded began with the establishment of the Total Abstinence Society. The promise, which the person made to abstain from alcohol, was known as 'The Pledge'.

5   Archbishop John MacHale (1791–1881), born in Tubbernavine, County Mayo, was the first Irish Roman Catholic archbishop of Tuam in County Galway, and was a prominent Irish nationalist. He, amongst others, agitated for many years in order to secure Catholic Emancipation in Ireland.

6   The Fianna cycle of tales is a body of prose and verse focusing on the exploits of the mythical hero Fionn MacCumhaill and his warriors in Fianna Éireann.

7   A well-known song based on the lament of the Virgin Mary on the death of her son Jesus Christ.

8   'Molly Malone' is a very popular Irish song describing the life of a beautiful fishmonger who plied her trade on the streets of Dublin, Ireland. Molly is said to have died young, of suspected fever. The song may have been based on a real historical woman who worked in seventeenth-century Dublin.

9   Michael Davitt (1846–1906) was a well-known Irish republican and nationalist. An agitator for Irish land reform, he was also an energetic

social campaigner, politician and journalist. He founded the Irish National Land League. Having been evicted from their smallholding in Ireland his family moved to England where he was brought up in Lancashire, in the heart of a poor Irish community who retained staunch nationalist feelings and a deep hatred of landlordism and the colonial class who then controlled Ireland. As a young man Davitt was strongly influenced by Ernest Charles Jones, the veteran Chartist leader, in particular his radical views regarding land nationalisation and the cause of Irish independence.

In 1865, Davitt joined the IRB and he soon became the organising secretary for both Northern England and Scotland. Under the guise of a travelling 'hawker' he organised the smuggling of a number of arms shipments to Ireland.

Davitt took part in the failed raid on Chester Castle in advance of the 1867 Fenian uprising in Ireland, but managed to evade the clutches of the law afterwards. He helped organise the defence of Catholic churches in Lancashire against the sectarian attacks of various Protestant groups the following year. In 1870, he was arrested in London while awaiting an arms delivery and was convicted of treason. He was sentenced to fifteen years penal servitude in Dartmoor prison. It was while incarcerated there that he concluded landownership – on the part of the ordinary people of Ireland – was the only solution to Ireland's woes and on release he moved to Ireland and re-joined the IRB. In 1879 he moved to his native Mayo where he became a major organiser in the movement for land agitation, i.e. 'The Land War'.

Today, Davitt is commonly credited with being one of the leading lights in the foundation of the British Labour Party and his strong support of socialism towards his latter years had its roots in the belief that Irish independence would only be achieved with the support of the British working class. Davitt died in a Dublin hospital in 1906.

10   'Booleying' was the Irish term for the transhumance of livestock. Transhumance is the seasonal movement of people with their livestock, typically to higher pastures in the summer and into the lower valleys in the winter.

11   Tradition has it that St Ciarán Mac Luaigne or Ciarán of Saigir was a bishop of the early Irish church and the first saint to be born in Ireland. He is said to have lived in the fifth century and to have been the patron saint of Ossory, now County Offaly and was a different historical figure from Ciarán of Clonmacnoise.

12 *Meitheal* is the Gaelic name for a work group and conveys the idea of 'community spirit' or 'connection with neighbour'. Traditionally, the term referred to groups of people – often neighbours – coming together to do agricultural work in a cooperative fashion, e.g. gathering hay or preparing for harvest. Each person helped their neighbours, who would then reciprocate in due course.

13 Boxty is a traditional Irish recipe made of potato pancake. There are many different recipes for boxty but all of them contain finely grated, raw potatoes. The mixture is fried on a griddle pan for a few minutes on each side, similar to a normal pancake. Boxty was such an essential aspect of Irish rural life at one point in time that poems such as the following were composed in relation to it:

> 'Boxty on the griddle,
> Boxty in the pan,
> If you can't make boxty,
> You'll never get a man.'

14 Poitín – illegally distilled Irish whiskey.

15 *Bean an Leanna* – (lit: 'the woman of the beer', i.e. the landlady).

CHAPTER 2: MY FIRST DAY AT SCHOOL

1 O'Malley the pig-merchant.

2 '*Fuist*' – 'whist' – an exclamation meaning 'Watch out' or 'Be quiet'.

3 *Ag súil le cúiteamh a mhilleas an cearrbhach* (it's always the 'next bet' that destroys the gambler).

4 It began in April 1898 and ended in August of that year, and the Treaty of Paris was signed in December.

5 Part of the imperial system of weights and measures: it is equal to fourteen pounds and to 6.350 kilograms. Eight stone make a hundredweight in the imperial system.

6 *Íosagán agus Sgéalta Eile* is a collection of four short stories for children published by Patrick Pearse in 1907. Pearse's stories were radical for their time since they deliberately adopted the form and technique of the modern short story, thereby counteracting the 'conservative' tendency of other Irish-language writers of the era who espoused more 'traditional' stories, often based on Irish folklore models. Patrick Henry Pearse (1879–1916), was born and raised in Dublin where he became a noted Irish teacher, barrister, poet, writer, nationalist and political activist. He was one of the

leaders of the Easter Rising in 1916 when he was declared 'President of the Provisional Government' of the Irish Republic. Both Patrick Pearse and his brother Willie were executed for their part in the Easter Rising along with fourteen of the other main protagonists. To this day, Pearse is considered by many as the embodiment of the 1916 rebellion, which set the way for a free and independent republic of Ireland.

7   *Conradh na Gaeilge* – a non-governmental organisation that promotes the Irish language in both Ireland and abroad. Founded in Dublin in 1893, by County Roscommon-born Douglas Hyde, later president of Ireland, its first newspaper was *An Claidheamh Soluis*, a broadsheet which included editors as notable as Patrick Pearse. Similar to the Gaelic Athletic Association, the League was a rallying point for Irish nationalists of different backgrounds and persuasions and it was under its auspices that many of the future Irish rebel leaders met and laid the foundations for future insurrection and the formation of groups such as the Irish Volunteers (1913).

8   Major John MacBride (1865–1916) fought in the 1916 Easter Rising and was executed by the British. Born in County Mayo, MacBride worked for a pharmaceutical firm in Dublin. He joined the IRB at a young age and was involved with Michael Cusack in the early days of the Gaelic Athletic Association (GAA). He emigrated to South Africa at the turn of the century where he fought in the Boer War with the Irish Transvaal Brigade. His military career proved very successful and he was appointed to the position of colonel in the Boer army. In 1903 he married Maude Gonne, a woman whose beauty was the inspiration for some of Yeats' most famous poems. They had one child, a son named Seán, who subsequently played a major role in Irish politics and public life. The marriage was not a happy one, however, and the couple later separated.

9   Arthur Alfred Lynch (1861–1934) was an Australian civil engineer, physician, journalist, author, soldier, anti-imperialist and polymath. He served as MP in the British House of Commons on behalf of the Irish Parliamentary Party, where he represented both Galway and West Clare at different junctures. Unlike the majority of his compatriots in Britain, Lynch fought on the side of the Boers side during the Boer War. A prolific author, Lynch wrote a large number of books ranging from poetry to philosophy.

CHAPTER 3: THE TEACHING CERTIFICATE

1 *An Claidheamh Soluis* was the most important Irish nationalist newspaper published in the early 1900s. It was published by the Gaelic League, with Eoin MacNeill as its first editor.

2 Fr Eugene O'Growney (1863–1899) was a scholar who became very interested in the Irish language while studying in the seminary at St Patrick's College, Maynooth. He was appointed professor of Irish at Maynooth in 1891 when he also became the editor of the *Gaelic Journal*. He was best known for his series entitled 'Simple Lessons in Irish', which were first published in the *Weekly Freeman*. O'Growney was one of the founders of the Gaelic League, set up in Dublin in 1893. He died from tuberculosis at the young age of thirty-six and is buried in Los Angeles, California. The Dublin office of the Gaelic League published *Tadhg Gabha* in 1902. Pupils learning to read and write Irish used it extensively.

3 Jeremiah O'Donovan Rossa (1831–1915) was a Fenian leader and a prominent member of the Irish Republican Brotherhood (IRB). Born in Rosscarbery, County Cork, he was both a rebel and a politician. In 1865, he was charged with plotting a Fenian rising and was tried by the colonial administration in Ireland, found guilty of high treason, and sentenced to penal servitude for life. He served his time in a number of English prisons including Pentonville, Portland and Chatham. Later in life, he emigrated to New York where he remained until his death in 1915. In August of that year, O'Donovan Rossa's body came home to Ireland and he was buried in Glasnevin Cemetery after one of the biggest funerals ever seen in Ireland. The graveside oration given by Patrick Pearse remains one of the most famous speeches in modern Irish history and served to garner significant support for the Irish Volunteers and the IRB. It ended with these memorable lines: 'They think that they have foreseen everything, think that they have provided against everything; but, the fools, the fools, the fools! — They have left us our Fenian dead, and while Ireland holds these graves, Ireland unfree shall never be at peace.'

4 The name Fianna Éireann (sometimes written as Fianna na hÉireann and Na Fianna Éireann) was used by various Irish republican youth movements throughout the course of the twentieth century. First formed by Bulmer Hobson, Fianna Éireann was originally set up as a sports organisation for young people (hurling) in West Belfast, in the year 1903.

CHAPTER 4: HOW I BEGAN WRITING IRISH

1   *Púcán* – traditional Connemara open sailing boat.

2   Seán Bán, an báiceara – White-haired Seán, the baker.

3   Ard-fheis – national convention.

4   Charles Lucas originally founded the *Freeman's Journal*, the oldest nationalist newspaper in Ireland, in 1763. It was associated with the radical strand of eighteenth-century Irish Protestantism and patriotism as represented by political figures such as Henry Flood and Henry Grattan. After 1784, the ideology of the journal changed, and under the editorial control of Francis Higgins (a British informer who was better known as the 'Sham Squire'), the publication adopted a much stronger pro-British and pro-colonial view of Irish political and social matters. By the nineteenth century, when it was the leading newspaper in Ireland, the journal had shifted position again and became more overtly nationalist. By the late-1800s, the journal was the principal supporter of Charles Stewart Parnell and the Irish Parliamentary Party within the Irish broadsheet industry. It had strong rivals amongst nationalist ranks: the *United Irishman* and *The Nation*, the latter founded by Thomas Davis. Amongst the pro-British establishment exemplified by the Anglo-Irish gentry, the 'unionist' newspaper *The Irish Times* had assumed precedence over the *Journal* by then also. The split amongst Irish Parliamentary Party members over the Parnell and Katherine O'Shea affair ate into the *Journal*'s readership even further as did the emergence of a more radical nationalism during the early decades of the twentieth century. The *Freeman's Journal* ceased publication in 1924, when it merged with the *Irish Independent*.

5   A liturgical feast on 29 June in honour of the martyrdom of the apostles St Peter and St Paul.

6   *Lint* – A fibrous coating of thick hairs covering the seeds of the bog-cotton plant.

7   Local people all wore home-spun clothes at this time, which included *báinín* sweaters and wide-brimmed black hats or fishermen's caps.

8   Páidín an Roisín – 'Paddy from Ros'.

9   Diarmuid Ua Duibhne was a son of Donn and a warrior of the Fianna in the Fenian Cycle of Irish mythology. He is famous as the lover of Gráinne, the intended wife of the leader of the Fianna, Fionn MacCumhaill. Diarmuid is a central character in the story *The Pursuit of Diarmuid and Gráinne*.

10   Red Hugh O'Donnell (1572–1602) was king of Tír Chonaill (County
      Donegal). He led a rebellion against English rule in Ireland from 1593
      and helped to lead the Nine Years' War against English occupation
      between 1595 and 1603.

11   The Land War was a period of agrarian agitation and unrest in rural
      Ireland between the 1870s and the 1890s. Many protests occurred aimed
      at bettering the position of tenant farmers with the ultimate goal of
      having Irish land redistributed from the landlords (especially absentee
      English landlords) to the tenants.

CHAPTER 5: WORKING AS A TEACHER

1   *Agam, agat* – prepositional pronoun – in this case – 'I have', 'you have', etc.

2   A weekly local newspaper published in Westport, County Mayo; John
      Redmond (1856–1918) was born in County Wexford, the son of a
      prominent Catholic gentry family. He was an Irish nationalist politician
      and barrister who served as an MP in the British House of Commons
      for many years. Leader of the Irish Parliamentary Party from 1900
      –1918 he represented the constitutional and conciliatory wing of Irish
      nationalist politics. An agitator for Irish Home Rule, Redmond saw his
      wishes granted under a 1914 Act which granted an interim form of self-
      government to Ireland, but the implementation of this act was suspended
      because of the outbreak of the First World War.

3   Tomás Bán Ó Conceanainn (1870–1946) was a writer and historian. A
      native of Inis Meáin, Aran Islands, he emigrated to America where he
      attended a number of colleges including Boston College. He graduated
      with a Masters in accountancy and set up a business in Mexico. He
      returned to Ireland in 1898 on a holiday but became involved with
      the Gaelic League and decided to stay. In 1905 both he and Douglas
      Hyde went on a fund-raising tour in America where they collected
      thousands of dollars for Irish-related cultural activities, money which
      they subsequently donated to help the victims of the 1906 San Francisco
      earthquake.

4   Midnight Mass.

5   *Sean-Shéamas Mac Giontaigh* – Old-Séamas McGinty.

CHAPTER 6: IN ERRIS

1   'Shoneen' or Shoneenism refers to Irish people who had an 'inferiority complex' and who imitated English ways and customs.

2   *Sinn Féin* was an Irish weekly nationalist newspaper edited by Arthur Griffith. It was published between 1906 and 1914, having replaced an earlier newspaper, the *United Irishman*. The *Sinn Féin* newspaper was suppressed by the British government in 1914.

3   An association set up to promote the manufacture of home-produced products for the Irish market.

4   Summer schools where Irish language and culture were taught, mainly to pupils from the more Anglicised parts of Ireland.

5   The Irish Parliamentary Party, more commonly called the Irish Party or the Home Rule Party was founded in 1882 by Charles Stewart Parnell, the then leader of the Nationalist Party. Until 1918 the IPP was the official parliamentary party for Irish nationalist MPs elected to the House of Commons at Westminster. Its two primary aims were the securing of legislative independence for Ireland and land reform.

6   The Black and Tans were composed largely of First World War veterans and employed by the Royal Irish Constabulary (RIC) between 1920 and 1921. Their aim was to suppress the rebellion then in full flow in Ireland and to target the Volunteers in particular. The Black and Tans were greatly hated and feared by the majority of Irish people and gained notoriety for their numerous and often random attacks on the civilian population.

7   The currach was a type of Irish boat with a wooden frame, over which animal skins or hides were once stretched. It is referred to as a *naomhóg* in Counties Cork and Kerry. Presumably the rock mentioned here was in the shape of a currach.

8   The Children of Lir is a well-known legend and many versions of the tale exist but its basic plot involves a number of children, the family of Lir – who are transformed into swans by their wicked stepmother Aoife, when she is unable to fulfil her murderous intentions in relation to the children. As swans, the children had to spend 300 years on Lough Derravaragh (a lake near their father's castle), 300 years in the Sea of Moyle, and 300 years on the Isle of Glora. To undo the spell, requires the blessing of a monk or a holy man. There are various endings to this legend, some happy and some sad.

9   Seán na gCapall – 'Seán of the Horses'.

10 Eoin MacNeill (1867–1945) was an Irish scholar, nationalist,

revolutionary and politician. He was a co-founder of the *Irish League*, the aim of which was the ongoing preservation and development of Irish language and culture. MacNeill became chairman of the council that formed the Irish Volunteers in 1913, prompted and encouraged by the Irish Republican Brotherhood (IRB). He later became chief of staff of the Irish Volunteers and held this position at the outbreak of the 1916 Easter rebellion, although he was strongly opposed to the idea of an armed rebellion. He was excluded from the planning of the Easter Rising but was arrested in its aftermath as part of the round-up of the rebels. Sentenced to life imprisonment, MacNeill was released in 1917. In 1921 he supported the pro-Treaty side and was appointed minister for education in the first Free State government. After his retirement from politics he became chairman of the Irish Manuscripts Commission and devoted the remainder of his life to scholarship, publishing a number of books on Irish history.

11 Piaras Béaslaí (1881–1965) was a member of the IRB and of Dáil Éireann and was also an Irish-language author and playwright. Born to Irish parents in Liverpool, England, he was baptised Pierce Beasley in 1881. He moved to Ireland at a young age where he worked as a journalist and freelance writer and became deeply involved with various nationalist-inspired groups including the Gaelic League. Along with Richard Mulcahy, Patrick Pearse and other members of the IRB, he instigated a 'revolt' within the Gaelic League which succeeded in removing the League's original founder, Douglas Hyde, in 1915. Béaslaí fought in both the Easter Rising and the War of Independence. During the latter he helped engineer the mass escape of Irish rebels jailed in Manchester. In the general election of 1918, Béaslaí was elected to the First Dáil Éireann as Sinn Féin representative for Kerry East. He was re-elected in a number of elections after this including the 1922 election where he was elected as a pro-Treaty Sinn Féin candidate. As with many of his colleagues, he devoted his later years to scholarship and literature in the Irish language, producing plays in Irish in the process. One book that he wrote in English related to his experiences during the War of Independence and the Civil War, *Michael Collins and the Making of a New Ireland* (1926).

CHAPTER 7: FIVE BLISSFUL YEARS IN CLIFDEN

1   The Ancient Order of Hibernians was founded in New York City, in 1836 and it still has its largest membership today in America. Originally formed by communities of American-based Irish immigrants, its primary aim was the protection of Catholics and their churches from the sectarian attacks and anti-Catholic bigotry common in many American cities during the nineteenth century. The order had a strong social conscience and sought to assist Irish Catholics who faced discrimination or harsh working conditions and it served as an important lynch-pin for the emergence of Irish-Americans in US politics. In Ireland the order's significance lay more in its ideological leanings and its function as a recreational association. Important too was the link it provided between the newer nationalist organisations of early twentieth-century Ireland and the long-established popular militant societies.

2   The leader of the Ancient Order of Hibernians (sometimes known as the Molly Maguires or Mollies) at this time, Belfast-man Joseph Devlin (Seosamh Ó Doibhlín) was a man of remarkable energy and political ability. Devlin was associated with the Dillonite wing of the Irish Party and under his stewardship the Ancient Order of Hibernians expanded very quickly throughout Ireland, north and south.

3   The All-for-Ireland League was a Munster-based political party which ran between 1909 and 1918. Founded by William O'Brien MP, it aimed to function as a new national movement intent on 'unifying' the various different Irish parties who sought consensus on the question of Home Rule.

4   William O'Brien (1852–1928) was a nationalist from County Cork. A journalist by profession, O'Brien became editor of *United Ireland* in 1881 and was imprisoned for his Irish Land League agitation. He was subsequently released under the Kilmainham Treaty and in 1883 he was elected to the Westminster parliament in which he served until 1918. After the Parnell split he worked for the reunification of the Irish Parliamentary Party. He did not stand for re-election in 1918 and declined a nomination to the senate of the Irish Free State, since he refused to accept the Treaty.

5   'Jumper' – presumably, a word referring to somebody who would 'jump' from one religion to the next depending on the prevailing social or economic situation. 'Souper' is a reference to the 'soup kitchens' run by some Protestant groups who wished to convert people from Catholicism

to Protestantism. Catholics who changed religious affiliation at this juncture were often said to have 'taken the soup'.

6   *Oireachtas* means 'gathering' in English. The Oireachtas is an annual national gathering which is often held over the course of a week and which incorporates competitions and exhibitions relating to Irish language, music and dance.

7   St Enda's school was an Irish-language medium secondary school for boys set up by Irish nationalist Patrick Pearse in Dublin in 1908.

8   Seán MacDiarmada (1883–1916) was one of the leaders of the 1916 Easter rebellion in Ireland. Born and reared in County Leitrim, he was deeply involved in Irish separatist and cultural organisations from a young age. In 1908 he went to live in Dublin where he was soon appointed to the Supreme Council of the IRB. In 1910 he was made a national organiser for the IRB, the same year that he became manager of the radical newspaper *Irish Freedom*, which he founded along with Bulmer Hobson and Denis McCullough. MacDiarmada contracted polio and had to walk with the aid of a cane. Because of his disability, he took little part in the fighting of Easter week, but remained at headquarters in the General Post Office (GPO). He almost escaped execution by blending in with the large body of prisoners rounded up after the rebellion but a British soldier identified him at the last moment. MacDiarmada was executed by firing squad on 12 May 1916. He was just thirty-three years of age. Seán MacDiarmada Street in Dublin's city centre is named after him as is MacDiarmada railway station in Sligo, and Páirc Seán MacDiarmada, the GAA stadium in Carrick-on-Shannon, County Leitrim.

9   The Irish Republican Brotherhood (IRB) was a secret oath-bound fraternal organisation dedicated to the establishment of an 'independent democratic republic' in Ireland during the nineteenth and early twentieth centuries. Its counterpart in America was the Fenian Brotherhood as organised by John O'Mahony. Both the Irish-based and the American-based wings of the movement would collectively be known as 'the Fenians'. Following on from earlier movements such as the *United Irishmen* (1790s) and the *Young Irelanders* (1840s), the IRB were the primary drivers for Irish republicanism and the campaigns to secure Irish independence as organised in the early 1900s, the Easter Rising of 1916 in particular.

10   *Naomh Pádraig* - Saint Patrick

11   *Púcán mór Rosmuc* (lit.) The Big Rosmuc Sailing Boat.

CHAPTER 8: HERE AND THERE IN CONNEMARA

1   Páraic Óg Ó Conaire (1893–1971) was born in Rosmuc, County Galway, in 1893. He excelled at school, winning a scholarship to study at St Enda's in Rathfarnham, Dublin. Ó Conaire qualified as a teacher after which he spent twenty years working as a travelling Irish-language teacher in a number of counties including Mayo, Offaly and Tyrone. He fought in the War of Independence and taught in Coláiste an Spidéil in the Connemara Gaeltacht. Between 1931 and 1958 he worked as a translator in the Irish government buildings at Leinster House, Dublin. He also worked as an Irish-language newsreader for Ireland's newly formed radio station Raidió Éireann. He was a talented writer and published a range of highly regarded novels and short stories in the Irish language.

2   The long-term result of centuries of conquest, confiscation and colonisation was the creation of a British landlord class who had granted little in terms of rights to an impoverished Irish tenantry comprising both Catholics and nonconformist Protestants. By 1921, the situation in Ireland had improved greatly with legislative measures ensuring that two-thirds of the land in Ireland had become the property of Irish tenants. The bulk of the remaining land was transferred to Irish ownership soon after the establishment of the Irish Free State in 1922.

3   *Ard Chomhairle* – national executive.

4   Daniel O'Connell, (1775–1847) known by many as 'The Liberator', was an Irish political leader of the first half of the nineteenth century. He was born in County Kerry and spent his life campaigning for Catholic Emancipation – the right for Catholics to sit in the British Parliament at Westminster – and for the Repeal of the Union between Ireland and Britain.

5   Cluad de Ceabhasa was born Claud Albert Chavasse in Oxford, England on 2 April 1885. His father was part of the British 'establishment' and was educated at Balliol before being appointed a Fellow of University College Oxford. Like his father, Cluad was something of a lifelong student and academic, entering University College Oxford in 1903, collecting his degree in 1909, but still being registered as a student there in 1916. He seems to have been very interested in the Irish language and culture from an early age and originally came to Ireland to stay with an uncle in Waterford, where he learned Irish from the locals. He was a founding member of Achill school, a summer school for the teaching of

Irish language and culture which ran for four years between 1910 and 1914 and which has seen a revival in recent years. De Ceabhasa became involved with Sinn Féin and the Irish national struggle and was interred in the Curragh for a year where he taught Irish to other prisoners. He was elected as Galway representative for Sinn Féin at the 1949 ard-fheis under the name Cluad de Ceabhasa. De Ceabhasa was a well-known 'character' around Galway city for many years, given his eccentric style of dress. He often wore a saffron kilt and a cloak and refused to speak English.

6   MacSuibhne, whose 'stomping grounds' were primarily Counties Galway and Mayo, was one of the last Gaelic poets in the west of Ireland who followed the older peripatetic tradition of the wandering poet, travelling from place to place and exchanging his 'art' for food and lodgings.

7   Michael Joseph Rahilly, often known as 'The O'Rahilly' was born in Ballylongford, County Kerry, and educated at Clongowes Wood in County Kildare. He attended University College Dublin before emigrating to the United States where he married. He returned to Ireland in 1909 and joined Sinn Féin. A big admirer of Arthur Griffith, he was also active in Conradh na Gaeilge, managing their journal *An Claidheamh Soluis*. He published the original article by Eoin MacNeill which proved the catalyst for the foundation of the Irish Volunteers. He supported MacNeill's attempt to abort the Easter Rising but once it was clear that the rebellion was going ahead he joined the garrison in the General Post Office. He was killed on 28 April 1916 while leading a charge down Moore Street in Dublin.

CHAPTER 9: DIVISIONS WITHIN THE VARIOUS NATIONALIST ORGANISATIONS

1   Croagh Patrick is about five miles from Westport in County Mayo. It derives its name from the Irish: Cruach Phádraig (lit.) 'St Patrick's Stack' and is known locally as 'The Reek', another word for 'stack'. The mountain has been a site of pilgrimage for Irish people since pre-Christian times. St Patrick, the patron saint of Ireland, reputedly fasted on the summit of Croagh Patrick for forty days during the fifth century.

2   Crom Dubh was a Celtic god in Irish mythology.

3   Ashe (1885–1917) was born in Lispole, County Kerry. He was a member of the Gaelic League, the IRB and a founding member of the Irish

Volunteers. He took part in the Easter Rising of 1916. He died as a result of a feeding tube piercing his lung, when being force-fed during a hunger strike.

4   *An Craoibhín Aoibhinn* was the pen-name of Douglas Hyde (1860–1949), a noted scholar of the Irish language who also served as the first president of Ireland between 1938 and 1945. Hyde was the founder of the Gaelic League, formed in Dublin, in 1893.

5   Ó Gaora said that he had the good fortune to run into Bulmer Hobson the previous evening who offered him a pass granting him permission to attend the graveside irrespective of whether Ó Gaora's Volunteer company were permitted to be in attendance or not.

6   George William Russell (1867–1935), who wrote under the pseudonym Æ (sometimes written AE or A.E.), was an Irish nationalist, poet and painter. He was also a mystical writer and had a strong interest in the theosophy movement.

7   Séamas Ó Súilleabháin was an Irish-language writer and translator who transcribed a great deal of Gaelic literature and song, including Fenian-related literature. He seems to have lived in County Limerick for some of his life where he earned his living as a schoolteacher.

CHAPTER 10: EASTER WEEK 1916

1   Ó Gaora said he had 'to admit that the police of this era were much more knowledgeable and well-trained than we Volunteers were with regard to the use of weapons'.

2   Ó Gaora says: 'This was the man whom we referred to as "The Butcher". Arbour Hill was where many of the leaders of the 1916 Rising, including Pearse, were buried after their execution'; General Sir John Grenfell Maxwell (1859–1929) was a British army officer and colonial governor. He arrived in Ireland on Friday 28 April 1916 as 'military governor' with 'plenary powers' under martial law – i.e. his understanding of martial law. During the week which ran from 2–9 May, Maxwell was in sole charge of trials and sentences – i.e. effectively trial without defence or jury. He had 3,400 people arrested and 183 civilians were tried. He also sentenced ninety of those people who were arrested to death. (*Source*: 'Shot in cold blood: Military law and Irish perceptions in the suppression of the 1916 Rebellion', in *1916, The Long Revolution*, Adrian Hardiman, pp. 225–249, Mercier Press (2007)).

3   Ó Gaora's 'summons was handwritten in pen on a piece of cheap paper'.

4   *Cú Uladh* (the 'Hound of Ulster') was the pen-name of Peadar 'Toner' Mac Fhionnlaoich (1857–1942), an Irish-language writer who was born in County Donegal. He wrote stories and plays, and regularly contributed articles to the Irish-language newspapers, including *An Claidheamh Soluis*. Éamon de Valera nominated him to the Irish senate where he served between the years 1938 and 1942. He was also president of the Gaelic League for a number of years.

5   George Noble Plunkett or Count Plunkett (1851–1948) was the father of Joseph Mary Plunkett, one of the leaders of the 1916 Rising.

6   Seathrún Céitinn (Geoffrey Keating) was a seventeenth-century Irish Catholic priest, poet and historian. He was born in County Tipperary *c.* 1569 and died in *c.* 1644. He studied at the University of Bordeaux in France but returned to Ireland in 1610 after which he worked in a parish near Cahir, County Tipperary. His most famous work, *Foras Feasa ar Éirinn* ('History of Ireland') was written in Irish and completed sometime around 1634. Based on the rich native historical and pseudo-historical traditions and ecclesiastical records, it is a history of Ireland from the beginning of time to the invasion of the Normans in the twelfth century.

7   The Irish-language organisation, *An Fáinne* (meaning 'The Ring' or 'The Circle' in Irish) was founded in 1911 by Piaras Béaslaí. *An Fáinne* was intended to promote the speaking of Irish and fluency in the language, with those non-native Irish speakers who became fluent in the language being awarded a gold ring lapel pin. During the early 1920s the majority of the people who earned their Fáinne did so while in prison and they were predominantly from the anti-Treaty side of the IRA.

CHAPTER 12: FREE ONCE MORE

1   The French family (sometimes written Ffrench), a wealthy landowning family in County Galway, are listed amongst the 'tribes' of Galway – i.e. the fourteen merchant families who dominated the political, commercial and social life of the city between the thirteenth and the nineteenth centuries. The Frenchs originally migrated to Ireland as part of various waves of Anglo-Norman settlers.

2   Thomas Derrig (1897–1956) was born in County Mayo, and attended University College Galway where he organised a battalion of the Irish

Volunteers. He was arrested and imprisoned for his part in the 1916 Rising and became a schoolteacher in his native Mayo upon his release. During the Irish War of Independence Derrig was interned in the Curragh where he was also elected a Sinn Féin TD for North Mayo and West Mayo. Derrig was on the anti-Treaty side during the Irish Civil War. Captured by the Free State army, he was shot by a CID detective while in custody and lost the sight in one of his eyes. Derrig was appointed minister for education in Éamon de Valera's first government of 1932. During the next twenty years, he alternated between the posts of minister for education and minister for lands in the Fianna Fáil governments of the era.

3   Ó Gaora says: 'Piaras MacCana died for the Irish cause while in an English prison. He was arrested in relation to the "German Plot" of 1918, may God have mercy on him.'

CHAPTER 13: NATIONALIST GROUPINGS IN COUNTY GALWAY

1   *Cumann* – association.
2   'O'Malley from Cois Fharraige'. Cois Fharraige is near Spiddal in County Galway.
3   A phenomenon whereby somebody would become incredibly weak while out on the hill or mountain, generally far away from home.

CHAPTER 14: A PRISONER ONCE MORE

1   The 'German Plot' of May 1918 was based on the 'alleged' theory that Sinn Féin were planning to open another military front in Ireland while the First World War raged. Claims for the existence of this 'plot' were spurious at best and many Irish nationalists viewed it as an excuse to round-up the most important leaders and 'foot-soldiers' of the republican movement and intern them. From a British point of view, the move proved counter-productive as the majority of the people interned were moderates within the Sinn Féin leadership and this allowed Michael Collins to consolidate his control of the organisation and organise it along more militant lines.
2   Séamus Quirke Road in Newcastle, County Galway, is named after him.
3   Charles Cornwallis (1738–1805), known as Earl Cornwallis, was a British army officer and colonial administrator. He was one of the leading

British generals in the American War of Independence and, in Ireland, he oversaw the military response to the 1798 Irish Rebellion and was a central figure in securing the union of Great Britain and Ireland.

4   Frongoch camp in Merionethshire, Wales, was a makeshift internment camp originally used to house German prisoners-of-war captured during the First World War. Before the Easter Rising of 1916, the German prisoners were moved and it was used as a place of internment for nearly 2,000 Irish republicans, including Michael Collins and Arthur Griffith. The camp, nicknamed 'University of Revolution' became an important military and cultural 'centre' for the dissemination of revolutionary ideas and strategies amongst the Irish rebels. The Irish rebels were released from Frongoch in December 1916.

5   *Teachta Dála* – (TD) member of the Irish parliament.

6   The Royal Irish Constabulary (RIC) was the main police force for most of the nineteenth and the early twentieth centuries in Ireland. It was an armed force, but Dublin had a separate civic police force, the unarmed Dublin Metropolitan Police, which patrolled Ireland's capital.

CHAPTER 15: A REPRESENTATIVE OF DÁIL ÉIREANN

1   Irish parliament.

2   Michael Collins (1890–1922) was born and reared in County Cork, he was minister for finance in the First Dáil of 1919. During the War of Independence he was director of intelligence for the IRA. He was also an important member of the Irish delegation during the Anglo-Irish Treaty negotiations. He was killed on 22 August 1922, during the Civil War. Supporters of Irish political party Fine Gael hold Collins' memory in particular esteem, many regarding him as their founder given his link to their precursor Cumann na nGaedheal and the pro-Treaty wing of Sinn Féin.

3   Fr Michael Griffin (1890–1920) was born near Ballinasloe, County Galway. Ordained at St Patrick's College, Maynooth in 1917, he served in the Galway diocese, primarily in Galway city. His murder was one of the most infamous incidents committed by the Black and Tans in Ireland. Fr Griffin was working as a curate in St Joseph's church, Galway when he was lured to his death by British forces on the evening of Friday 14 November 1920. Another man, an alleged informer, went missing and was presumed dead. His disappearance was reported to the

Black and Tans, and it was claimed that the alleged murderer (an Irish republican) had confessed to Fr Griffin. The Black and Tans lured the priest out of his house on false pretences and tortured him before they killed him. It was almost a week before his body was discovered in a bog near Barna and his funeral, attended by many thousands of people, generated huge international attention, partly because Fr Griffin had refused, under torture, to break the seal of the confessional. In 1948, a group of Galway GAA enthusiasts gathered to form a football club which they named Fr Griffin, a club which is still active in many competitions to this day.

4   Tomás Bairéad was born on a small farm near Moycullen. He joined the Irish Volunteers in 1913. He began his writing and publishing with the local newspapers in Galway and in 1922 he got a post with the *Irish Independent*, writing on politics. He rose through the ranks and became the *Independent*'s editor in 1945. Bairéad was a close friend of Máirtín Ó Cadhain who, recognising his talent from an early stage, urged him to leave and focus more closely on his writing. He won the Irish Academy of Letters Award in 1938. His two best-known books were *Cumhacht na Cinniúna* (1953) and *An Geall a Briseadh* (1968).

CHAPTER 16: THE WAR OF INDEPENDENCE

1   Ó Gaora says: 'Speaking of tea-drinking reminds me of an afternoon a group of us spent in Pearse's cottage, in Rosmuc, years ago. The conversation had turned to the question of stamps for some reason when Pearse suddenly announced that he could see the day coming when Irish stamps would be in the Irish language. "Wouldn't that be a fine thing?" he said. That this might actually one day happen still seemed like a pipe dream that afternoon in Rosmuc. A few decades later, Pearse's vision did come to pass and the Irish language was printed on the Irish stamp (printed as 'Éire'), albeit that the revival of the Irish language has yet to be realised.'

CHAPTER 17: TAKING THE FIGHT TO CONNEMARA

1   The morning of Bloody Sunday (21 November 1920) saw an IRA operation lead to fourteen deaths. Twelve of those shot dead were British agents/informers while two were Auxiliaries. In revenge, British forces

fired indiscriminately on a crowd at a Gaelic football match being held in Croke Park and killed fourteen Irish civilians. Later that evening, three IRA prisoners being held in Dublin Castle were beaten to death by their British captors, allegedly whilst trying to escape.

2   Ó Gaora says: 'We didn't actually succeed in destroying the barracks – we didn't have the explosives necessary to blow up a fortress as solid as that barracks in Clifden.'

3   18 April was the date of the ambush.

4   'Anybody on whom a monetary fine was imposed for collaboration, only had this done so after the case against them was overwhelmingly strong.'

5   This is a reference to British politician, Sir Oswald Mosley, (1896-1980), who was known principally as the founder of the British Union of Fascists. A member of the British aristocracy, Mosley had Irish links having married into the Anglo-Irish gentry. Unusually, given his background, Mosley became a prominent British supporter of the cause of Irish independence.

6   His and Tomás Ó Cadhain's houses were regularly used as 'safe houses' by our men during these years.

7   'Sliabh Gortach'. Induced by desolate or wild surroundings including bog which renders somebody confused as to the direction they are travelling in. In the past there were many superstitions as to what might induce this condition in somebody, including the possibility that a person had unwittingly infringed upon an enchanted place, a fairy-fort, for example.

Bibliography

Ambrose, Joe, *Dan Breen and the IRA* (Cork, 2006)

—— *Seán Treacy and the Tan War* (Cork, 2007)

Augusteijn, Joost, *From Public Defiance to Guerrilla Warfare: the experience of ordinary Volunteers in the Irish War of Independence, 1916–21* (Dublin, 1996)

—— (ed.), *The Irish Revolution, 1913–23* (New York, 2002)

Barry, Tom, *Guerrilla Days in Ireland* (Dublin, 1989)

Bennett, Richard, *The Black and Tans* (London, 1976)

Borgonovo, John, *Spies, Informers and the 'Anti-Sinn Féin Society': The intelligence war in Cork city, 1920–21* (Dublin, 2007)

Brennan, Michael, *The War in Clare, 1911–21* (Dublin, 1980)

—— *Land and Revolution: nationalist politics in the west of Ireland, 1891–1921* (Oxford, 2005)

—— 'The Easter Rising in Galway', in *History Ireland*, 14, 2 (2006), pp. 22–5

Coleman, Marie, *County Longford and the Irish Revolution, 1910–23* (Dublin, 2006)

Comerford, James J., *My Kilkenny IRA Days, 1916–22* (Kilkenny, 1978)

Conlon, Lil, *Cumann na mBan and the Women of Ireland, 1913–25* (Kilkenny, 1969)

Coogan, Oliver, *Politics and War in Meath, 1913–23* (Dublin, 1983)

Costello, Francis, *The Irish Revolution and its Aftermath, 1916–23: years of revolt* (Dublin, 2003)

Dalton, Charles, *With the Dublin Brigade, 1917–21* (London, 1929)

Davis, Richard, *Arthur Griffith and non-violent Sinn Féin* (Dublin, 1974)

Deasy, Liam, *Towards Ireland Free: the West Cork Brigade in the War of Independence, 1917–21* (Cork, 1973)

Doherty, Gabriel and Keogh, Dermot (eds), *1916: The Long Revolution* (Cork, 2007)

Dwyer, T. Ryle, *Tans, Terror and Troubles: Kerry's real fighting story, 1913–23* (Cork, 2001)

Farry, Michael, *Sligo, 1914–21: A chronicle of conflict* (Meath, 1992)

—— *The Aftermath of Revolution: Sligo, 1921–23* (Dublin, 2000)

Fitzpatrick, David, *Politics and Irish life, 1913–21: provincial experience of war and revolution* (Dublin, 1998)

Gallagher, Ronan, *Violence and Nationalist Politics in Derry city, 1920–23* (Dublin, 2003)

Griffith, Kenneth and O'Grady, Timothy, *Curious Journey: an oral history of Ireland's unfinished revolution* (London, 1982)

Hall, Donal, *World War One and Nationalist Politics in County Louth, 1914–20* (Dublin, 2005)

Hopkinson, Michael, *The Irish War of Independence* (Dublin, 2004)

Joy, James (ed.), *Victory and Woe: the West Limerick Brigade in the War of Independence* (Dublin, 2002)

Joy, Sinéad, *The IRA in Kerry, 1916–21* (Cork, 2005)

Macardle, Dorothy, *The Irish Republic* (Tralee, 1968)

MacCarthy, Jack (ed.), *Limerick's Fighting Story from 1916 to the Truce with Britain: told by the men who made it* (Tralee, 1965)

MacCiarnáin, Séamus (ed.), *The Last Post: the details and stories of republican dead, 1913–75* (Dublin, 1976)

Maher, Jim, *The Flying Column: West Kilkenny, 1916–21* (Dublin, 1987)

O'Callaghan, John, *Revolutionary Limerick: the republican campaign for independence in Limerick, 1913–21* (Dublin, 2010)

O'Callaghan, Michael, *'For Ireland and Freedom': Roscommon's contribution to the fight for independence, 1917–21* (Roscommon, 1964)

Ó Conchubhair, Brian (series ed.), *Dublin's Fighting Story, 1916–21: told by the men who made it* (Cork, 2009)

—— *Kerry's Fighting Story: told by the men who made it* (Cork, 2009)

—— *Limerick's Fighting Story: told by the men who made it* (Cork, 2009)

—— *Rebel Cork's Fighting Story: told by the men who made it* (Cork, 2009)

O'Donnell, Ruán (ed.), *The Impact of the 1916 Rising: among the nations* (Dublin, 2008)

O'Donnell, Stephen, *The Royal Irish Constabulary and the Black and Tans in County Louth, 1919–22* (Louth, 2004)

O'Donoghue, Florence, *No Other Law: the story of Liam Lynch and the Irish Republican Army, 1916–23* (Dublin, 1954)

O'Hegarty, P. S., *The Victory of Sinn Féin* (Dublin, 1924)

O'Mahony, Seán, *Frongoch: university of revolution* (Dublin, 1987)

O'Malley, Ernie (ed.), *Rising Out: Seán Connolly of Longford,* ed. Cormac K. H. O'Malley (Dublin, 2007)

—— *The Singing Flame* (Dublin, 1992)

—— *Raids and Rallies* (Dublin, 2001)

—— *On Another Man's Wound* (Dublin, 2002)

Ó Duibhir, Liam, *The Donegal Awakening: Donegal and the War of Independence* (Cork, 2009)

Ó Ruairc, Pádraig, *Blood on the Banner: the republican struggle in Clare, 1913–23* (Cork, 2009)

Ryan, Desmond, *Seán Treacy and the 3rd Tipperary Brigade* (Tralee, 1945)

—— *The Rising: The Complete Story of Easter Week* (Dublin, 1949)

Ryan, Meda, *Tom Barry: IRA freedom fighter* (Dublin, 2003)

—— *The Real Chief: Liam Lynch* (Cork, 2005)

Twohig, Patrick J., *Blood on the Flag – Autobiography of a Freedom Fighter* (Cork, 1996) [translated from *B'fhiú an braon fola* by Seamus Malone]

Ward, Margaret (ed.), *Unmanageable Revolutionaries* (Dublin, 1983)

—— *In Their Own Words: women and Irish nationalism* (Dublin, 1995)

Index